AVOIDING GOVERNORS

T0327287

RECENT TITLES FROM THE HELEN KELLOGG INSTITUTE
FOR INTERNATIONAL STUDIES

Scott Mainwaring, series editor

The University of Notre Dame Press gratefully thanks the Helen Kellogg Institute for International Studies for its support in the publication of titles in this series.

Barry S. Levitt
Power in the Balance: Presidents, Parties, and Legislatures in Peru and Beyond (2012)

Sérgio Buarque de Holanda
Roots of Brazil (2012)

José Murilo de Carvalho
The Formation of Souls: Imagery of the Republic in Brazil (2012)

Douglas Chalmers and Scott Mainwaring, eds.
Problems Confronting Contemporary Democracies: Essays in Honor of Alfred Stepan (2012)

Peter K. Spink, Peter M. Ward, and Robert H. Wilson, eds.
Metropolitan Governance in the Federalist Americas: Strategies for Equitable and Integrated Development (2012)

Natasha Borges Sugiyama
Diffusion of Good Government: Social Sector Reforms in Brazil (2012)

Ignacio Walker
Democracy in Latin America: Between Hope and Despair (2013)

Laura Gómez-Mera
Power and Regionalism in Latin America: The Politics of MERCOSUR (2013)

Rosario Queirolo
The Success of the Left in Latin America: Untainted Parties, Market Reforms, and Voting Behavior (2013)

Erik Ching
Authoritarian El Salvador: Politics and the Origins of the Military Regimes, 1880–1940 (2013)

Brian Wampler
Activating Democracy in Brazil: Popular Participation, Social Justice, and Interlocking Institutions (2015)

J. Ricardo Tranjan
Participatory Democracy in Brazil: Socioeconomic and Political Origins (2015)

For a complete list of titles from the Helen Kellogg Institute for International Studies, see http://www.undpress.nd.edu

AVOIDING GOVERNORS

Federalism, Democracy, and Poverty
Alleviation in Brazil and Argentina

TRACY BECK FENWICK

University of Notre Dame Press

Notre Dame, Indiana

Manufactured in the United States of America

Library of Congress Cataloging-in-Publication Data

Names: Fenwick, Tracy Beck, 1975– author
Title: Avoiding governors : federalism, democracy, and poverty alleviation in
  Brazil and Argentina / Tracy Beck Fenwick.
Description: Notre Dame, Indiana : University of Notre Dame Press, 2015. |
  Series: The Helen Kellogg Institute for International Studies | Includes
  bibliographical references and index.
Identifiers: LCCN 2015032992 | ISBN 9780268028961 (paperback) | ISBN
  0268028966 (paper | ISBN 9780268079802 (web pdf))
Subjects: LCSH: Central-local government relations—Brazil. | Central-local
  government relations—Argentina. | Decentralization in government—Brazil.
  | Decentralization in government—Argentina. | Federal government—Brazil.
  | Federal government—Argentina. | Public welfare administration—Brazil.
  | Public welfare administration—Argentina. | BISAC: POLITICAL SCIENCE /
  Public Policy / Social Policy. | SOCIAL SCIENCE / Poverty & Homelessness.
Classification: LCC JS2411 .F46 2015 | DDC 362.5/5610981—dc23
LC record available at http://lccn.loc.gov/2015032992

To my mother—Iris, mi tulipán,
and mis muchachos, Rolando, Félix, and Samuel

CONTENTS

TABLES

FIGURES

ABBREVIATIONS

This list is selective. Acronyms are also identified in the text.

ANSES	La Administración de Seguridad Social
AUH	Asignación Universal por Hijo
CBA	Ciudad Autónoma de Buenos Aires
CCTs	Conditional Cash Transfers
IBGE	Instituto Brasileiro de Geografia e Estatística
IBOPE	Instituto Brasileiro de Opinião Pública e Estatística
IMSS	Instituto Mexicano del Seguro Social
INDEC	El Instituto Nacional de Estadística y Censos
IPEA	Instituto de Pesquisa Econômica Aplicada
LBA	Legião Brasileira de Assistência Social
LRF	Lei de Responsabilidade Fiscal
MDS	Ministério de Desenvolvimento Social
PJJHD	Programa Jefes y Jefas de Hogares Desocupados
SP	State of São Paulo

POLITICAL PARTIES, ARGENTINA

Alianza	Alianza para el Trabajo, la Justicia y la Educación
FPV	Frente para la Victoria
PJ	Partido Justicialista
UCR	Union Cívica Radical

POLITICAL PARTIES, BRAZIL

ARENA	Aliança Nacional Renovadora
PFL	Partido Frente Liberal

PMDB	Partido do Movimento Democrático Brasileiro
PSDB	Partido da Social Democracia Brasileira
PT	Partido dos Trabalhadores

ACKNOWLEDGMENTS

I am grateful to many people who have assisted me in writing and researching this book over the past decade. My interest in Latin American politics, and more specifically Argentine politics, began in Lomas de Zamora Este in 1992, where I lived as an exchange student attending El Colegio de San Agustín in Temperley and the Faculdad de Filosofia y Letras at the University of Buenos Aires. My goal—to understand the local reality and the factors that determined the ways things were and still are—has never ceased over the years.

My interest in municipalities and in decentralization, however, did not begin in South America or within a federal system of government. In 2003 I worked on a Cooperación Española–financed project with FLACSO (Facultad Latinoamerican de Ciencias Sociales) in the Dominican Republic. Here, I was part of a research team interviewing mayors who had no political power, no fiscal resources, and little administrative capacity to deal with the draconian governing challenges they faced—problems that were not local. My supervisor, Haroldo Dilla, during one of our long trips back to the capital, with me asking him incessantly, "*¿Pero Cómo?*," joked in his Cuban way that there were two types of social scientists: those who had read his book *Descentralización Municipal en la Republica Dominicana*, and those who had not. I read it, and I have never looked back.

This project would not have been possible without the ongoing academic and emotional support from a multitude of people and institutions, from which I have greatly benefited. First of all, I want to thank my two doctoral supervisors, Laurence Whitehead and Timothy J. Power, and my two examiners, Nancy Bermeo and Anthony Hall, for their patience and encouragement throughout my time at the University of Oxford as a student and into my early academic career. Special thanks to Laurence for his uncanny ability to elucidate, to Tim for constantly encouraging me to "move beyond the bark" in order to see the forest, and to Nancy for believing in my research and its potential. St. Antony's College and the Latin American Centre of Oxford were generous with their support and time, for which I am indebted. Special thanks are also due to Dan Kelemen, Leslie Bethell, and Aaron Schneider for excellent (and tough) comments and for their early guidance during the formative and more rebellious stages of my research. This book would not have been possible without the research guidance and advice of Daniel Béland of the University of Saskatchewan, who generously provided me with a postdoctoral fellowship at the Johnson-Shoyama Graduate School of Public Policy when I returned to Canada, and who has supported me ever since. Thanks also to Rianne Mahon and many members of the ISA-RC19 group of Social Policy for pointing out important perspectives that I had failed to observe, observations that later enriched my research.

In Brazil, I benefited immensely from the guidance and contacts provided by CEBRAP (Brazilian Centre of Planning and Analysis) and the Social Policy Group (POLIS) of the Pontifícia Universidade Católica de São Paulo, headed by Aldaísa Sposati. Particular thanks are due to Celina Souza, who guided me daily and read my work for over a month at the Universidade Federal de Bahia, to Eduardo Marques, Marta Arretche, and Argelina Figuereido, all for offering ideas and careful guidance during my fieldwork in Brazil, and to Eduardo Suplicy for sharing his optimism. My research in São Paulo would not have been possible without the gracious hospitality of my dear friends Paola Ricci, Henrique Teixeira, and Janet Salmona. Thanks also to Bianca Begnozzi and Antonio Telles for their interest in my project and their assistance and to Osvaldo Pavanelli for allowing me to use his image on the cover.

In Argentina, I am indebted to Gabriela Ippolito, the late Guillermo O'Donnell, and Juan Manuel Abal Medina for their encouragement and fieldwork assistance. I also thank Rebecca Weitz-Shapiro and Fabiola Carcar for sharing their ideas and contacts. My stay in Argentina was made more pleasurable by my two long-standing surrogate families in Lomas de Zamora: Alfredo, Helena, Mercedes, and Victoria Pintos, and Carlos, Elvira, Pablo, Mariano, and German Balancini. My interest in Argentine politics began at the Pintos family's kitchen table, where this topic has been endlessly discussed and has flourished for over twenty years. I am particularly indebted to Helena for inciting my passion for Argentina politics, and I thank her deeply.

I express special thanks for comments, feedback, and support on the Argentine section of this book to Edward Gibson, Carlos Gervasoni, Alberto Fohrig, and Marcelo Leiras. On the Brazil section, thanks to Tyler Dickovick, Alfred Montero, Wendy Hunter, David Samuels, Oswaldo Amaral, Elaine Licio, Kênia Parsons, and Lena Lavinas, plus the large and influential network of U.S.-based Brazilianists whom I have been privileged to meet over the years at numerous conferences and small workshops. For the international policy perspective, many thanks to Brian Wampler, Kathy Lindert, and her colleagues at the World Bank for the updates and a productive exchange of ideas, and to Santiago Levy at the Inter-American Development Bank for his candidness. Thanks are also due to Rebecca Holmes and Rachel Diprose for their feedback and expert comments on two chapters related to emerging CCTs outside of Latin America that were eventually excluded from the current volume. To my colleagues and supporters at the Australian National University who helped make this book a reality, in particular to John Uhr and Keith Dowding, who were solid sounding boards, I appreciated your tips, guidance, and encouragement.

This book has a long and winding history that began when I was a doctoral candidate in politics at the University of Oxford in 2004, when interest in CCTs was nonexistent. My earlier publications in *Latin American Research Review* (44, no. 1 [2009]) and *Journal of Politics in Latin America* (2 [2010]) are covered in portions of chapters 2 and 3. Portions of an article held in copyright by Sage Publications, published in *Global Social Policy* (13, no. 2 [2013]), appear in chapter 7. I thank these journals for extending permission to reprint some of that text.

I am very grateful for having had the chance to work with the University of Notre Dame Press. The reviewers were incredibly generous in their time and comments, making this a much better manuscript. Special thanks to Stephen Little and Scott Mainwaring, to the entire Faculty Board of the press for their support of this project, and to the entire team at the press for their hard efforts.

Last but not least, I thank my husband Rolando; my ability to be a mother during this journey and to reach my career goals has been due to your selfless compromises and enduring support for all that we strive to accomplish together. Thanks to my mother Iris for her constant support and strength, my father Geoff for his silent approval, and my sister Joanne and her husband Dean for their love and support over the years—it has been a long road. To my Mexican in-laws and their extended family who have accepted my entry into the Ochoa-Hernandez-Montero clan, *gracias*!

The last paragraph I have saved for the children, because the social programs that fascinate me are intended to promote their development and society's future equality. The logic of inequality in our current world perpetuates an unjust society. Institutions and politics still fail to fully represent the interests of children and secure their futures. Therefore, to my loving sons, Félix and Samuel, to my international godchildren, Mora, Holden, and Charlotte, and to my niece, Sadie, may you all sit down together one day and see your similarities more than your differences. A just society is ultimately our responsibility.

CHAPTER 1

The Politics of Alleviating Poverty and Why Federalism Matters

Latin American federalism is a rapidly growing area of research. Recent studies of federalism, including in this region of the world, have emphasized the ability of this governing system to provide institutional incentives to key stakeholders at various levels of government, to structure unique electoral strategies, and to determine policy outcomes, government effectiveness, and the quality of democracy (Abrucio 1998; Arretche 2000 and 2012; Calvo and Medina 2001; Eaton 2004a; Filippov, Ordeshook, and Shvetsova 2004; Gibson 2004 and 2012; Rodden 2006; Samuels 2003; Spiller and Tommasi 2007; Ward, Rodriguez, and Mendoza, 1999; Wibbels 2005). The important reemergence of federalism in Latin America is juxtaposed against the *Zeitgeist* of a decade of democratic experimentation that led to government decentralization—the transfer of political power, fiscal resources, and policy responsibility to subnational levels of government.

In recent years, a plethora of comparative studies applying both instrumental and substantive perspectives has contributed to explaining the origins and consequences of decentralization in Latin America (Dickovick 2012; Montero and Samuels 2004; O'Neill 2004; Oxhorn, Tulchin, and Selee 2004; Souza 1997; Willis, Garman, and Haggard 1999; Wilson et al. 2006). Much of this literature has emerged out of a "growing disappointment with decentralization and federalism, especially among developing countries" (Rodden 2004, 481). It conceptualizes decentralization as a political process and thus evaluates it on the contingency of those processes that are determined by the relevant political and electoral incentives, an approach that began with Willis and colleagues' heavily cited 1999 article, "The Politics of Decentralization in Latin America." The new political-institutional or electoralist approach asserts that decentralization (or recentralization; Eaton and Dickovick 2004; Eaton 2014) is a product of political incentives at all levels and their resulting political relationships (Montero and Samuels 2004, 20).

There is, however, an important distinction to be made between the concepts of decentralization and federalism. Whether centralized or decentralized, federalism is based on a territorial distribution of powers, a distribution that cannot be altered without mutual agreement (Requejo 2001, 115). Decentralization initiated under a unitary system of government that disperses power outward is based on the presupposition of unilateral, centralized power. Because of the territorial dimensions of federalism, both government performance and democratic quality are determined by multiple tiers of government that, more often than not, compete for both institutional and political power. This new approach to understanding Latin American federations has been aptly described by González as "the power distributional approach" (2008, 212).

The main question that I explore in this book is, broadly, how federalism impacts a national government's ability to deliver targeted social policy goods. The question is framed comparatively in the context of contemporary Brazil and Argentina. I provide an analysis of how these two federations differ from each other, why their differences matter, and for what policy outcomes. Brazil and Argentina each offer important lessons to other countries, federal or not, both within the region and beyond, about how to broaden social agendas using targeted social policy initiatives. Federalism matters in Latin America for policy outcomes because in three out of four of the region's federations, which also include the region's largest populations—Mexico, Argentina, and Brazil—national governments have been unable to resolve their most important social and economic problems without interacting with one or both levels of subnational government.[1] During recent democratic periods in all three of these countries, it has not been so much the case that subnational actors were dependent on the federal center, but rather that national governments have in fact been dependent on subnational actors both to pursue national executive preferences and to carry out important national policy objectives.

In contrast to other more advanced industrial countries, decentralization in Latin America was not simply synonymous with either neoliberalism or the idea of a shrinking state. The topic of government decentralization has been tremendously important to our ability to understand both the transition and the consolidation of democracy in most Latin American countries. In an effort to move beyond decentralization, however, the emphasis here is on the impact of each level of government, within a multi-tiered governing system, on the ability to deliver targeted social welfare, set within what I broadly label as a "social investment agenda." The social investment agenda has now fully integrated Latin America's Conditional Cash Transfer programs (CCTs), which deliver small amounts of cash to households in return for their fulfillment of conditions linked to human capital investments, into its policy recommendations. This agenda rests on three pillars: first, learning is fundamental to the success of future societies and their economies; second, social spending designed to break the intergenerational transmission of poverty should be promoted; and third, investing in socially vulnerable individuals, particularly children, is beneficial for the community as a whole in the future (Giddens 1998; Esping-Andersen et al. 2002). With its origins in European social policy circles, the advocacy for a new social investment welfare state to confront today's and tomorrow's risks has obviously become more global in nature (Jenson 2010). Traditionally, however, in Latin American–oriented research, social inequality and poverty have persistently been considered critical issues in Latin American development because of their deleterious effects on the rights of citizenship and the quality of democracy. As James Malloy stated in the early 1990s, "the real issue however is not one of 'political will' but one of governmental capacity; the ability to define, implement, and sustain social policies" (1993, 221).

By focusing on targeted social welfare—specifically, CCTs designed to alleviate poverty and prevent the intergenerational transmission of poverty through investing in human capital—I examine the impact of federalism on the subsequent development and performance of national CCTs in two neighboring countries. From a policy perspective, this social reform area is recognized as being nationally oriented and is increasingly conceived from a rights-based approach. The performance of CCTs in each country, however, has varied. Therefore, the empirical goal of this study is to examine why Brazil and Argentina experienced differing outcomes from similarly designed CCTs, beginning during the administrations, respectively, of President Luiz Inácio Lula da Silva (2003–2011) and President Néstor Kirchner (2003–2007). It does so by privileging the role of domestic factors. In theory, the programmatic ideas, policy goals, and discourses that led to pioneering policy experimentation in Latin America and the eventual formulation of coherent policy instruments to reduce poverty (CCTs linked to human capital investments) have roots beyond regional actors and arose from multiple sources, including the World Bank. In practice, however, both the capacity of a national government to implement a CCT program and the political willingness of subnational levels of government to deliver and enable its polity-wide success are domestically determined. An international policy perspective alone cannot explain the divergent outcomes observed across the two cases presented here, or the varying outcomes of CCTs more generally in the developing world.

CONDITIONAL CASH TRANSFER PROGRAMS IN BRAZIL AND ARGENTINA

The evolution, development, and performance of CCT programs in Brazil and Argentina have been mixed. Brazil's highly celebrated national program, Bolsa Família, has been very successful in terms of the number of households included, the territory and social groups covered, and its empirically established ability to reduce poverty. The year 2013

marked ten years since this powerful national social program and popu-
larly supported poverty alleviation initiative was introduced by former
Brazilian president Inácio Lula da Sílva. In part due to both Brazil's
importance in the region and its prominence in producing innovative
policy ideas (interview Levy 2013), Bolsa Família has overshadowed the
success of the earlier implemented Mexican national program Progresa-
Opportunidades-Prospera, which is today both smaller and more specifically targeted. In fact the Mexican CCT was the first national CCT
that integrated health, education, and nutrition conditions into a single
social program designed to alleviate poverty through human capital investments (Aguiar and Araújo 2002, 70; Sugiyama 2012; Fenwick 2013;
interview Levy 2013). Today, however, within international development circles, Brazil's Bolsa Família is increasingly considered the gold
standard to emulate throughout the developing world.

Within three years of Bolsa Família's introduction it had reached
its intended target. By 2006, poverty alleviation benefits were being
delivered to more than 11 million households in all 5,564 Brazilian
municipalities. The program was maintained following the election of
Brazil's current president, Dilma Rousseff, in 2010. Rousseff launched
her own umbrella program, called Brasil Sem Miséria (BSM), with the
goal of combatting extreme poverty in Brazil by expanding the coverage
of Bolsa Família for socially vulnerable families. By 2014, 14.1 million
families were receiving this CCT (MDS 2015).

Brazil's poverty alleviation strategy and the flagship programs
within it, such as Bolsa Família, can be characterized by both continuity and gradual change. In terms of program design, rules, and processes, Bolsa Família has been seldom changed since its introduction
over a decade ago, when it replaced Bolsa Escola. Even though each
of these two national CCTs was administratively unique, Bolsa Família
complemented President Fernando Henrique Cardoso's previous CCT
program and did not represent a wholesale policy departure. The small
changes that have been made to Bolsa Família under Brazil's current
president, Dilma Rousseff, have evolved as add-ons. Within Rousseff's
Brasil Sem Miséria, new complementary policy initiatives, particularly
in the area of productive inclusion, are being grafted onto the otherwise
stable framework of Bolsa Família. These new initiatives are intended
to further Brazil's long-term social goals and to encompass a broad

cross-sector strategy that facilitates a household's ability to "exit" from receiving publicly provided financial assistance.

In contrast with Brazil, Argentina's first attempt at implementing an integrated national CCT program, backed by international financing and technical support, that was part of President Néstor Kirchner's governing agenda (2003–2007), performed poorly in terms of territorial coverage, public visibility, and the number of beneficiaries included. Three years after its implementation, this CCT, called Programa Familias, delivered benefits to only 372,000 households in 232 municipalities.[2] By 2010, it was replaced by a completely new centralized initiative called Asignación Universal por Hijo (AUH) under Argentina's current president, Cristina Fernández de Kirchner.

Argentina's poverty alleviation efforts since 2003 have been volatile and characterized by unsustainable short-term initiatives. AUH effectively replaced Argentina's largest CCT, a labor-based program designed for unemployed heads of households (Programa Jefes y Jefas de Hogares Desocupados, or PJJHD), and a second human capital-based CCT, Programa Familias. The most recent national program is distinct from the two previous initiatives because of its evident centralization and the ambiguous nature of its conditions, which are linked to human capital investments that are to be provided at the subnational level. AUH's ability to avoid both governors and mayors has facilitated its rapid and extensive implementation, yet the program's goal to reduce the intergenerational transmission of poverty through human capital investments necessitates intergovernmental policy collaboration that is not clearly visible. AUH stands out as a "state-centric development strategy that privileges the redistribution of resource rents to the poor" (Jenson 2010, 62), and thus arguably does not represent an approach to social policy that rests on the pillars of a now global social investment approach.

The current study, elaborated from an institutionalist perspective, will examine why the CCT experience was so successful during the administrations of President Lula in Brazil from 2003 through 2010, and was less successful for President Kirchner in neighboring Argentina from 2003 to 2007, and then under President Fernández de Kirchner from 2007 to 2010. It will additionally explore how the outcomes of these programs set the stage for either their "continuity and change" or their "termination." Each of these countries initially chose to adopt

CCTs that invested in human capital as a solution to visibly growing poverty toward the end of the 1990s. CCTs fall within the social policy area of noncontributory social protection. CCTs, in particular with their emphasis on linking conditionality to income assistance, are conceived throughout this study as a fundamental part of the emerging social investment perspective that has its roots in both Europe and Latin America. The goal of this focused comparison, which will be first constructed through two within-case analyses and then considered in comparative perspective, is to answer the following research questions:

1. Why were CCTs nationalized from the subnational levels, and what were the intended political effects of nationalized poverty alleviation programs?
2. What explains the extensive territorial distribution of Bolsa Família Brazil, in contrast with Argentina's parallel underperformance with Programa Familias?
3. How does each program's performance impact on its stability and future policy development?

CHALLENGING THE IDEA OF "ROBUST" FEDERALISM

Beyond this book's empirical goals, its broader objective is to challenge the idea of "robust" federalism. In general terms, robust federalism simply refers to a federal democracy where subnational levels of government have sufficient power (structural, institutional, and political) to undermine the federal center. Brazil and Argentina are both highly decentralized, presidential federal republics. This book will contend, however, that varying structural, institutional, and political factors have shaped the ability of each national government to execute its policy objectives in the area of poverty alleviation, objectives which matter for future generations because they are designed to reduce the risks of social vulnerability and deepen social citizenship rights for those groups that have been perpetually excluded. The central hypothesis forwarded in this research is that within some federal countries, municipalities can facilitate the national government's ability to carry out its desired policy goals within what is otherwise a robust federal system.

Each country studied here is an example of a robust (sometimes referred to as "strong") federal system, where subnational levels of government can constrain the ability of the federal government to deliver collective welfare goods and to carry out national policy objectives. In such multi-tiered structures of government, targeted social policy objectives may be set at the center, but the success of such a strategy will be determined by institutionally derived political interactions and the fiscal incentives linking the various levels of government. The center may seek uniformity of outcome by trying to bypass the core federal unit's executives, "governors," thus avoiding the "undermining constraints" of federalism. But for this to occur, I suggest, certain conditions must be present. I argue that three key explanatory factors shaped the performance of these national CCTs and their subsequent stability. The first is the constitutional recognition given to subnational levels of government. The second concerns the fiscal rules that regulate subnational finances. The third is the extent of majoritarianism present in each democratic system.

This study makes constant use of David Samuels and Scott Mainwaring's theoretical contributions to federalism, which they developed primarily to explain the outcomes of economic reform in Brazil and, more generally, to distinguish federal systems (2004, 87). The intended theoretical contribution of the present book is to build on the continuum of weak to strong federalism that these authors proposed, by adding another institutional variable of federalism which has become increasingly relevant to the politics of policymaking and policy outcomes in federal systems. My intended contribution is developed from a social policy perspective and is designed primarily to explain the outcomes of national efforts to alleviate poverty using CCTs. Samuels and Mainwaring defined their continuum of weak to strong federalism without recognizing either the strength of municipalities in terms of fiscal, administrative, and political resources (distinct from those of the states) or their ability to exercise this power independent of governors. This is not to say that a federal system that nationally recognizes municipalities as a distinct order of government from the core federal units (states and provinces) is not strong; but it does mean that a modified proposition that includes the strength of municipalities and their ability to exercise this strength autonomously from the core federal units may have considerable explanatory value in the context of contemporary Latin American federations.

The findings of this research do not coincide with the valuable arguments put forward by Stepan (2004), which suggested that Brazil and Argentina were equally "robust" from a veto-players approach; this is an approach that neither I nor Samuels and Mainwaring apply. This study questions Stepan's earlier proposition "that the greater the number of institutional veto players, the more difficult it is to redress poverty and inequality via a polity-wide welfare system" (2004, 333). Stepan classified both Brazil and Argentina as having four institutional veto players (the president, each chamber of Congress, and some member states that have policy implementation vetoes). Within Stepan's approach, Brazil is always considered more constraining than Argentina, because it does not have a political party that can reduce the number of its veto players (2004, 341). Counting veto players facilitates *large-n* cross-national analyses across federal and unitary countries. Such an approach does not demonstrate, however, the dynamic ways in which these identified veto players can interact uniquely to either avoid the undermining constraints of federalism or make them more constraining. There are nuanced, yet important, differences across federal systems. Weak governors can become stronger when united with mayors, weak presidents can become stronger when united with mayors, and strong governors can become weaker when mayors are bolstered by a stronger central government. By distinguishing municipalities as a separate actor, a dynamic intergovernmental relationship is represented; indeed, there is shown to be a power struggle between multiple levels of government and their electorates, not just a dichotomously framed, two-level game of the national level versus the subnational.

This research focuses specifically on the ability of the federal government to encourage municipalities to promote a national policy objective to "redress poverty via a polity-wide [targeted] welfare system," using nationally financed and designed noncontributory CCTs. A country's ability to minimize poverty is considered a precondition to pursuing a broader social investment strategy (Esping-Andersen et al. 2002). The current study does not intend to evaluate the impact of such programs on the reduction of poverty as such, or its impact on human capital indicators.[3] Rather, it sees federalism as a system of constraints and incentives that shapes the willingness of various levels of government to complement national policymaking by carrying out its intended policies. As suggested by Dickovick (2006), municipalization was a second-best strategy in a federal system such as Brazil's, where further recentralization was not institutionally feasible. It will be shown within this research that decentralization to the municipal level in Brazil provided a policy opportunity that resulted in effective and efficient targeted social policy outputs that were widely distributed throughout its territory, policy outcomes that previously would have been considered unattainable. This study asserts that this policy opportunity was not readily available to the federal government in neighboring Argentina, regardless of what Stepan identified as "a partisan-based political party" (2004, 341). The national government in Argentina does not have the opportunity within its federal system to easily avoid governors and thereby distribute CCTs without their intermediation. Strong federalism impedes national government capacity in Argentina in key public policy domains.

In contrast with Brazil, CCTs in Argentina from 2003 to 2010 were compromised by the ambiguous constitutional status of municipalities, a weak system of federal regulations over subnational finances, and the levels of majoritarianism inherent to its democratic system (particularly at the provincial level). These factors worked together to constrain the ability of the Argentine government to implement its policy preferences and deliver its program polity-wide, thus impeding program performance and its subsequent stability. A party-based coordinative mechanism in a federal system such as Argentina's does not encourage the kind of intergovernmental collaboration that is required to implement and sustain a national social program such as Programa Familias under examination here, predominantly because Argentina has one of the most decentralized party systems in the world and because municipalities are de facto captured by the provincial level for political ends. They have few incentives, either political or fiscal, to collaborate directly with the national government in order to reduce the intergenerational transmission of poverty, and thus may choose to limit its territorial distribution or be apathetic toward the program's goals. It should be underscored that an agenda to reduce the intergenerational transmission of poverty is fundamentally *supply*-driven.

In Brazil, the success of similarly designed and financed national CCTs has been facilitated by the constitutional distinction afforded to municipalities that enables them to act independently of the states in adhering to national policy objectives; by subnational fiscal regulations that do not necessitate municipal political capture for local fiscal survival; and by what is, relative to Argentina, a consensual model of democracy.[4] All three of these factors limit the ability of governors to punish politically or fiscally those municipalities that choose to cooperate with the federal government in implementing powerful social initiatives such as CCTs, for which governors cannot claim the credit or control the effects. Of great importance, the intergovernmental policy-based cooperation that is evident in Brazil's emerging social investment agenda has evolved and has now been sustained through an alternation in power between two opposition parties and three presidents. Moreover, it does not currently exhibit high levels of volatility.

Historically, in both Brazil and Argentina, governors have exercised enough power to seriously undermine and destabilize the governability of each country. Moreover, subnational representatives in both national congresses have traditionally represented the interests of the governors and/or their local political parties or subnational factions that are territorially based—something that rarely occurs in Mexico, where the federal system is much more vertically integrated and where political parties are heavily nationalized. Thus the ability of governors to monopolize patronage within their territories in strong federal systems such as Brazil and Argentina is very important because it has traditionally fueled that power, which in turn they have used as leverage over the federal government to obtain more "pork." The point is that national CCTs and any other targeted national social welfare programs that distribute what Shugart (1999) broadly calls "national collective goods" cannot easily be used for subnational patronage, specifically "when users understand that the program falls outside of their [local officials'] influence" (Hunter and Sugiyama 2013, 54). Therefore, states in Brazil and provinces in Argentina are unable to claim credit for national CCTs, so their incentive to cooperate is moot. Governors in Brazil and Argentina, however, are able to impede national credit-claiming by obstructing program implementation or by politically manipulating programs for themselves, when the distribution of national collective goods falls inside their direct influence or, alternatively, when it goes through mayors, who are administratively, fiscally, and politically beholden to powerful governors. These historically entrenched realities provide the national government with a motive to avoid governors when they want to distribute collective welfare goods without political intermediation. Operating as an autonomous actor in any federal system, mayors cannot directly undermine the president's preferences because they do not have formal representation in the national congress. Municipalities can, however, greatly assist with the enabling of CCTs in their territories, particularly with programs that have *supply*-side inputs requiring at least subnational acquiescence, in a large federal country that covers vast amounts of geographical territory.

The central hypothesis of this research moves away from the earlier developed wisdom in the literature that Brazil is a center-constraining federation (Souza 2002; Samuels and Mainwaring 2004; Stepan 2004). Instead, this study contributes to the emerging consensus that Brazil is in fact governed from the center (Figueiredo and Limongi 1999; Cheibub, Figueiredo, and Limongi 2009) and has even been currently classified by some as relatively centralized (Dickovick 2012; Arretche 2012; interview Arretche 2006). It suggests that extensive early decentralization and what many Brazilian political scientists have labeled as a "consensus-like democracy" or, more recently, a "power-sharing model" (Amorim Neto 2009)[5] have facilitated the president's ability to avoid governors in order to extensively distribute a poverty alleviation program territory-wide, enhancing both the center's credibility and consolidating the role of municipalities along the way.

RESEARCH DESIGN

The book uses the strategy of paired comparison to draw out key relationships among variables in two similar federal systems. It also builds a "focused comparison" based on a specific social policy area—that of noncontributory social protection—to show why, and for what, the relationships among the identified variables matter. From a methodological perspective the study of this book is made up of three major parts: description, including theoretical framing of the cases and establishing the relevance of the chosen policy focus; within-case analysis, based on causal process tracing and empirical testing; and, in conclusion, cross-case analysis. This research strategy is intended to generate new or alternative explanatory factors using a strategy of "dual process-tracing" that is designed "to reduce the possibility that a supposed determining variable is as critical as it might seem from a single-case study alone" (see Tarrow 2010, 244). Although I clearly argue that municipalities matter for the successful performance of CCTs, the institutional mechanisms that connect this structural factor to the policy outcomes examined remain political.

Like many studies in the comparative social sciences, I utilize a certain degree of methodological pluralism, while consciously trying to avoid the "messy center" where anything goes. This study has tried to remain true to the tradition of comparative democratization research, which stipulates that "all separate national realities require equivalent consideration" (Whitehead 1996, 357). Therefore, each national case is carefully built and examined through a within-case analysis before it is compared. I assert, however, that the broad comparative research strategy I have chosen "does not pose a major problem from the standpoint of scholars concerned with selections bias" (Collier, Brady, and Seawright 2004, 87). Although there is variance in the outcomes I am trying to explain, the variance in the explanatory factors is not as extreme as the national constitutions would have us believe. The constitutional recognition of municipalities cannot, as a single factor, explain the willingness of mayors to complement national policymaking or their own institutional strength. The main difference between this institutional variable in the cases selected is that municipal autonomy in Brazil is recognized by the national constitution, and in Argentina it is "expected" by the national constitution to be recognized by provincial constitutions. I do not consider this to be the kind of extreme variance that comparative-methods scholars believe can lead to "over-claiming."

The data for the case studies were originally obtained during two separate stages of fieldwork in each country from 2005 to 2007. The data have been continuously updated, and during recent years I have interviewed many interviewees a second or third time. The international perspective was further explored in June 2013, during a flurry of substantive interviews conducted in Washington, DC.[6] The empirical chapters are based on semi-structured interviews with key stakeholders at all levels of government, together with conversations with and observations of many technical bureaucrats working with the programs on a day-to-day basis (when I have used any direct quotes from interviews at this bureaucratic level, they are labeled as "anonymous") and the analysis of primary documents of government data, national statistics, and national media sources. The empirical analysis relies on straightforward descriptive statistics and simple odds ratios. National statistical databases were also utilized, although the majority of program data cited were directly supplied from the directorates of the responsible offices. All interview material and government-supplied program data were triangulated across a variety of ministerial offices at multiple levels of government to ensure their accuracy.

Brazil and Argentina were chosen for comparison because of their similarities. Each has three levels of government, national, state/provincial, and municipal, as well as a bicameral national legislature elected by proportional representation and an executive presidential system. As highlighted within the central argument, from a federal perspective both of these countries are classified as strong federal systems (Mexico, for example, is not). They do, however, have unique institutional characteristics that only become visible through a comparative study such as this one. Where they most stand apart is in the variation that can be found by disaggregating the subnational layer into two separate levels— that of the core federal units called states in Brazil and provinces in Argentina, and that of the local level, which I will refer to throughout the book as municipalities.[7] It will be emphasized throughout, however, that the importance of municipalities in Brazil is determined by much more than simply their constitutional recognition. The varying degrees of majoritarianism found within these democratic systems have a clear effect on the willingness of municipalities to collaborate with the federal government and, ultimately, on social policy outcomes, a finding that will be shown to be counterintuitive to the dominant literature.

A large number of cross-national analyses rely on the aggregation of municipalities to the core federal units (states and provinces) to constitute what is referred to in the literature as "the subnational." This practice is flawed because it assumes that municipalities are unable to have any effect independent from the provinces or states within a federal system. Therefore, when this book refers to subnational levels, it is referring to them both, and it is used in the plural because in all federal countries there are at least two levels, if not more, of subnational government. Thus when the term "subnational" is applied, it is to be understood in ordinary terms as a contradistinction to national. Most frequently, each level will be referred to separately. One of the main conceptual goals of this study is to show how the frequent practice of aggregating the subnational level into one unified actor has limited the scope of our comparative explanations. I aim to establish that when municipalities are recognized as a distinct level of government from the core federal units, we find that they can assist the president in avoiding some of the undermining constraints of a strong federal system.

In terms of alternative arguments and explanations, there are several; however, the case selection of Brazil and Argentina eliminates most of these by design. In terms of social and economic context, both countries have weathered constitutional reforms that have changed their federal structures, and each has attempted fiscal reforms in order to correct the macroeconomic instability that was partly produced by perverse subnational spending during the 1980s and early 1990s. Most important for this book's policy significance, both countries have persistent problems of emerging poverty resulting from a decade of macroeconomic policy experimentation that left each government in a situation of social deficit toward its citizens. Addressing this deficit was confronted in similar ways by both national governments. Since the late 1990s, each country has experimented with various CCTs at all levels of government, designed and financed from both national and subnational resources, and supported by various political parties of diverse ideological and partisan basis—all with varying successes in alleviating poverty and in enabling the future-oriented goals of such programs.

Although it could be argued additionally that the municipal origins of CCTs in Brazil facilitated the local promotion efforts inherent to Bolsa Família's success, this is a tautological argument that is very difficult to sustain. Many of these earlier subnational CCTs also continue to operate today—the City of São Paulo, for example, promotes three CCTs, local, state, and federal.[8] Moreover, the City of Buenos Aires designed and financed a CCT program that began in 2004, Ciudadanía Porteña, which is both highly successful and has been sustained over alternations of executive power.[9] This local CCT, however, has not been diffused throughout Argentina, and it did not increase the city's willingness to either promote or enable Programa Familias, which the city deemed "incompatible" with the majority of its self-financed, noncontributory social protection programs (interview Pucciarelli 2006; interview anonymous Ministerio de Desarrollo Social 2006; interview Ibarra 2006).

Equally difficult to sustain is an ideologically based argument to explain the performance of national CCTs. First, there was no single political party or ideology in Brazil that could claim credit for the early innovations, nor was it the case that the municipalities that adhered to Bolsa Família during its implementation and expansion phases were uniquely governed by the PT (Partido dos Trabalhadores, or, the left of center "Workers' Party"). The PT did not govern the majority of states and municipalities where Bolsa Família was distributed. Second, the ideological differences between Lula and the two Kirchners were not great; true, as a political party Brazil's PT is much more programmatic than Argentina's PJ (Partido Justicialista), but the PT has never governed the majority of Brazil's 5,564 municipalities, all of which autonomously adhered to Bolsa Família by 2009. In fact, if ideological or partisan considerations were driving the performance of CCTs measured in terms of their territorial distribution, then this should be best exemplified in Argentina, where even though the provinces are institutionally heterogeneous, the PJ controls far more provinces and municipalities than the PT could ever imagine.

What about each nation's concerns with poverty? Citizens in Latin America care increasingly about poverty and inequality, and Brazil and Argentina are no exceptions. Both countries shared similar levels of public perceptions regarding poverty around the time of the inception of CCTs. According to the 2004 Latinobarometro survey, both Brazil and Argentina considered poverty to be the fourth most important problem in each country, after violence, unemployment, and lack of income security.[10] Additionally, according to the World Values Survey (1995–1998), which was conducted around the time that social protection policy began to take priority in each of the two countries selected for analysis, over 75 percent of citizens in each country believed that "the poor are poor because society is unjust." This is over ten percentage points higher than the region's average.

Also in a parallel process, following democratization each country faced rampant inflation and macroeconomic instability, problems that were then effectively resolved. Because of their geographical proximity and export commodity dependence, important external factors that could present alternative explanations for their policy outcomes were equally a challenge in both of these selected cases—that is, in experimental terms it is not possible to say that one case was exposed to a stimulus to which the other was not. In both countries, the potentially positive effects of government decentralization and local democratization could not be achieved until critical issues of macroeconomic stability were resolved. While it is certain that Argentina's ability to achieve this important goal was more tenuous than Brazil's, it was nonetheless achieved not once but twice. It would be extremely difficult to assert, based on these two selected cases, that macroeconomic instability explains why either Argentina or Brazil could not easily encourage municipalities to promote a national social program designed to alleviate poverty. Each country faced inflation and then stabilized its currency successfully during the mid-1990s.

Voter turnout, which is compulsory by law in both countries, is in fact quite high compared to the rest of the region. According to Diaz and Payne (2007, 252), the average turnout in the presidential elections from 1990 to 2004 was 80.7 percent in Argentina and 81 percent in Brazil. These two countries stand apart, however, in terms of what the Inter-American Development Bank's Network on Public Policy Management and Transparency called the "Bureaucratic Merit and Functional Capacity Indexes" (Stein et al. 2005, 68–69). On a 0–100 scale, Brazil stands out as the highest in the region on each index, with over 80 points on merit and 60 on functional capacity. By contrast, Argentina has just over 50 points on the merit index and fewer than 50 on the functional capacity index, which still places it within the top five countries of the region (Stein et al. 2005, 69). The use of patronage in Argentina's bureaucratic appointments weakens both its merit and its capacity, although in this regard it is well ahead of Mexico, which has still managed quite successfully to deliver poverty alleviation benefits in absolute terms following a top-down strategy that was dependent on "congressional" collaboration.

It is because of similar domestic and regional governing challenges that it is feasible to establish a general empirical proposition, based on a cross-case analysis of these two selected countries both classified as strong federal systems, that has wide theoretical implications for both federal theory and public policy studies.

SIGNIFICANCE AND OVERVIEW

An important area of targeted social welfare was chosen as the focused comparison in the current book because of the observable variation on the outcome variable: Brazil's Bolsa Família successfully dismantled, reformed, and transformed Bolsa Escola, and it continues today under current president Rousseff; whereas Argentina's Programa Familias (2002–2009) was not able to successfully dismantle, reform, and transform the Program for Unemployed Heads of Households (PJJHD) as intended, and it was discontinued in 2009. Both the institutional determinants of these programs' outcomes and the policy feedbacks that emerged from them provide an important lens for viewing how federalism affects the ability of a national government to invest socially and to pursue social development in general. Federalism does not necessarily entail a "race to the bottom" in social welfare, and decentralization does not necessarily equate to a shrinking state and weakened national capacity. Important lessons can be learned from nations experimenting with these particular social programs, that is, with CCTs, and can be applied to other important emerging social policy areas linked to a social investment agenda, such as universal early childhood care and education. Targeted social welfare depends on both the ability of a central government to pursue it as a national policy objective, and the willingness of local governments to promote and monitor such policies on the ground.

From an international development perspective, the consensus is that CCTs originating in Latin America are an effective and coherent policy instrument that is part of a global social investment agenda.

Nevertheless, the success of the intended future-oriented goals of a CCT, which are also tied to expanding the social rights of citizenship, is dependent on the ability of a national government to ensure its territorial distribution and to guarantee the type of subnational collaboration that is required to promote access (demand-side and supply-side). The intended outcomes and the sustainability of CCTs are therefore determined by domestic factors and actors and not by international policy prescriptions.

By highlighting a contrast between these two federal cases, a key finding of this study is that broad institutional, structural, and political variables are more important to pursuing a national social investment agenda than the technical design of specific programs. Contrary to the mainstream interpretations of Brazilian politics and institutions, this study shows that federal arrangements in Brazil have contributed to the relative success of its CCTs. In Argentina, in contrast, the structural, political and fiscal incentives for intergovernmental policy-based cooperation have not been adequate, at least thus far, to consolidate a CCT program that is based on human capital investments designed to achieve future-oriented goals.

The next chapter explores the origins and the rise of CCTs in Latin America and then demonstrates from a theoretical perspective how a federal system of government can constrain the ability of the center to realize its goals of delivering collective welfare goods polity-wide. In a more systematic way, it then builds the central argument by introducing further the three key explanatory factors. Chapters 3 and 4 present the Brazilian case. Chapter 3 extensively traces the politics of the evolution and development of noncontributory social protection policy and then empirically analyzes the territorial distribution of Bolsa Família itself. Chapter 4 confronts the claims put forward in chapter 2 against the empirical evidence from Brazil. Chapters 5 and 6 present the Argentine case; they are designed to mirror the Brazilian chapters. The concluding chapter, chapter 7, returns to the explanatory factors and their propositions in order to review the model in light of the empirical analysis and to highlight lessons learned and potential areas (and approaches) for future research.

Federalism, the Welfare State, and the Rise of CCTs in Latin America

The quality of democracy, then, depends on social democracy,
on long-sustained policies of social protection and solidarity.
—Rueschemeyer, "Addressing Inequality"

Conditional cash transfer programs, broadly defined, are social programs that transfer small amounts of cash to socially vulnerable families, who are usually selected through some form of means testing. In return, program recipients must meet certain conditions that are linked to fulfilling human development goals in the areas of health, education, and nutrition. It is specifically the conditions themselves that are intended to break the intergenerational transmission of poverty, not the actual transfer of cash. CCTs are a form of noncontributory social protection, a policy area that in theory sits within the jurisdiction of local governments because of its association with social assistance, yet in practice can operate, and has operated, at all three levels of government in most federal countries. These national social programs have played a considerable role in expanding social policy regimes in Latin America to cover families outside of the formal labor market. They are also an integral part of a global social investment agenda that prioritizes social policy for its ability to "protect" the weak and vulnerable (children, women, and the poor)[1] and to promote social "inclusion" and "cohesion."

In this chapter I first briefly explain the rise of CCTs in Latin America in the context of this book and discuss some of the myths surrounding this policy idea. Next, by demonstrating from a theoretical perspective how "strong federalism" can constrain the ability of a national government to expand its social policy regime and to guarantee the basic rights of social citizenship, I will argue that measuring the territorial distribution of authority is insufficient for understanding who does what, how, and why in a federal system of government. Finally, I suggest that municipalities can facilitate the ability of the national government to deliver targeted social policy goods and to pursue a social investment strategy, if certain political and institutional conditions are present.

The interactions between federalism and the growth of the welfare state are well documented. With particular reference to the developed world, studies of federalism and the welfare state form an integral part of institutionalist-based explanations of change and, more often than not, of the institutional "ratchet effect," where federalism has been shown to hinder both retrenchment and the development of "new" welfare states.[2] Although macro-quantitative and macro-qualitative studies have often elucidated the ability of federalism to limit welfare state expansion, micro-qualitative research has shown that it is very difficult to draw general conclusions about the impact of federalism on the welfare state because of institutional variation between countries and between policy sectors within a given country (Béland 2010b, 60). Moreover, increasing attention is being paid to the reciprocal relationship between the two, where federalism shapes the growth of social policy, and the development of social policy impacts the growth and identity of the state.[3]

Until quite recently, the concept of the welfare state, as it is has been employed in the institutionalist literature mentioned above, was seldom found in the Latin American literature (Huber and Bogliaccini 2010, 644). Particularly, the concept of noncontributory social protection, a key component of any modern state that provides a basic social safety net to citizens attached to the social rights of citizenship, has seldom had a place in the Latin American literature.

Traditionally, in Latin America's wealthier countries, such as Argentina, Brazil, Chile, and Uruguay, social protection was linked to formal social insurance policy, a policy area that was never associated with eliminating poverty or redistributing wealth, but was rather about incorporating the urban middle class and working class into the state— a state that has both a strong colonial and a patrimonial heritage (Malloy 1993; Collier and Collier 1991). Of great importance is the fact that social policy regimes in Latin America have previously been tied to a social citizenship discourse, but access to these social rights has not been equally granted to all members of society and all territories within the nation. Entrenched historical inequalities thus deepened during the early stages of social policy expansion in Latin America.

It is therefore imperative to understand that in contrast to federal countries in Europe and the New World, where the emphasis is on the ability of federalism to provide diversity in social policy (self-rule) in conjunction with uniformity (shared-rule), in that order of importance, in Latin America a "social investment welfare state"[4] and the social policies that constitute it must emphasize the ability and capacity of a central state power to ensure similar programs and benefits to all citizens regardless of where they reside. More often than not, the ability of Latin American federalism to provide diversity in public policy has resulted in entire territorial entities having little or no access to real income, goods, and services. This has denied entire groups of society the access to social rights, or, as Stephens puts it (2010, 513), "the right to active participation in society."

The capacity of federal governments in Latin America to provide social protection and break the intergenerational transmission of poverty is dependent on intergovernmental policy collaboration, collaboration that for a plethora of reasons has been difficult to guarantee. Therefore, it needs to be reiterated that the goal of this research is to evaluate how federalism affects the ability of a central government to pursue a national social investment agenda that is intended to expand social citizenship rights, not how federalism enables diversity in public policy, reflecting the preferences of regional communities and cultures (Banting 1995). This is a key distinction between studies of federalism and social policy in the developed world and studies rooted in the developing world; a priori, the central state's ability to deliver basic social rights should be guaranteed before regional diversity ought to be encouraged.

The ability either to deliver targeted social welfare or, stated otherwise, to ensure access to those with the most need to basic social services in any system where power is formally divided among multiple levels of government, requires intergovernmental collaboration. The idea that social policy framed as a national social investment can be designed and implemented by avoiding both governors and mayors will be shown in this book to be both false and unsustainable over the long term. The policy inputs (supply-side) of any social investment initiative within a *decentralized* federal or nonfederal context, and their quality— a factor that is fundamental to achieving the desired policy outputs, which include higher levels of educational attainment, basic nutrition, and health—require local collaboration. This is particularly true when conditionality is not punitive but rather used as a mechanism that necessitates the intervention of local actors and social assistance networks when compliance is not met. It is for this reason that domestic variables have been emphasized for policy outcomes, and not the transnational actors and processes that are often highlighted in CCT research.[5] Evaluating the impact of these programs will not be explored in this book. Many systematic and influential studies have already been conducted on this question (including Hoddinot, Skoufias, and Washburn 2000; Barrientos and Lloyd-Sherlock 2002; Vinocur and Halperin 2004; Handa and Davis 2006; Ronconi et al. 2006; Lindert, Skoufias, and Shapiro 2006; Parker, Rubalcava, and Terurel 2008; Soares, F. V., Ribas, and Osório 2010).[6] Suffice it to say, when properly targeted, CCTs have been empirically shown to reduce poverty and generate a downward pressure on inequality measures. Impact evaluations of CCTs in reducing the intergenerational transmission of poverty, particularly in the area of education, remain inconclusive. Their expected future-oriented outcomes are increasingly recognized in international social policy circles as being linked to the *quality* of the social services provided.

Poverty and inequality additionally pose considerable threats to the quality of democracy in developing countries. Economic inequality is inextricably tied to the degree of both social and political equality. Poverty means not only a lack of economic resources but also a loss of political voice (Rueschemeyer 2004, 83). The ability of all citizens to use their political voice is of fundamental importance to the practice of any democracy. Moreover, the inability of any government to provide some degree of income security to a large number of its citizens calls into question the efficiency and effectiveness of that government in "protecting" and "delivering" the political and social rights of citizenship inherent to liberal democracy. It should also be noted that adequate minimum income protection is a critical precondition for an effective social investment strategy that seeks to reconcile social and economic goals (Hemerijck 2012, 49). For Esping-Andersen et al. (2002), "high social protection" is a fundamental pillar of an active welfare state because it is inextricably tied to the right to participate.

In Brazil and Argentina, social protection appeared on the federal agenda in the late 1990s, subsequent to macroeconomic stabilization, when it became clear that low inflation and the reduction of social expenditure, both part of the *Zeitgeist* of neoliberal economic policies in the 1980s, could not protect a substantial proportion of each country's citizens. According to Lloyd-Sherlock, sound development strategies such as neoliberalism failed to produce the intended long-term results of social welfare because "policymakers were unable to take into account key intervening variables such as unforeseen external shocks, political factors, and the consistency of implementation" (1997, 22). The macroeconomic stabilization and low inflation that were achieved in both Brazil and Argentina during the mid-1990s did produce short-term positive effects for poverty reduction. Lloyd-Sherlock's prediction, however, was correct. National policymakers in both countries had not taken into consideration the effects that unforeseen shocks and political factors would have on the lower earners of each society in the late 1990s, and on those permanently excluded groups whose inclusion in an ever-changing labor market seemed even more remote.

SOCIAL PROTECTION AS A PROACTIVE SOCIAL POLICY

An emerging consensus among international development specialists and development agencies, such as the Inter-American Development Bank and the World Bank, and among national governments in Latin America and Europe is that social protection policies must be developed and strengthened to reduce the intergenerational transmission of poverty. Poverty alleviation is a strategic area of social policy from a political perspective because it has long been held that both the amount of poverty and inequality in a country and the impact of policy on these factors are important indicators of national policy success (Saunders 2010, 526). From an economic perspective, poverty and inequality are also considered bad for any economy. The Institute of Development Studies at the University of Sussex defines social protection as follows:

> Social protection describes all public and private initiatives that provide income or consumption transfers to the poor, protect the vulnerable against livelihood risks, and enhance the social status and rights of the marginalized; with the overall objective of reducing the economic and social vulnerability of poor, vulnerable and marginalized groups.[7]

I apply this definition throughout my research, although I am only interested in the politics of *publicly* provided social protection goods that are considered to be social investments, as opposed to passive welfare expenditure. Additionally, when I use the term "social protection," I am referring only to *noncontributory* social protection schemes. This means simply that the beneficiaries of such schemes have not made a formal payroll or tax contribution providing them with an automatic "entitlement" to benefits such as formal social insurance. Thus, at no point in this book does "social protection" imply formal social insurance or traditional social assistance.

In Latin America, the idea of framing noncontributory social protection policy within the context of a liberal rights discourse that is attached to a theory of the state is relatively novel. Outside of the region, the idea of a "social service state"[8] became prevalent in Western Europe around the end of the nineteenth century in the form of "poor laws." Notwithstanding this, the provision of social rights remained detached from the concept of citizenship until the later development of the idea of a universal right to real income (Marshall [1950] 2006). The delivery of social protection "goods" analyzed within this research derives from this concept of a universal right to real income, goods, and services, which is not proportionate to the market value of the claimant, but rather is attached to the status of citizenship within a democratic context. Nevertheless, CCTs are a form of noncontributory social protection whose benefits are "targeted" to the most vulnerable and are generally based on some form of "means testing," which makes them fundamentally part of a neoliberal welfare model.

During most of the 1980s and into the mid-1990s, Latin America's economic growth was negative, leading to dramatic cuts in social spending and fueling "new" poverty (see table 2.1). Gradually, a "liberal-informal welfare regime" emerged in Latin America, which relies on individuals and families making private provision for themselves (Barrientos 2004, 146). This regime, however, remains both informal and weak as it struggles to provide a basic public safety net that "ensures all citizens should attain at least to the prescribed minimum, either by their own resources or with assistance if they could not do it without" (Marshall 2006, 37).

For structural, political, and strategic reasons, continual progress has been made in Latin America since the late 1990s toward achieving

Table 2.1. Social Insurance Coverage, Poverty, and Growth Rates in Federal Latin America

	Formal Social Insurance Coverage in Federal Latin America (%)		Poverty Rates (%)		Average Annual Growth in GDP per Capita (%)
Country	1980	1998	1981	2002	1980–2004
Argentina	69.1	20.2	8	35	0.3
Brazil	87	34.5	43	30	0.53
Mexico	42	8.2	29	33	0.64
Venezuela	49.8	8.6	22	43	−0.87

Source: Barrientos 2004.

Marshall's social citizenship goal by including socially vulnerable families that are not part of the formal labor market. Such progress has been predominantly made through targeted social welfare programs such as CCTs, which originated in Brazil at the municipal level and were first developed nationally in Mexico. Today, countries throughout the region have all implemented varying forms of CCTs attached to human capital investments intended to break the intergenerational transmission of poverty.

Cash transfers can be both conditional (offering "cash for work," or depending on health or education requirements) or unconditional (for the elderly, disabled, and extreme poor). Within this research, only conditional ones are being considered. It is specifically the conditions themselves that are dependent on supply-side policy inputs (falling within various subnational social policy jurisdictions within a decentralized federal context) that are intended to break the intergenerational transmission of poverty. That is, it is not the delivery of cash per se that breaks the intergenerational transmission of poverty; rather, it is the knowledge the child obtains from attending school, the protective vaccination a child receives, or the access to basic health services that drives the virtuous circle of inclusion that is expected to break the permanent exclusion created by illiteracy, malnutrition, and chronic illness. Even though it is accepted in the literature on the welfare state in the developed world and within more liberal-oriented international development communities that welfare conditionality is intended to induce behavioral change, in small and medium-sized municipalities in Brazil in particular, program conditionality is linked in practice to solving more pragmatic problems.[9] Welfare conditions, when tied to the often badly needed receipt of cash, however small the amount, create a demand for access to basic social services that was previously absent and, equally, the need for a local supply of such services. It is for this reason that the local monitoring of conditions is more important than their national enforcement. Why did a user fail to comply with a CCT requirement? Is it because their child suffers from an untreated chronic illness, or because the school is too far from the child's home, or has no books or even teachers? Welfare conditionality, in a developing context, can uniquely transmit knowledge downward, but it can also send knowledge upward to national ministries of health, education, and social development. Given the importance of local service providers and the role of local actors in supplying information as to why individual human development investments may be locally constrained, it becomes very difficult to conceive how national governments can "go it alone" when it comes to investing socially across territorially diverse areas that are institutionally, administratively, historically, ideologically, socially, economically, and culturally defined.

THE DEVELOPMENT OF CCT PROGRAMS IN LATIN AMERICA

Latin American countries, in particular Brazil and Mexico, were pioneers in developing CCTs as a way to target socially vulnerable families and to develop a minimum social safety net for these households. The first large-scale national CCT was launched under President Ernesto Zedillo in 1997, under the name of Progresa (Mexico), followed by Bolsa Escola (Brazil), launched by President Fernando Henrique Cardoso in 2001. These two original CCT programs can be considered indigenous to each country in the sense that they were initially designed and financed without the help of development banks (Handa and Davis 2006, 514). The motivating foundational idea, however, which was to target poverty with human capital investments, has its roots beyond the region and should be considered transnational. Of equal importance, the subsequent country-level developments that led, in Mexico in 2002, to the expansion of CCTs from rural to urban coverage and, in Brazil in 2003, to the expansion of CCTs from a compartmentalized (education only) to an integrative approach (health, education, and nutrition) were heavily influenced by transnational policy actors and networks, backed by international financing and "globalized" through international media proliferation.[10] As can be witnessed in the World Bank's *World Development Report 2012: Gender Equality and Development*, this policy instrument has currently become so entrenched that highly influential development agencies (somewhat alarmingly) have reduced social policy and social protection discussions almost exclusively to CCTs, with a focus on sub-Saharan Africa (see Razavi 2012).

Following the "municipal era" of CCT development in Brazil (1995–2001), numerous other countries in the region created national programs based on the idea of using cash transfer programs to confront poverty; these included Mexico (1997), Honduras (1998), Colombia, Costa Rica, and Nicaragua (2000), Brazil and Jamaica (2001), Argentina and Chile (2002), Ecuador (2003), and the Dominican Republic, El Salvador, Paraguay, Peru, and Uruguay (2005).[11] In 1995, this policy instrument was first experimented with in two Brazilian cities, Brasilia and Campinas, and then propelled throughout the country.[12] Today, a broad consensus has been reached among international organizations and national governments throughout the developing world that CCTs are an effective policy instrument to alleviate poverty (Barrientos 2004; Handa and Davis 2006; Razavi 2012). This consensus and the rate of emulation and spread of CCTs are largely attributed to the early and rapid successes of national-level CCTs in Mexico (1997) and Brazil (2001) and their established positive impact—which, beyond providing high promise, garnered international support. According to Weyland's theory of policy diffusion (2007, 8), "the representativeness heuristic induces policy-makers to jump on the bandwagon of a diffusion process." Aside from Weyland's idea, which essentially means that CCTs represent an available solution to a pressing problem, the normative idea behind CCTs is symbolically embedded in a rights-based framework that is appealing to the international community. Thus, beyond being framed by words such as "targeting efficiency" and "program effectiveness," the arguments for CCTs are also framed using the discourses of citizenship and social justice. These normative frameworks, plus the fact that CCTs have been empirically shown to reduce poverty, have enabled the idea of CCTs to become both nationally appealing and internationally legitimate.

THE MYTHS AND ORIGINS OF CCTS

There are many myths surrounding the origins of CCTs. The programmatic ideas, policy goals, and discourses that led to pioneering policy experimentation in Latin America and the eventual formulation of coherent policy instruments to reduce poverty from a social investment perspective have their roots beyond regional actors and arose from multiple sources. As Béland and Orenstein (2013) assert, beyond the role of financial loans and material interests in policy diffusion and transnational influence, ideational processes play a major role in shaping domestic policy development. In the case of CCTs, former Brazilian president Fernando Henrique Cardoso clearly stated in a televised interview that although the actual subnational and eventual national program experiments of Bolsa Escola were Brazilian, the basic idea of combining short-term poverty alleviation with long-term human capital investment came from within the World Bank during the 1980s, following the failure of a neoliberal discourse.[13] This earlier discourse objected to almost any state intervention in development policies. Its eventual failure was parallel with the rise in legitimacy of a newer discourse centered on ideas of human capital development and the idea of a "third way." These latter ideas were foundationally based on the work of key development economists such as Amartya Sen and social theorist Anthony Giddens.

This new interpretive framework for understanding poverty was heavily propelled and supported in the developing world by international institutions such as the World Bank, the Inter-American Development Bank, and a host of UN bodies such as UNICEF and UNESCO. These agencies reached a broad international consensus during the 1990s over what the World Bank termed a "two-pronged approach" to social protection: economic growth combined with investment in poor people's human capital—human capital that would be expanded through investments in basic health and primary education, and via well-targeted safety nets provided by the state (Lipton and Ravallion 1995, 2571). Therefore, it is feasible to claim that the overarching goals that guided social protection policy and motivated states in Latin America to experiment with CCTs in the mid-1990s amounted to a broadly conceived transnational policy paradigm, which was based on the idea of targeted cash transfers and investing in human capital to alleviate poverty for future generations.

Nevertheless, the actual techniques and the specific policy instruments used to develop targeted social safety nets came from Brazil and Mexico. Brazil's first documented experimentation with such programs began during the mid-1990s. The intellectual background of Mexico's national CCT program Progresa (1997) can be found in the work of Santiago Levy's 1991 paper, "Extreme Poverty in Mexico: A Policy Proposal." Levy, an economist and the former director of Social Security in Mexico (IMSS), was a key actor in the design of former Mexican president Carlos Salinas's National Solidarity Program, PRONASOL (1988),[14] and the central architect of Zedillo's Progresa, later renamed by President Fox's administration as Opportunidades (2002). This CCT has since been renamed Prospera by President Enrique Peña Nieto (2014).

From a policy perspective, the general aim behind publicly supported CCTs in Latin America is twofold. They are intended to promote social inclusion, drawing on a liberal rights-based perspective (Barrientos 2004), and to alleviate poverty now and in the future, drawing on a social investment perspective (Jenson and San Martin 2003). From a political perspective, the goals of such programs are also twofold. They are intended to address, first, a large social deficit that amassed during a decade of economic stagnation, which began as early as 1982 in Mexico and subsequently spread south (failure of the market).[15] And, second, they are intended to create a direct relationship between the government and its citizens that bypasses political intermediaries who, by patronage and corruption, reputedly often prevent benefits from reaching the people who require them most (failure of the state).

From a development perspective, the successful implementation of social protection programs in the developing world is dependent on three key factors in order to be considered effective. These are (1) adequate and sustained financing; (2) administrative and management capacity; and (3) political commitment (Devereux and Gorman 2006). All three factors within a federal system are determined by multiple levels of government often competing within a game, which is unique to each country. Within my research, I use Filippov, Ordeshook, and Shvetsova's definition of federalism because it assumes the existence of democracy. They define federalism as

> a government structure that can be characterized by multiple layers (national, regional, and local) such that at each level the chief policy makers—presidents, governors, mayors, legislatures, judges—are elected directly by the people they serve, or, are appointed by public officials thus directly elected at that level. (2004, 9)

Achieving a national social policy goal within a political system where multiple levels of government share authority becomes a dual challenge. First, federalism requires national legislative cooperation in order to pursue executive policy preferences, and second, it requires subnational levels of government to carry out or to promote national policy objectives. My research is most interested in the latter problem. According to the late Richard Simeon,

> Governments [national, regional, and local] are interdependent, so that initiatives taken at one level have immediate consequences for the other. The programs available to citizens, and the tax burdens to pay for them, are a combined product of what all the governments do. This suggests that any re-thinking or restructuring of public finances or the welfare state which is to meet the needs of citizens requires a coordinated effort with all the governments working together.[16]

Simeon was referring to Canada, but the theoretical rationale can be applied to all federal systems of government. To enable the delivery of social protection as a national policy objective requires a strategy of multilevel governance, whereby multiple tiers of government and policy sectors cooperate. Once a national government has made the decision to offer social investment goods to alleviate its citizens' poverty, its success, measured by its ability to territorially distribute these goods nationwide, will be determined by the institutional characteristics of that country's political order and the political willingness of key political actors. As stated simply by George Tsebelis, "if different characteristics of political systems are significant it must be because of the effects they have on policy outcomes" (2000, 441).

Empirically in this research, I identify varying policy outcomes from two national CCTs in Brazil and Argentina. Since both countries have federal systems of government, the difference is to be found *within* federalism itself. The reasons why municipalities promoted or failed to promote a national policy objective designed to alleviate poverty will be explored in depth. The broader theoretical questions embedded within this specific policy focus are, What are the varying political and institutional characteristics of each federal system that have affected the ability of each national government, both in theory and in practice, to achieve its *ex-post* policy objective? How does this impact the stability of these policy objectives? And what general lessons can be drawn for other strong federal systems or heavily decentralized countries experimenting with CCTs?

FEDERALISM AS A SYSTEM OF CONSTRAINTS

In 1964, William Riker stated in the preface to his seminal work that federalism emanates from one source but exists across many diverse institutional and cultural settings. The one source he had in mind was the Constitution of the United States of America, whose ratification during 1787–1788 was well documented in the eighty-five newspaper editorials known as the Federalist Papers. The main dilemmas of federalism can be found in this collection, primarily in James Madison's paper no. 10.

This paper addressed one of the public's central concerns (or, stated otherwise, complaints over federalism) that "our governments [states] are too unstable, that the public good is disregarded in the conflicts of rival parties, and that measures are too often decided, not according to rules of justice and the rights of the minority party, but by the superior force of an interested and overbearing majority" (Ball 2006, 40). In other words, two of the main theoretical concerns about federalism that Madison identified were that it *could* lead to government instability, because the pursuit of public goods was compromised by party-based competition, and that policy decisions were made by a powerful majority and not by the minority groups within the polity, which could lead to factionalism. Madison contended that the threat of factionalism could be cured by the ability of the union (central government) to control its effects. Thus the early concerns of federalism were over how to control factions so "that the public voice pronounced by the representatives of the people, will be more consonant to the public good" (Ball 2006, 44). The answer, to repeat, could be found in the ability of the central authority to control the effects of factionalism.

Riker's theoretical concern, in contrast to Madison's, was about the ability of the central authority to encroach upon the constituent units. His answer was the power of the states: "What is important about federalism is the constitutionally assured potential for local [state] governments to distrupt, this is how they act as a restraint on the federal government" (Riker and Schaps 1987, 74). Although the principle of "disharmony" is admired by many federal theorists, particularly in countries with significant ethno-linguistic divisions, it also challenges the ability of the central government to provide what Shugart calls "broad national collective goods" (1999, 54). The ideal goal of federalism, at any rate in the twenty-first century, is to simultaneously enable the central state to provide national collective goods in the name of public interest, while still allowing constituent units and other groups within the federation to be represented and, ideally, to have localized input.

Today (and historically during democratic periods), Brazil and Argentina are considered "strong" federal systems because their core federal units compete continually with the central government for greater autonomy over governing their territories. This competition reduces the leverage of the national government over its subnational tiers. Theoretically, this makes federalism more robust, because the central government is structurally restrained from encroaching upon its units (Riker's concern). However, its units must also be prevented from disregarding the public good by undermining and free-riding on the center (Madison's concern). These theoretical considerations led to what Figueiredo and Weingast identify as the two dilemmas of federalism: (1) the *general dilemma*—what prevents the central government from destroying federalism by overawing its units, and (2) the *local dilemma*—what prevents subnational units from undermining federalism through noncooperation and free-riding (2005, 104). They additionally contend within the tradition of equilibrium institutionalism that both dilemmas must be resolved together, because resolving only one will exacerbate the other, leading to suboptimal outcomes (Figueiredo and Weingast 2005).

Federal systems of government are based on the territorial fragmentation of power. This fragmentation of power makes it difficult for a nonconsensual will to form and to be sustained. Fragmentation accomplished through an official territorial division of power, however, requires "the cooperation of different institutions, accountable to different constituencies, before significant policy shifts can be made" (Bednar, Eskridge, and Ferejohn 2001, 230), policy shifts that ultimately affect the general public. In practice, not all of the institutional contexts of a federation engender such intergovernmental cooperation. The central argument of this book, therefore, depends on the assumption that Brazil and Argentina are both strong federal systems that have had difficulties during the most recent democratic period in preventing subnational units from undermining the national government through free-riding and noncooperation, and from disregarding the public good. From a theoretical perspective, the local dilemma is inherent to the "politics of governors" in Brazil and Argentina.

In all federal systems, the center and its constituent units bargain over the allocation of federal powers. During democratic periods in both Brazil and Argentina, governors have demonstrated that they have the ability to capture national legislators within their parties, or those representing their states, in order to exert pressure on the center to achieve their desired ends—which have not always been virtuous. This power struggle among federal units can lead to what Filippov, Ordeshook, and Shvetsova call "undesirable bargaining" or "non-institutionalized bargaining" and can destabilize the larger institutional setting that is required to ensure gradual change as a society evolves and new circumstances arise (2004, 68–76). In Brazil, because of a highly fragmented and relatively undisciplined multiparty system, among other factors, gubernatorial influence over national legislators has historically constrained the center's ability both to pursue required political and economic reforms and to deliver public goods. The power of governors historically weakened governability. In Argentina, where the power of governors emanates from a provincially organized and a more disciplined party system, the effect on the federal center has been similar. Governors have contributed at various times in Argentina's democratic history to destabilizing the larger political institutional context. For example in the late 1980s and 1990s, powerful governors in both Brazil and Argentina contributed directly to worsening economic crises and ultimately to hyperinflation (Eaton 2004b, 143).

Therefore, when I imply that municipalities, recognized as a distinct order of government (under certain institutional conditions), can facilitate the ability of the national government to either regulate or provide public goods (avoiding governors), I am referring to strong federal systems that are struggling with the local dilemma of federalism (center-constraining) and that exhibit high degrees of Samuels and Mainwaring's institutional variables. These four variables were the resource base of subnational governments, the power of governors, the articulation of subnational interests in the national legislature, and the policy jurisdiction of subnational governments (2004, 101–2). The unique challenge for strong federal systems is to reduce the salience of the local dilemma, or at least move toward the middle of the continuum.

FEDERALISM AS DECENTRALIZATION

One of the key structural features of a federal system of government is the division of power across multiple levels of government and, more generally, at least some degree of formal decentralization. How independent these multiple levels of government are in relation to one another, however, is not prescribed theoretically. The dynamic relationship among two or more levels of government is determined in federal and federation-like nations[17] by processes of evolving intergovernmental relations that swing like a pendulum between centralized and decentralized power—power that is usually measured as the territorial distribution of authority.

Intergovernmental relations have been most commonly examined in the literature on Latin America using the concept of government decentralization, especially during the 1990s. These studies defined decentralization as a shift in authority from the national toward the subnational (regional and local), on the basis of measurements of fiscal, political, and policy autonomy. With these empirical measurements as benchmarks, many authors sought to understand the political determinants of decisions to transfer authority in order to gauge the real intergovernmental distribution of power (Souza 1997; Willis, Garman, and Haggard 1999).

More recently, authors have suggested improvements to the various subconcepts of decentralization in order to refine their measurements. There is a consensus that fiscal decentralization could be measured more accurately by including additional empirical measures, such as "subnational revenue autonomy" (Schneider 2003; Rodden 2004). Including measures of revenue and own-source income definitely improves the ability of researchers to gauge the complexity of fiscal relations. In Latin America, finance does or did not always follow function; there is a frequent contradiction between centralized revenue arrangements and decentralized subnational expenditure responsibility.[18]

As for policy decentralization (equally referred to as administrative decentralization), an analysis of the extent of authority in social areas such as health and education does not always allow us to understand whether the rulers of subnational units have greater influence over health care and education simply because the Constitution says they do. Earlier theorists tried to overcome this problem by introducing the concepts of "deconcentration, delegation and devolution" (Rondinelli 1980), although such terms are rarely used today to understand the complex dynamics of administrative decentralization. Others, such as Rodden, have questioned the validity of measuring policy decentralization altogether, concluding that "the decentralization of policy autonomy is rarely addressed by empirical scholars because it is difficult to measure" (2004, 486).

In terms of measuring political decentralization, our traditional measure—free and direct regional and local elections—is also now somewhat outdated, given that nearly all Latin American countries have such elections. Within what is now, for the most part, a region of consolidated procedural democracies, this measure does not adequately capture the degree of subnational political autonomy.

The de facto political issues behind the territorial distribution of power in Latin America are not easily assessed using rigidly defined empirical measurements of decentralization. To do so would be to assume that democracy and the market in Latin America are played out on a formal field where all the constituent units of a federation and the national government play by the same rules. It has been well documented that even when the president has control over the constituent units, as in Mexico and Argentina during the neoliberal economic era of the 1990s, some units continued to exist as subnational authoritarian enclaves that had greater influence over the affairs of their territory than did the national government (Fox 1994; Gibson 2004).[19] In the cases of federation-like Bolivia and federal Mexico, it has been asserted that it is the nature of local politics and local parties that determines the success of government decentralization, and not the other way round (Singer 2004). Perhaps the entire concept of decentralization has been a misplaced one for understanding the realities of many Latin American countries.

Below the surface of formal governance in Latin America exist diffuse patron-client networks (Malloy 1993, 223), which historically have been predominant at the subnational levels. The frequent aggregation in macro-quantitative cross-national studies of both the local and core federal units of government into one category referred to as "subnational" is a grave empirical error committed in our research. The existence (or, should I say, persistence) of weak governing structures and informality in Latin America means that a great deal of complex politics can be concealed within this misleading concept.[20]

In addition to the context of what politically determines policy reforms, we need to pay equal attention to the "political incentives" to carry out social sector reforms that involve lower levels of government, and whether they are fiscally and administratively sustainable.[21] In all of the federal systems of the Americas—Mexico, Argentina, Brazil, Venezuela, the United States, and Canada—multiple levels of government are interdependent in varying ways. Political initiatives taken at any one level have immediate consequences for another. How can the constraints of federalism be overcome to create an active welfare state that is based on both social protection and social promotion? How can equality of access to basic social rights be sustained in territorially decentralized systems of government, where lower levels of government may not have either the political or fiscal incentives, or the capacity to guarantee these rights or the quality of social services provided? Answering these questions will provide us with a more insightful understanding of how social policy regimes are institutionalized in federal systems of government, compared to a macro-quantitative analysis of decentralization that is based on the aggregation of subnational data into a single category. Moreover, because federalism describes a set of institutions that make policy, the best way to compare federalism cross-nationally is through comparing policy (Bermeo 2002, 102).

The policy outcomes I have selected for cross-national comparison are the territorial distribution in two countries of noncontributory welfare benefits. The main finding will be that more uniform results occur in Brazil owing to the scope for "avoiding governors" in that country, whereas in Argentina, such avoidance was not possible; the territorial distribution of antipoverty programs is accordingly less uniform in Argentina and cannot rely on intergovernmental collaboration in the

future to guarantee either equality of access to national social investments or the quality of associated social services. This suggests municipalities can facilitate the national government's ability to carry out
its desired policy goals, particularly in providing access to basic social
rights when tied to targeted cash transfers. To account for this finding,
we need to extend the analysis beyond the formal and structural concepts discussed so far, to take into account differences of institutionally
derived political dynamics and of municipal government authority.

WHY MUNICIPALITIES DO OR DO NOT COLLABORATE WITH NATIONAL POLICY OBJECTIVES

Much progress has been made by academics in explaining the varying outcomes of decentralization in Latin America at both the national
level (Fox 1994; Abrucio 1998; Falleti 2003; Samuels and Mainwaring
2004; Stepan 2004) and the subnational level (Eaton 2004a; Gibson
2004, 2012; Wilson et al. 2006; Grindle 2007; Montero 2008). Less attention has been paid to the municipal level (Nickson 1995; Gómez 2003;
Dickovick 2006; Grindle 2007). As noted already, Brazil and Argentina
are both highly decentralized "strong" federal systems where varying
political, institutional, and structural factors have shaped the ability of
each national government to implement its desired public policy goals.

Most evident within a paired comparison of these two countries's
federal systems is the emerging capacity in Brazilian federalism to avoid
state governors and use municipalities as the prime agents of the national
government (Dickovick 2006; Borges 2007; Fenwick 2009; Cheibub,
Figueiredo, and Limongi 2009). This research suggests that municipal
collaboration contributed to the ability of the Brazilian government (the
união) to avoid governors during its noncontributory social protection
policy expansion (2003 to 2010) and to promote its benchmark CCT
program, Bolsa Família. Additionally, it has been argued that successful
redistributive initiatives such as CCTs can create policy feedbacks that
effect electoral and individually based political participation in a positive manner (Campbell 2002). It then follows that these powerful "new"
constituencies serve to "lock in" policy. But for this to occur here or elsewhere, national social investment initiatives must be federalized toward

the municipal level without being blocked by powerful governors who have an incentive to either use them for their own political gain or block them; or, they must emanate directly from the core federal units, who have a direct political incentive to guarantee outcomes. This is not to imply that mayors are more trustworthy than governors; according to Hunter and Sugiyama's 2013 survey of three municipalities in the northeast of Brazil, 65 percent reported that politicians buy votes in their city (50). However, Bolsa Família is a national social program, and therefore far fewer respondents in the same survey, 14.9 percent, reported that they thought it was used for local vote buying, even though municipal officials help both in expanding this CCT locally and in monitoring users' compliance with its conditions. The main point is that national governments have far fewer incentives to take punitive measures against governors in federal systems, because governors have a far greater capacity to undermine (i.e., destabilize) national governments. Moreover, governors have little political interest in, and few incentives to promote, a national policy initiative that furthers the idea of "shared-rule" within their territory. In Argentina, I argue that municipal collaboration is less likely because it is impeded by the ability of the provinces to directly capture local units of government and by the governor's preferences, thus undermining a mayor's incentives to directly promote national policy incentives—no matter how virtuous.

Using three explanatory factors, I explain the variance in how, following the macroeconomic stabilization in both countries, federalism affected the national government's ability to implement two similar national CCTs, both *within* Brazil and Argentina and *across* them in comparative perspective. The three factors I propose and the corresponding propositions relating to why municipalities collaborate or fail to collaborate with national policy goals are shown in table 2.2 and discussed below.

National Recognition of Subnational Levels of Government

Federalism is a system of government that represents the *de jure* territorial division of units of government and the separation of powers between the legislative, executive, and judicial branches. The nature of executive-legislative relations is not the focus of this book, and is a topic

Table 2.2. Factors that Impede or Encourage Municipalities with Respect to Promoting National Policy Goals

Factor	Brazil	Argentina	Proposition
National Constitutional Recognition of Subnational Levels of Government			
Recognition of constituent units; status of local units ambiguous	No	Yes	Municipalities are creatures of the states and/or provinces. Mayors are constrained from bypassing governors.
Local government recognized as a distinct level of government from the states and/or provinces	Yes	No	Municipalities can autonomously adhere to national programs. Three-level federal system.
Rules Regulating Subnational Finances			
Market-regulated subnational finances (soft budget constraints)	No	Yes	Governors will overspend where access to external market credit is permissible. Municipalities can be fiscally captured by states and/or provinces through extending credit. Fiscal incentives for direct national-local policy collaboration impeded. Inflation and monetary pressure exacerbates this fiscal behavior and its political consequences.
Legally regulated subnational finances (hard budget constraints)	Yes	No	Through regulating public policy spending responsibilities and setting subnational budget targets, national-local policy collaboration is fiscally encouraged. A stable and favorable economic context facilitates the political credibility of these transactions.
Political Regime Type			
Majoritarian model of democracy	No	Yes	Single-party cabinets, executive leverage over congress, and national two-party dominance encouraging the logic of punishment and reward federalism. Local promotion of national policy objectives is thus politically difficult, fiscally risky, and can be impeded by governor politics.
Consensual model of democracy	Yes	No	Large presidential-led multiparty governing coalitions encourage mayors to promote national objectives demanded by public.

only minimally reflected upon; my primary interest here lies with the territorial divisions of government within the national constitution and the formal protection it affords them, among other institutional variables that determine the extent of municipal agency. The national recognition of local government autonomy is a required yet insufficient explanation of de facto local power.

What sort of constitutional design might alleviate the practical difficulties of constructing and maintaining a federal democracy is a crucial question, which has been rigorously addressed in Bednar, Eskridge, and Ferejohn's "A Political Theory of Federalism" (2001). According to these authors, the division of constitutionally recognized levels of government maintains a stable and credible decentralized political structure. Building on this proposition, I suggest that national constitutional recognition of municipalities as distinct from the states/provinces prevents these core federal units from usurping the powers of the local level for their own ends. The ability of the core federal units to "capture" local units of government within their territory (control their boundaries) has been a significant part of the story of subnational party stability in many federations, which does not necessarily lead to optimal policy outputs or democratic quality.[22]

The number of constitutions within a federal system also varies. For example, in a federal country such as Canada there is only one constitution, the national one, and no formal constitutions for either provinces or municipalities, but provincial autonomy is given constitutional status in that constitution. The US and Argentine national constitutions recognize and protect the core federal units of government, known in the United States as states and in Argentina as provinces, but these units also have their own constitutions. The question of municipal autonomy in all three of these federal countries is left to the discretion of the core units. In these federal systems, municipalities are creatures of the states and provinces, thus restricting the ability of municipalities to define and act on municipal interests or to engage in nonhierarchical arrangements. All three of the aforementioned federal constitutions are relatively old: United States (1787), Argentina (1853, reformed in 1994),[23] and Canada (1867, repatriated and amended in 1982).[24]

The cases of Mexico and Brazil are, from a constitutional perspective, somewhat different, primarily because of their official recognition of a third level of government.[25] Municipalities are formally included and protected as official constituent units of the federation. This constitutional recognition permits municipalities *de jure* to be political competitors for authority with both the national government and the states, and gives them the *de jure* authority to engage directly with either level. Mexico has had three constitutions (1824, 1857, and 1917, with the third reformed in 1984). In terms of reforms, the 1984 version of the constitution was significant because it nationally recognized municipalities as a distinct order of government, although admittedly the 1857 constitution did formally recognize *municipios libres* (Graham and Rowland 2006, 46). Brazil has had seven national constitutions since her independence (1824, 1891, 1934, 1937, 1946, 1967, and 1988). It was only the last, fully rewritten constitution of 1988 that recognized municipalities as an official third tier of government, distinct from the states.

The *de jure* allocation of territorial autonomy is a structural and static variable. It is a way to explain organizationally induced relationships between levels of government. This makes it possible to begin to understand how distinct levels of government within a federal system work together and to whom are they subordinate (Carroll and Shugart 2007). These territorial divisions are fundamental to understanding what Madison called the "distinct exercise of different powers of government." In order for them to become operational, "each department should have a will of its own; and consequently should be so constituted, that the members of each should have as little agency as possible in the appointment of the members of the others" (Madison, Federalist Paper 51, 1787; in Ball 2006, 251). Using Madisonian logic, one can see how the authority of local government is impeded when its autonomy is not protected by a national constitution and its existence is subordinated to the authority of the core federal units: provinces or states.

Some federal countries have chosen to provide municipalities with constitutional protection as independent entities, but they must still bargain for any real governing authority. Their independent status formally provides them with the ability to bargain and engage with other competing levels of government, providing even greater strength to a federal system in resisting both national and state/provincial aggrandizements of power. Just as the opportunism of the national government is best constrained by fragmenting its power (Bednar, Eskridge, and Ferejohn 2001, 231), so the opportunism of the core federal units is also best constrained by fragmenting their power through municipalization. This theoretical proposition increases the institutional safeguards of federalism because it prevents governors from undermining and free-riding on the national government.

Similar to the territorial distribution of authority discussed previously, this institutional variable sheds light on the amount of formal political opportunity embedded within subnational units by disaggregating them. Nevertheless, the potential to use this political opportunity (namely, constitutionally autonomous municipalities in Mexico) can be compromised by both political and electoral incentives, which de facto reflect "deeper distributions of power within the political system" (Beer 2003, 188). Therefore, it is possible to understand the role of municipalities within a federation only by taking into consideration both their constitutional status *de jure* and the deeper actual distributions of power resulting from the rules regulating subnational finances and the dynamics of each political regime type, which I have classified broadly as majoritarian versus consensual.

Rules Regulating Subnational Finances

Subnational finances are an integral part of understanding the politics of any federal game and how core federal units and municipalities can either facilitate or impede national policy objectives. Macroeconomic instability within a country can exacerbate the fiscal behavior and political consequences linked to the actors who are bound by these rules. Beyond the required political will and the administrative capacity required by subnational levels of government to carry out national policy objectives, successful policy outcomes are also determined by how and by whom it is financed. The rules regulating subnational finances can have a deleterious effect on the behavior of these two lower levels and on their ability to respond to local needs.

Political economists specializing in fiscal federalism have been primarily concerned with the relationship between federalism and economic outcomes, that is, the consequences for the overall macroeconomic performance of a federation of how policy is financed and who finances it (Tommasi, Saiegh, and Sanguinetti 2001; Rodden,

Eskeland, and Litvack 2003). Increasingly, attention is being paid to how the rules governing subnational finances build certain incentives into the political system that may ultimately be negative for overall democratic quality (Benton 2009; Bonvecchi and Lodola 2011).

The consequences of recent processes of fiscal decentralization on economic performance in Argentina and Brazil and elsewhere in the Americas have been well documented (among others, see Bird and Vaillancourt 1998; Dillinger and Webb 2002; Guigale and Webb 2000; Rodden and Wibbels 2002; Eaton 2004a; Haggard and Webb 2004). The public choice theory–prescribed virtues of fiscal decentralization did not have much success in Latin America or elsewhere in reducing the size of the state, increasing market competitiveness and efficiency, or promoting economic growth. Instead, fiscal decentralization weakened macroeconomic performance and resulted in unsustainable debts, high inflation, and low economic growth (Dillinger and Webb 2002). The only exception among the federal cases in the Americas is Mexico, where growth in subnational spending did not pose a major threat to Mexico's macroeconomic stability (Guigale, Trillo, and Oliveira 2000).[26]

Mexican exceptionalism has been attributed most frequently to the limited capacity of Mexican states and municipalities to borrow funds in the first place, and also to the 1995–1996 international bailout packages that enabled the Mexican federal government to make discretionary transfers to rescue heavily indebted states without incurring higher domestic costs. Mexican fiscal decentralization seems to have been extremely cautious, this country having perhaps learnt from the examples of Argentina, Brazil, and Canada, which suffered more recessionary effects.

One of the principal debates on issues of fiscal decentralization in federal countries revolves around how to manage and regulate subnational spending and debt. The revenue capacity of both the core federal units and local levels of government is often limited by reduced tax-raising capacity. Specifically at the local level, a heavy reliance on local taxes based on property and consumption means that revenue will fluctuate substantially according to market trends.

Ideally, the ability of these governments to manage their spending should be regulated by market discipline. In practice (particularly in less developed countries), this may not be an ideal solution. Market-based regulations are known as "soft budget constraints." They are designed to enable subnational governments to regulate themselves through strict market discipline. Three federal countries in the Americas, Argentina, Brazil, and Canada, attempted this mechanism during the 1980s, at significant social cost by the end of the 1990s (Guigale, Trillo, and Oliveira 2000; Rodden, Eskeland, and Litvack 2003).

There is an alternative, rules-based approach to using market discipline to monitor the capacity of lower levels of government to pay debt and to avoid excessive debt. Such an approach has been implemented, to varying degrees, in Brazil and the United States, as well as other federal countries outside of the Americas. It normally entails that national governments limit subnational borrowing capacity, regulate public sector spending, enforce bankruptcy and fiscal responsibility laws, and encourage private risk-rating. The rules-based approach is commonly referred to as "hard budget constraints." This budgetary regulation approach has the advantage of improving transparency and impartiality and, most importantly of all, encouraging the minimization of political bargains and discretionality (Guigale, Trillo, and Oliveira 2000, 257).

For the current research, what is important is how, and to what extent, hard budget versus soft budget approaches facilitate or impede the willingness of municipalities to promote national policy goals. What political incentives are created by either approach at varying levels of government? And how do they affect the two dilemmas of federalism, of preventing the national government from destroying federalism by encroaching on its constituent units, and of preventing the constituent units from undermining the national government (Figueiredo and Weingast 2005, 104)?

Soft Budget Constraints

The term "soft budget constraints" was first coined by Janos Kornai, and was intended to highlight the economic behavior of socialist economies (1980). "It applies figuratively to a specific, comprehensive social syndrome found in economic reality" (Kornai, Maskin, and Roland 2003). A soft budget constraint, within the context of rules regulating subnational finances, refers to the responsibility of the subnational governments to cover their budget expenditures out of their allotted central government transfers and their own source revenues. If the subnational government fails to cover its budget, it cannot survive without outside fiscal intervention. This is how, in the Latin American context, national government fiscal interventions arising from soft budget constraints at the subnational level weakened overall national macroeconomic performance during the late 1980s and early 1990s. The national government, within the context of soft budget constraints, plays a supporting fiscal role to lower levels of government—in essence, it bails them out or rescues them financially in order to avert a national fiscal crisis.

Beyond economic performance, the "soft budget syndrome," as Kornai terms it, affects political behavior and intergovernmental relations (see figure 2.1). Political motives often induce a national government to extend fiscal support to a needy lower level of government because of its past political support, or because of patronage connections that it would lose if it did not. The national government may, in certain political contexts, be responsible or protective of a subnational level. Such causality is based on the assumption that the supporting institution, in this case the national government, is hierarchically superior to the supported "budget constraint organization," that is, the subnational units of the federation (Kornai, Maskin, and Roland 2003).

Soft budget constraints affect the behavior of key stakeholders because they create a "mentality" that, according to the dominant theorists, is the basic condition of the syndrome. This mentality is developed over time and based on collective experience: "Will the national government bail us out when we spend too much?" The only way a national government can "harden" soft budget constraints is with some institutional change that provides such threats with credibility. The abstract argument of this research suggests that core federal units of government will change their behavior only when a change in the territorial distribution of power modifies the vested interests of the national government to lend its patrimonial support to these units that have traditionally benefited from *not* playing by the rules of the federal bargain.[27]

Hard Budget Constraints

Hard budget constraints refer to a situation where subnational levels of government will not receive outside support to cover their excessive spending and will thus be obliged to reduce or terminate an activity

Figure 2.1. Link between Politics and the Soft Budget Syndrome

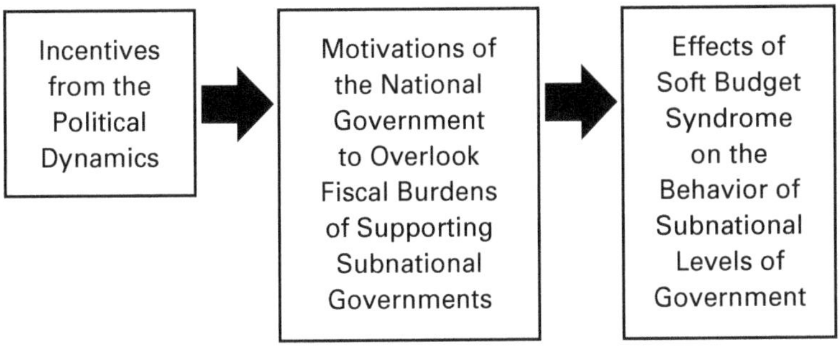

Incentives from the Political Dynamics	⮕	Motivations of the National Government to Overlook Fiscal Burdens of Supporting Subnational Governments	⮕	Effects of Soft Budget Syndrome on the Behavior of Subnational Levels of Government

Note: This figure is based on Kornai, Maskin, and Roland's (2003) formal theory of the causality of a support organization in a budgetary constraint organization.

if the deficit persists (Kornai, Maskin, and Roland 2003). As already alluded to in the above section, the threat of hard budget constraints induces a change only when it becomes credible. A threat is credible when constraints are both enforceable (*de jure*) and in the vested interests of the national government (*de facto*). Several institutional characteristics present in Latin America, however, distort the threat of such constraints. Cronyism, populism, clientelism, and "un-institutionalized federal bargaining" and macroeconomic volatility all weaken the potential effect of hardening budget constraints.[28]

The theoretical advantage of hard budget constraints over soft budget constraints is that the former make it more difficult for governors to hold mayors fiscally hostage, because mayors cannot rely on politically aligned governors to cover their expenses—at least not with funds destined to cover social expenditures. It weakens the co-dependent relationship between the intermediate (politically induced) and local levels of government (fiscally induced). This budgetary regulation approach also has the advantage of improving transparency and impartiality and encouraging the minimization of political bargains and discretionality (Guigale, Trillo, and Oliveira 2000, 257). Most importantly, hard budget constraints provide a fiscal incentive for subnational levels of government to accept nationally financed policy that provides an alternative local fiscal resource.

As the authors who review the rich literature on "soft budget constraint syndrome" themselves admit, from a theoretical point of view it seems that hard is "good" and "soft" is bad (Kornai, Maskin, and Roland 2003). It should be emphasized, however, that this is just a starting point for the task ahead. There are valid political and social reasons why a national government would opt for soft budget constraints. Why and how a national government plays this game will become clear only in the light of a more complete understanding of the political incentives for intergovernmental collaboration and the constitutional recognition of subnational levels of government.

Political Regime Type

This explanatory factor is not intended to classify either Brazil or Argentina as an ideal type of either a majoritarian or a consensual model of democracy. Such statements in both cases would be empirically incorrect and a serious exaggeration. Rather, it is meant to point out a crucial difference between these two political regimes along Lijphart's "executive-parties" dimension—an important distinction between the two that becomes highly visible within a comparative strategy. The "executive-parties" dimension was one of the two key dimensions used by Lijphart (1969; 1984) to distinguish majoritarian from consensual models of democracy. The other was the "unitary-federal dimension," which is clearly moot within these two cases.

An alternative approach to understanding how federalism as a governing system constrains the center is Tsebelis's veto player approach (1995). According to Stepan (2004, 324), who extended this approach to compare federal systems, "Argentina and Brazil are the only democracies in the world to have four 'robust' electorally generated institutional veto players." Hence the use of this approach does not really enable us to see either the differences, or distinguish the governing logic, between these two models of democracy. For this reason, I use Lijphart's approach to contrast the governing logics not between a unitary and a federal system, but *among* federal systems.

Broadly stated, Lijphart's "executive-parties" dimension was characterized by a concentration of executive power, single-party majority cabinets, executive-legislative relations where the executive is dominant, and a party system where the number of effective parties hovers at around two, or where it exhibits an "integrated federal party" that can reduce the number of veto players (Filippov, Ordeshook, and Shvetsova 2004). These authors defined integrated parties (or integrated party systems) as those in which "politicians at one level of government bear an organizational relationship to politicians at other levels"; the essential commodity between them is a shared *party label* (2004, 190). Other Lijphart factors, such as unidimensional versus multidimensional party systems and electoral rules, are beyond the purview of this study.

In a highly decentralized federal system, the strength of majoritarianism varies across levels of government. Logically, however, a political regime will be more majoritarian when electoral rules and the party system encourage political parties and candidates from multiple levels of government to rely on each other for their survival and success. If party systems are also decentralized, they will have an even greater constraining effect on the national government's ability to realize its policy goals because, in this context, the national-subnational party-based relationship is symbiotic. By contrast, if the national level controls the majoritarianism inherent to the system, it is reasonable to expect that it *ought* not to have many problems (all others things being held constant) in convincing lower levels of government to carry out its policy objectives. In the presence of a vertically integrated federal party system, majoritarianism along the executive-parties dimension can coordinate national and subnational policy interests in such a way that it can reduce the kind of legislative fragmentation that is believed (among other things) to delay policy reforms.

A consensual model of democracy is quite the opposite since it is normatively based on compromise. It is characterized primarily by executive power-sharing in broad multiparty coalitions, an executive-legislative balance of power, a higher number of effective parties at the national level, and proportional representation. In the traditional political science literature, the dominant wisdom is that a majoritarian model of democracy enables more effective national governments and more uniform policy outputs. Stated quite simply, decision-making authority is in the hands of fewer actors, who theoretically represent the "majority" of citizens. This assumption, however, has lost credence in recent years, particularly in light of the theoretical development of the *intraparty* dimension of political parties, where compromise and concessions are made within the confines of elite internal party forums. It still theoretically holds that consensual models of democracy are considerably more representative, but the hyper-representation they create can slow down the policymaking process.

The characteristics of the policy solutions to alleviate poverty that reduce its intergenerational transmission are both cross-sectorial and interjurisdictional. A decentralized federal system of government, therefore, requires intergovernmental (and interparty) cooperation to carry out a national poverty alleviation strategy that is based on active social investments, as opposed to passive social expenditure. The attributes of each country's political regime contribute to the amount of political will across levels of government and the intergovernmental cooperation that can be expected to achieve such a policy goal. For the purpose of comparison, I reduce and synthesize many party and electoral system variables into a single category and refer to them as a majoritarian or a consensual model. This is a very broad categorization that reduces many complex variables into a simple dichotomous framework. I believe, however, that it offers a successful analytical strategy, particularly when comparing two presidential federal countries whose differences are otherwise quite subtle.

In summary, the ability of a national government to socially protect the weak and vulnerable within a strong system of federal government does not depend on any single explanatory factor, but rather on the interaction of a number of domestic factors. Federalism is a political system built on complex and overlapping relationships between multiple levels of government. In order for any level of government (central, core, or local) to block policy implementation through apathy or to opt out in any policy area, it must have constitutional recognition: the first explanatory factor. It must also have fiscal and political incentives to promote a policy objective that emanates from an external level of government. Municipal willingness to promote national policy objectives is thus motivated both by the rules regulating subnational finances and by the dynamics of the political regime type: the second and third explanatory factors. All three of these factors can interact in important ways and lead to varying policy outcomes. Nevertheless, I suggest that these three key explanatory factors help to explain how a national government can overcome the undermining constraints of strong federalism in key policy areas.

CHAPTER 3

Avoiding Governors
and the Success of CCTs in Brazil

Poverty is a widespread phenomenon in Brazil. Although economic growth rates from 1950 to 1980 were high, household poverty rates remained problematic throughout these years of industrial development, always hovering, according to ECLAC historical statistics, around 39 percent. In 1987, household poverty continued to afflict 40 percent of the nation (ECLAC 2003). The combination of positive economic growth rates and consistently high household poverty rates, spanning over forty years, led to the counterintuitive realization in Brazilian policy circles that economic growth had a minimal impact on poverty, particularly in view of the fact that poverty rates had remained relatively constant before and after the so-called "lost decade" of the 1980s. Unlike other Latin American countries during these same years, poverty in Brazil could not be attributed to a lack of government social expenditure. It was due rather to a "transmission problem" (Camargo and Barros 1993, 61). Government expenditure did not reach those families facing the

greatest vulnerability at the local level.[1] This policy transmission problem in Brazil is both historically and federally derived, constituting a
major policy challenge. This challenge is believed by many specialists of
Brazilian politics to be linked to a deeper problem of "institutionalizing
an effective capability to govern at all" (Malloy 1993, 221).

By 1989, Brazil was a fully-fledged democracy for the first time in
its history, with universal suffrage and free and fair elections at all levels of government. Poverty, inequality, and social exclusion, however,
remained problematic as Brazil moved into the current democratic
period. Particularly from 1990 to 2000, the first decade following democratization, social progress was slow. The Gini Index for inequality
remained a static 0.60 over the decade, while the poverty rate in 1999
was 33.3 percent of the total population (Silva 2008). The editor of the
Cambridge History of Latin America, Leslie Bethell, once asked if Brazilian democracy can be healthy, if it can function, and if it can survive
in the long run, when a third of its population lived in conditions of
extreme poverty, ignorance, and ill health (Bethell 2000, 14). It proba-
bly could not; and without a doubt, greater income equality remains
an uphill battle. However, gains have been made—a fact that is now
empirically undeniable.

The number of people living in poverty in Brazil fell from 61 million in 2003 to 39 million in 2009 (IPEA 2010). This decrease was determined both by a mixture of labor and social policies and by a context
of stable economic growth. In 2013, only 21.4 percent of Brazilians live
in poverty, less than a quarter of the total population. There is no doubt
in the research of any scholar who works on contemporary Brazil that
public policies in several key sectors (macroeconomic, labor, and social)
contributed to these social gains. Which ones mattered more, minimum
wage policy or cash transfers, is another debate with no clear empirical
answer. Notwithstanding, CCTs played an important role in improving the lives of the poorer sectors of the population, particularly those
within the informal sectors, given that only 34.3 percent of actively employed Brazilians over the age of fifteen held formal wage employment
in 2004 (de Andrade et al. 2010).

The central goal of this chapter is to show how social protection
as CCTs evolved in Brazil and to put forward empirical evidence that
Bolsa Família was successfully territorially distributed and promoted

in all municipalities, based on the explicit targeting of this highly applauded program. The Brazilian story of CCTs as a mechanism to both protect and promote the socially vulnerable is about "politics as learning" combined with "politics as power." The unique political and historical circumstances that facilitated the original CCT experimentation at the subnational level in Brazil during the early 1990s was created out of both necessity and opportunity. The post-1988 period of radical decentralization had left many cities in a state of draconian need in terms of social services that were no longer nationally provided, as well as with new political and administrative opportunities to provide these services. The new opportunities emanated from the national constitution, which had been completely rewritten in 1988. Out of this period of Brazilian history a plethora of influential policy ideas was generated. The most successful one, the use of CCTs to promote both social inclusion and to reduce the intergenerational transmission of poverty, received the prestigious award for outstanding achievement in social security in 2013 from the International Social Security Association based in Geneva. This award is intended to recognize Brazil's outstanding contribution to the promotion and development of social security at the national and international level. It is also intended to encourage other governments to adopt this initiative. It should be evident by the end of the chapter, however, that Brazil's evolution in social protection was a uniquely domestic affair, facilitated by Brazilian policy entrepreneurs and political-institutional incentives.

THE EVOLUTION AND POLITICS OF SOCIAL POLICY AS CCTS IN BRAZIL

Social protection policy—the ability to protect poor, vulnerable, and marginalized groups in society through the delivery of social goods—is a fundamental extension of a democratic governing system. It also represents an area where, in Brazil and beyond, "the control of social agencies and programs represents a strategic political resource" (Castro Guimarães 1993, 79; interview ibid. 2006). Traditionally originating in the Vargas years (1930 to 1945), national government initiatives in this policy area were motivated by the political desire to increase the power-generating capacity of the national government (Malloy 1993). The Vargas regime substantially expanded contributory social protection benefits to citizens who had made payments through the formal labor market. The use of formal social insurance schemes to incorporate the working classes into the governing apparatus during this period of Brazilian history is an example of corporatism and "controlled social inclusion." Here, "controlled social inclusion" refers to a political process whereby societal demands for social welfare and equity are moderated through diverse state strategies, particularly populism (Oxhorn 1995).

During the 1980s, a more informal version of controlled inclusion remained prevalent, but for different reasons. Social protection policy at this time can be characterized in Brazil as

> an uncoordinated mass of programs heavily concentrated in the federal government; fragmented, discontinuous action; glaring ineffectiveness in terms of the results obtained and the impact produced among the target population; and above all, the strongly clientelistic approach adopted in implementing such programs. (Draibe 2004, 88)

An artificially imposed, majoritarian political model contributed to what Draibe called the "clientelist approach adopted in implementing social programs," because the Party of the Brazilian Democratic Movement (PMDB) relied on delivering patronage and clientele networks to win subnational elections and to maintain its leverage over the national executive (Mainwaring 1995b, 388). This party, which is commonly classified as a centrist ideological catch-all party, dominated subnational electoral politics from 1982 to 1990. During this period, "the use of public resources was crucial in determining internal organizational control in catchall parties" (Mainwaring 1995b, 388). The importance of the PMDB for the national government's ability to deliver social goods was further exacerbated when José Sarney became president (1985–1990) by default following the death of opposition leader and elected president Tancredo Neves (PMDB), who died before he could assume office. Sarney was a weak president both because of the way he assumed the presidency and because of the fact that he formerly represented ARENA, the military regime's official federal party.

Sarney forged a successful relationship with state governors (twenty-two out of twenty-three governors were PMDB in 1986), on whom he relied because of their ability to generate subnational support for the government and their control of extensive political clienteles. The composition of the federal cabinet between February 1986 and March 1990 was very much dominated by two political parties, the PMDB and the PFL. During these years, only 14 percent of federal cabinet ministers were without partisan affiliation (Amorim Neto 2007, 58), and a majoritarian model of democracy dominated.

Despite the democratic climax in March 1990 with the inauguration of the first democratically elected president, Fernando Collor de Mello (PRN), democratic consolidation in Brazil was far from complete. The decade-long fiscal crisis that complicated democratization was not resolved until 1994, when a successful stabilization package, known as the Plano Real (Real Plan), was implemented under de Mello's replacement, President Itamar Franco (1992–1994). The gradual nature of these two parallel political and economic processes delayed the implementation of many progressive public policy reforms that had been voted through the National Constituent Assembly of 1987.

For example, title VIII, articles 203–204 of the 1988 Constitution institutionalized social assistance to the poor and vulnerable as a public policy. However, this policy intent must be juxtaposed against the backdrop of increasing interparty competition arising out of the first direct presidential elections in 1989 and the subsequent gubernatorial and legislative elections of 1990. The 1990 elections decreased the monopoly of the PMDB at the subnational level. These changing voting patterns created a political opportunity to make significant changes in the way social protection policy was conceptualized. Following President Collor de Mello's impeachment in September 1992, social policy experimentation at the subnational level began to advance.

The original draft of the "new national policy on social assistance" was defeated in Congress in 1991. Social assistance policy thus remained under the Legião Brasiliera de Assistência Social (LBA), the centralized agency for this social policy area since the 1940s. Traditionally, the presidency of the LBA was an honorary position reserved for the nation's first lady, and so from 1990 to 1991 the LBA was controlled by Rosane Collor de Mello, who, like her husband, would be charged with embezzling funds (*Folha de S.Paulo*, June 17, 1991, front cover). A significant part of LBA revenues came from private donations. This fact isolated social assistance programs from state and municipal involvement, even though they operated at that level as well (Arretche 2000).

After Itamar Franco assumed the presidency of Brazil in late 1992, the Organic Law of Social Assistance (LOAS) was passed by Congress on December 7, 1993. Of particular importance was the municipalization of social assistance. Article 15 vested the execution of all programs confronting poverty in the municipalities, Article 1 stated that social assistance and public transfers must guarantee self-realization to citizens. The intended political effect of this rights-based conceptualization of social protection was to generate a direct relationship between the state and citizens in situations of social vulnerability, with as little political intermediation as possible, particularly following the publicly denounced politicization of the LBA that had led to its termination.

Aside from the negotiations in Congress from 1992 over the newly proposed legislation, the realization of social protection policy framed as a public responsibility was dependent on the resolution of the economic crisis and the recovery of the administrative and financial capacity of the government (Castro Guimarães 1993, 85). Draconian high inflation rates limited the implementation of the new reforms, particularly given that the average yearly inflation rate from 1990 to 1994 was 1,625.8 percent (World Bank Indicators). This fiscal crisis slowly began to be resolved during 1993–1994, following the implementation of the Real Plan that finally succeeded in reducing inflation by 1995 to 77.6 percent. These two parallel economic and political processes were important for social protection policy, because they provided for approximately six years of *locally based* experimentation (1995–2001).

In 1995, the federal government eliminated the LBA and replaced it with the National Secretariat of Social Assistance (SNAS). The creation of this new, responsible agency greatly facilitated the institutionalization of noncontributory social protection policy. The SNAS embraced social inclusion as a right, and thus conceived of social security and social assistance as means to an end rather than ends in themselves. Embraced as a "right," the regulation, production, and operation of social protection policy was consolidated as a public responsibility. This moving of social assistance from a private framework (based on private philanthropy, the Catholic Church, first ladies' fundraising, and so on) to a public conception enabled a universal expansion of benefits that would no longer rely on an individual's monetary contribution or private networks (interview Sposati 2006). Finally, the long reform processes in the area of social protection that had been initiated in 1988 began to take effect after 1995.

This same year, the first two experimental noncontributory cash transfer programs became operational in the Federal Capital of Brasília and in the Municipality of Campinas, São Paulo State—both of which were funded by own-sourced revenues. The ideas behind these programs had been circulating for some time, beginning, initially, in Brasília under the auspices of Cristovam Buarque. In a highly influential paper in 1987, Buarque proposed a social program that would give scholarships to keep the poorest children in school by the government guaranteeing a minimum income to poor families as an incentive to provide education to their children (Aguiar and Araújo 2002). He adamantly opposed, however, the idea of the government providing a basic income to the poor without conditions that would link it to additional social policy goals such as education.

In 1991, São Paulo Senator Eduardo Suplicy (PT-SP) launched the idea of the Basic Guaranteed Income Project, which was also based on achieving minimum social rights for all Brazilians. His project, unlike Buarque's, was not explicitly linked to conditionality. His law was passed by the Senate as "Bill 80" but has yet to be fully implemented. In 1993, economist José Márcio Camargo (PT) suggested changing Suplicy's project into a program that would increase a family's income but would be dependent on school attendance, as had been suggested earlier in Brasília by Buarque (Suplicy 2002, 135).

Each of the local CCT programs implemented in 1995 was an experiment in dominant policy ideas that had been circulating in left-wing academic circles during the 1980s. They were also the product of progressive subnational experimentation, facilitated by revenue increases for both the states and municipalities. The program in the City of Campinas was grounded in a rights-based principle of basic income, while that in Brasília was based on the condition of school attendance. The Campinas program called Renda Mínima was not based on conditionality but was only provided to families with children under the age of fourteen "in school," and provided R$35 to each eligible household per month. It was implemented by Mayor José Magalhães Teixeira of the PSDB (interview Suplicy 2006).

The second program, implemented by Buarque (PT) in 1995 as the elected governor of Brasília, was based on the School Stipend program he had conceived in 1987. This program was dependent on school attendance, and guaranteed R$100 to each family residing in the Federal Capital who earned 50 percent (or less) of the minimum wage and had children under the age of fourteen. Following the success of these programs, similar CCT initiatives began to emerge after 1995 in many other municipalities and states, such as Ribeirão Preto, Belém, Belo Horizonte, Caixas do Sul, Goiânia, Rio Grande do Sul, Mato Grosso, and Acre, among others (Suplicy 2002). According to Sugiyama's (2013) empirical analysis of the determinants of this diffusion process, electoral competition did not spur it; rather, ideological and sociological motivations compelled local elites to emulate Buarque's initiative. It should be noted, however, that in 1998 the federal government provided a fiscal incentive called the National Minimum Income Guarantee Program to poor municipalities by covering 50 percent of their costs in providing a local CCT program linked to school attendance. Although Brazil is an institutionally uniform federation, where all twenty-six states (plus one federal capital) and 5,564 municipalities have the same political, administrative, and fiscal competencies, during the 1990s subnational CCTs were distributed based on where a citizen resided.

NATIONALIZATION OF CCTS
UNDER PRESIDENT CARDOSO, 1995–2002

The two consecutive administrations of President Fernando Henrique Cardoso (PSDB) that began in January 1995 and ended on December 31, 2002, prioritized macroeconomic stability. Cardoso sought to alleviate "economic problems," "inflation/high prices," and "job instability," all considered in Latin America to be some of the country's most important problems (Mainwaring, Scully, and Vargas Cullell 2007). Ironically, what was an initially successful macroeconomic stabilization pushed

Brazil into a period of critical uncertainty from external economic shocks, leading to the eventual devaluation of the currency in 1999. This currency devaluation also resulted in a subsequent decrease in per capita household income (FGV 2006).

As a consequence, the credibility of the national government in the eyes of a large portion of the electorate fell. The Real Plan had been a key factor in the federal government's credibility. In an effort to address the short-term negative effects of the sudden currency devaluation on the poorer segments of the Brazilian population, the federal government launched the first national CCT program designed to alleviate both immediate and longer-term poverty. This program maintained the same name as the originally conceived city program in Brasília—Bolsa Escola. Based on conditionality, this national program, created in 2001, was considered worldwide to be an example of good social programming. It provided R$15 to each child attending school, up to a maximum of R$45 per family (three children). The number of beneficiaries in this program peaked at 5,106,509 families in December 2002.

The nationalization of Bolsa Escola led to the eventual extinction of most subnational CCTs designed to alleviate poverty. The end of many of these programs was related to the same economic reforms that had motivated their nationalization. The lack of fiscal resources to finance subnational initiatives and the magnitude of subnational debt caused by the drastic reduction in inflation since 1995 had had severe effects on the administrative capacity of subnational federal units. Within this fiscal context the opportunity to auto-finance local programs became constrained. According to Patrus Ananias, the ex-mayor of Belo Horizonte and Lula's former minister of social development in the national government (2003–2010), any mayor or governor may continue to remain outside of a national cash transfer program and develop localized social programs, "as long as you can pay for it" (interview Ananias 2006).

Minister Ananias has clearly laid out how a hardening of subnational budget constraints, beginning slowly in 1995 and culminating in the "Fiscal Responsibility Law" in 2000, provided municipalities with new fiscal incentives to adhere to national policies that they could no longer maintain autonomously, and which the states could no longer finance. Increasingly, earmarked national grants financed by federal revenues became necessary to finance the provision of subnational social services (Rezende 2007). Local autonomy to formulate social protection policy was thus compromised by an external restriction related to new fiscal rules. The fact that this earlier sequence of progressive state and municipal policy experimentation had contributed to the eventual success of national poverty alleviation programs, however, is worth emphasizing.[2] Cardoso's national programs were built upon the experiences of the "municipal era" of CCTs.

From a policy perspective, Bolsa Escola was superior to earlier local CCT initiatives for two reasons. First, it was accessible to all citizens earning below half of the minimum salary throughout the entire country, which made it universal by design. Second, it was associated with, and supported by, another policy area that was also designed nationally, namely, education. Its impact in alleviating poverty was, however, narrow because it targeted only families with school-age dependents, and because it was framed as a social investment initiative in education intended, among other things, to combat child labor.

Therefore, the Cardoso administration created two additional noncontributory CCTs to alleviate poverty, targeted at additional families in conjunction with different policy sectors. The first program was Bolsa Alimentação, also created in 2001 and administered by the Ministry of Health. Using an electronic card system, this cash transfer program provided from R$15 to R$45 to pregnant and lactating women, or to families with children from six months to six years old, in order to assist them in purchasing basic food stuffs. It was conditional on regular attendance at prenatal care facilities, compliance with vaccination schedules, and health education. The second program, Auxilio Gás, was created in 2002 and administered by the Ministry of Mines and Energy. It provided a monthly stipend of R$7.50 to low-income families to assist them in purchasing cooking gas to support nutritional needs; it was conditional on being registered within Bolsa Escola.

Although internationally applauded, these social programs faced many internal organizational challenges. The stipulation of municipal execution of social assistance programs created obstacles to administrative cost-sharing and program monitoring, given that there are more than 5,500 municipalities of varying sizes and institutional capacities, a problem compounded by the fact that no unified federal database existed at the time.

Most importantly, the PSDB's three programs were not easily institutionalized because of the challenges of integrating three ministries across multiple levels of government, which were, as ever in Brazil, controlled by varying interparty cabinet factions. This ministerial characteristic, emanating from Brazil's consensual model of democracy, made compartmentalized social programs vulnerable to both vertical and horizontal intra-bureaucratic conflict. The coexistence of three cash transfer programs targeted at the same citizens created cross-sector conflict, described as "chaotic" by public administrators from various intergovernmental implementing agencies (interviews Pochmann 2006 and Sposati 2006). It has been suggested in various interviews with senior policy experts that the causes of weak coordination during this period, which initially extended into the new PT administration, were policy-oriented and driven by intra-bureaucratic conflict rather than ideology.

Although poverty rates dropped by only 2.1 further percentage points during President Cardoso's eight years in office, compared to the level following the original decrease achieved by the Real Plan in 1994 (see figure 3.1), President Cardoso left the federal government stronger than when he had taken office in 1995. The Second Real Report suggests that the major gain in social welfare under Cardoso resulted not from social policy but from the stabilization of individual incomes that came from macroeconomic stabilization (FGV 2006, 11).

Successful macroeconomic stability, however, had an effect on future policy development and outcomes. It created a new opportunity for centralized policy authority because of the increased regulation of decentralized spending and the increased credibility of the national government. This eliminated much of the vice observed in earlier municipal and state behavior after 1988, which had undermined federal government performance. Most importantly, the macroeconomic stability Cardoso achieved during his two administrations (1995–2003) had reduced the "uncertainty factor" that previously made national social policy planning and its implementation so difficult (FGV 2006).

As shown in figure 3.1, poverty rates began to drop again after the PT administration's inauguration in January 2003. During President Lula's first term (2003–2006), he prioritized the expansion of the purchasing power of Brazilians through both minimum wage increases and

Figure 3.1. Poverty Rates in Brazil during CCT Expansion, 1992–2006

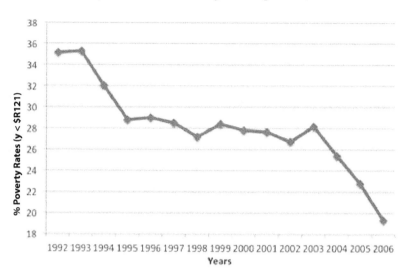

Source: FGV 2006.
Note: This report asserts that poverty rates fell between 1993 and 1995 from 35.3 percent to 28.8 percent, concurrent with the implementation of the Real Plan; and then again in 2003–2005, from 28.2 percent to 22.7 percent, representing an overall decrease in the proportion of Brazilians below the poverty line of 19.18 percentage points, comparable to the previous drop between 1993 and 1995 of 18.47 points.

targeted social policy. Similar to the previous PSDB administration, the PT was also addressing issues that mattered to its key supporters, who historically had come from the poor and working-class segments of society, particularly in the southeast of the country.

According to a credible public opinion survey of voters taken in 2002 (IBOPE 2002), of the fifty-two campaign promises Lula made prior to his election, the main three that the public believed he could accomplish in his four-year term were alleviating hunger, misery, and poverty (24 percent); creating jobs (17 percent); and raising the minimum salary (10 percent). In contrast, only 0–1 percent of the public expected he could (or would) fulfill the remaining forty-nine campaign promises. On the basis of public expectations, Lula's government had a clear mandate to prioritize poverty alleviation. Before he even took office, this issue was visibly on the federal agenda. The national government's new initiative was called Fome Zero (Zero Hunger) and Bolsa Família, a CCT program created to both alleviate hunger, misery, and poverty in Brazil and to fulfill a promise Lula had made earlier to Brazilian voters.

TRANSFORMATION AND EXPANSION OF CCTS UNDER PRESIDENT LULA (PT), 2003–2010

The goal of Lula's first administration (2003–2006) was to create a new flagship CCT that would unite and replace the three programs of Cardoso's government, that is, Bolsa Escola, Bolsa Alimentação, and Auxilio Gás, as well as a fourth one that Lula himself launched in his initial days in office, called Cartão Alimentação. Bolsa Escola was effectively discontinued and replaced by Bolsa Família starting in 2003 (see table 3.1). Current recipients of Bolsa Escola voluntarily transferred to the new program, which had an inherent incentive given that it was no longer uniquely dependent on the presence of school-age children.

The integration of Bolsa Escola with the other three social protection programs into a single CCT designed with a centralized administrative structure can be considered an example of "continuity with change." The endogenous changes that occurred between the two programs of Bolsa Escola and Bolsa Família over the course of roughly a decade, however, signified a shift toward a broader social policy approach that brought in new actors through the inclusion of new sectors—health, nutrition, education—and of families in extreme poverty who did not have dependent school-age children. Moreover, the design and structure of Bolsa Família improved upon three weak points in the other programs comprising the earlier compartmentalized phase of national CCTs (2001–2003). First, it resolved intra-bureaucratic chaos (ambiguity) by

Table 3.1. Scope of Bolsa Escola, 2001–2006

Year	2001	2002	2003	2004	2005	2006
Total Families	4,794,404	5,106,509	3,771,199	1,452,061	839,853	49,268
Proportion	100	107	89	30	18	1

Source: Ministério de Desenvolvimento Social.

integrating the program into a single responsible federal ministry, the Ministério de Desenvolvimento Social (MDS). A central office within the ministry was responsible for running the program. Second, it reduced the administrative costs to the government and facilitated user access to available goods from the local level on up, by deepening and consolidating a decentralized system of registration for eligible households, accessible at the municipal level and delivered through a single electronic bankcard. Third, the straightforward design of a single mass integrated social assistance program in Brazil was adapted to the circumstances of Brazil's unique political-institutional configuration, which by 2003 was clearly consolidated.

Bolsa Família is designed to serve each family via one application method, one responsible local office, one payment, and one federal registry. As a uniform and easily implemented social program, it is appealing to municipal authorities, who have varying levels of institutional capacity. Municipal heterogeneity had not been previously recognized in Brazilian federalism, which is institutionally symmetric across all levels of government. This territorially based heterogeneity can and does lead to widespread inequality of access to basic social services and service quality. Administrative changes to CCTs from Cardoso to Lula facilitated the ability of municipal governments to register, monitor, and successfully promote CCTs to eligible households within their territories. Mayors could communicate with only one federal government ministry, liberating them from negotiations with cabinet ministers from multiple political parties, who are often controlled by powerful state-based brokers.

The Ministry of Social Development (MDS) was newly created by President Lula in 2004 specifically to organize, administer, and execute national programs for social development and social assistance. Lula was also frequently present in person in the central office that administered Bolsa Família, as reported by a senior World Bank official who worked at the ministry during the early registration phase (interview Lindert, Fruttero, and Silva 2013). A unified federal administration, housed within one ministry, facilitated the ability of the national government to directly oversee the expansion and implementation of Bolsa Família. According to the ministry's coordinator of Bolsa Família (who also worked on Bolsa Escola), "previously it was the same families who would be eligible for the four redistributive programs, but they would have to go through four separate bureaucratic processes in order to register and present themselves to four separate local offices in order to meet the required conditionality" (interview Fonseca 2006).

Now operating as a single poverty alleviation program, Bolsa Família could efficiently use the centralized federal registry Cadastro Único to store all of the information about lower-income families in Brazil. The consolidation of this data registry, which was originally created for Bolsa Escola in 2001 and transferred to the MDS's architecture under Bolsa Família, strongly influenced the future development of Brazil's national poverty alleviation strategy. Families are registered in the database at the municipal level from the bottom up and are then selected automatically for eligibility by the MDS. In order to reach the government's 2006 target of 11.1 million families, the MDS was inputting data on up to 100,000 new families a day into the Cadastro Único database, much of which arrived at the office in paper form in brown envelopes from remote municipalities (interview anonymous MDS 2006). Monthly payments are given to families conditional on the requirements stipulated by a single office. The reported administrative cost of delivering one benefit payout is estimated at 6 percent of its total value: R$3.66 per household per month (interview Fonseca 2006). This efficient administration is fundamental to the program's public reputation and its targeting performance.

In terms of its success, by 2006 all municipalities in Brazil had voluntarily adhered to this program, allowing the federal government to reach its initially intended target (in 2003) of 11.1 million socially vulnerable families (MDS). With an average family size of four in Brazil, approximately 44 million citizens were included in this program during Lula's first term.[3] The importance Bolsa Família has been given by the national government can be seen in the resources that were allocated to it. The federal government's annual budget for income transfer programs nearly doubled from R$3.36 billion in 2004 to R$6.39 billion in 2006. As a means-tested targeted social program, it provided immediate available resources to 99.9 percent of the households in the nation whose monthly per capita income was below R$120 per month up until 2008, and then up to R$140 thereafter. The expansion of direct income transfers to the poor positively addressed a problem that citizens from across diverse parties expected Lula to resolve when they voted for him in 2002 (IBOPE 2002).[4]

It is therefore evident that the story of Bolsa Família is also a story about "politics as power." It is now well established that Bolsa Família had a feedback effect on electoral and individually based political participation in the 2006 presidential elections, an effect that certainly also had a "lock-in" effect on the program's continuity under Dilma Rousseff, and would be expected to apply under any future elected president. Exactly *how much* it mattered in explaining Lula's 2006 victory and whether it mattered more than other labor politics, such as the rise in minimum wage, however, is still open for discussion (Power and Zucco 2013).

Lula had a political motive to transform and expand Bolsa Família into a bigger and better CCT because he was elected in 2002 on this basis. The PT wanted to provide a monetary amount per month that would allow millions of households in Brazil to rise above the poverty line. The PT under Lula won the second round of the 2002 presidential election with 61.3 percent of valid votes. His electoral strength provided him with a clear mandate to improve upon government performance by reforming social policy and addressing pressing public issues. As previously mentioned, 24 percent of voters surveyed expected Lula to alleviate poverty. Of those surveyed, however, 22 percent identified with the right of center Partido Frente Liberal (PFL), now known as Democratas (DEM), 21 percent with the centrist social democrats (PSDB), 22 percent with the catch-all PMDB, and 32 percent with the left of center Partido dos Trabalhadores (PT) (IBOPE 2002). Given that this specific issue had broad multiparty support, it was paramount to the success of the incumbent national administration and its governing coalition that it deliver on the social promises it had made to voters during presidential campaigning. What mattered for the PT's success was continuing the policies that worked in Brazil, such as monetary and macroeconomic policy, and improving in other public policy areas where the government's results were still unclear.

Although it can be asserted that Bolsa Família contributed to the "comparative popularity and greater regional advance of Lula and his government," this does not provide conclusive evidence that this targeted social policy represents the "unfolding of the old story of using the government to build clientelistic support" (Hunter and Power 2007, 9), particularly given that over 50 percent of Brazilians surveyed in 2010 not only approved of Bolsa Família but also wanted it to expand (Ames et al. 2013). It does suggest, however, that Bolsa Família's territorial penetration remains the best explanation for increased voter turnout in poorer northeastern states (Hunter and Power 2007, 20). This can be classified as a policy feedback on individual political behavior. In the northeast, voter turnout in 2006 compared to the second round of 2002 increased by 4.6 percentage points (TSE 2006). According to Hunter and Power (2007, 20), the penetration of Bolsa Família into the lower segments of society was the best explanation for voters returning to the polls: "The bottom line is that Lula's social policies appear to have boosted enthusiasm and turnout among Brazil's poor majority in 2006." These voters were particularly swayed by the fact that poverty in Brazil dropped from 28.2 percent to 22.7 percent during 2003–2005, representing an overall decrease in the proportion of Brazilians below the poverty line of 19.18 percent (FGV 2006). Moreover, the national government's ability to improve upon and expand the previous administration's programs and to create a highly visible CCT that bypassed governors contributed to strengthening the conviction within a large segment of the population that the federal center was fair, responsive, and valuable.

In 2006, the average benefit provided per family was R$61, an amount that was often not large enough to push a family across the line from either extreme poverty to poverty, or from poverty to non-poor. Even though this average amount has increased gradually over time (in 2011 it had reached R$70), according to Soares and Sátyro (2010) the program only reduced (absolute) poverty by 1.6 percentage points. They argue, however, that its greatest impact is on the reduction of the poverty gap (18 percent), the reduction of the severity of poverty, and the downward pressure on the inequality rate, of which according to Soares, Souza, et al. (2010), 16 percent from 1999 to 2009 can be attributed to Bolsa Família. It is clearly acknowledged in the literature that Bolsa Família's impact on poverty and inequality has been modest.

Although the ability of CCTs to reduce poverty and inequality is of great importance, the central argument of this chapter is that the secret behind the success of Bolsa Família measured in terms of its territorial distribution—a factor that is clearly linked to the powerful policy feedback effects it generated in 2006—lay in the ability of both the national government and municipalities to avoid the control or interference of powerful state-based governors in its implementation. As a redistributive social program based on bottom-up registration that was designed to be carried out at the municipal level, Bolsa Família avoided the kind of negotiation between the executive-legislative branches that has come to epitomize Brazilian politics. State-based power brokers are not able to claim credit for these targeted social investment expenditures because the resources completely bypass their level of government. This is not to say that governors do not have alternative means to stay in the patronage-game, through traditional paths such as elite control of the state's apparatus, control over public employment, unequal land tenure, and control over capital in public companies—a system of vote-buying and material rewards distribution that clearly still exists, post–Bolsa Família, in many Brazilian states (Montero 2010). What it does mean is that targeted social programming that cuts out the so-called middleman reduces the ability of state-brokers to use *these* specific funds to generate patronage.

The widespread success of Bolsa Família promoted a strengthened relationship between citizens and the national government, mediated through municipalities, which become the prime agents of the federal government in social service delivery. This equally represents a new political relationship that many authors have asserted contributed to Lula's electoral victory in 2006 (Hunter and Power 2007; Nicolau and Peixoto 2007; Zucco 2008; Soares and Terron 2008; Castro, Licio, and Renno 2009). The biggest losers in Bolsa Família were the twenty-seven governors whom the federal government cut out, by building on and expanding national poverty alleviation initiatives without their involvement. This meant that these states could not claim credit or control the electoral effects of these social initiatives. This is a fact that matters greatly in a political system where individualism and personalism are important parts of subnational election campaigns. The direct credit for Bolsa Família was given almost entirely to the federal government and to Lula, generating important feedbacks for electoral and individually based political participation. According to recent survey research on public opinion in the 2010 presidential elections, 80 percent of respondents attributed Bolsa Família to the federal government (Ames et al. 2013, 38).

Municipal participation, however, was also fundamental to this program's success and contributed to generating its electoral effects.

This new relationship of direct national-local policy collaboration was predominantly linked to the fact that the design and implementation structure of Bolsa Família focused on implementation and promotion at the municipal level. Although mayors in Brazil in the past were entirely beholden to state governors (Ames 1995; Samuels 2003), the hardening of budget constraints and the increasingly centralized control over subnational expenditure in the post-millennium context liberated large and medium-size municipalities from excessive fiscal dependence on the states, making them somewhat less beholden.

The economic and fiscal reforms of the previous PSDB administration gave municipalities a new fiscal incentive to collaborate with the federal government in many social policy areas because such collaboration increased their share of the national government's earmarked grants. As a technical advisor to the Secretariat of Social Assistance in the City of São Paulo claimed, "Bolsa Família shows up in our fiscal accounts; although the money does not go through them, the total amount transferred into our territory is included on our balance sheets" (interview anonymous Secretaria de Assistência Social 2006). Stated simply, CCTs also entailed bringing small economic inputs into their municipalities, new revenues to cover their administrative costs, and increased employment in social sector areas that are required by the program to fulfill recipient conditions.

Municipalities had little to lose by participating and by supporting the federal government, given that their main responsibility after 1988 was to be the federation's primary social services provider, and given that after 2000 this responsibility was legally enforceable through fiscal regulations imposed by the national government. By 2004, municipal social expenditure in the areas of health, education, and social assistance exceeded that of the states.

THE SUCCESSFUL TERRITORIAL DISTRIBUTION
OF BOLSA FAMÍLIA

Brazilian federalism after 2000 provided incentives for mayors to carry out national policy objectives. The key permissive condition that helped the national government realize this policy objective was the constitutional recognition of municipalities as an order of government distinct from the states; this constitutionally allowed states to be bypassed. By 2006, all 5,564 municipalities and the Federal District in Brazil had cho sen autonomously to adhere to this national social program, without the interference of state governors. The obvious winners of this program's success were the federal government and the president. Municipalities, which were able to claim credit for the program's local existence, bene fit most from the small economic benefits that flow from the program into the local economy, plus the fiscal incentives that are given to the local bureaucracy for its efforts and for improving the supply-side in puts. The losers of Bolsa Família from 2003 to 2010 were state-level ac tors and bureaucracies.[5]

The importance of the small economic inputs for municipalities generated by the program's cash allowances is greater than many in ternational observers expect (interview Marques 2006). Rosa Marques (2004) identified groups of municipalities in the northeast where 45 percent of total families within the territory received the family stipend; in the north this figure was approximately 20 percent for some groups, in the southeast it ranged between 15 and 29 percent, and in the wealth ier south it was much less. What does this mean? Marques calculated how much of the disposable revenue in the municipality was repre sented by the aggregate monetary amount of the Bolsa Família stipends. She then compared these numbers with the federal transfers from other social programs, such as SUS (Sistema Única de Saúde), and the revenue from ICMS, the value-added service and merchandise tax. The results were surprising: Marques identified small municipalities with low HDI (Human Development Index ratings) where up to 43 percent of the municipality's disposable income came from this one social program. For example, the Municipality of Vitória de Santo Antão (Pernambuco) received 40 percent of its disposable income (calculated based on own-source revenues and transfers) from Bolsa Família. This was 289 per cent more than what had been transferred to the municipality to finance the unified system of health called SUS. Marques's study found similar results in numerous municipalities in different regions throughout the nation. Subsequently, Figueiredo, Torres, and Bichir (2006, 181) have used a similar research method, based on a household survey taken in 2004 within the municipality of São Paulo (SPM); they asserted that for 14 percent of families receiving cash transfers in SPM, this represented their total family income. Whichever way the economic benefit is calculated or analyzed, increasing evidence exists that significant economic inputs are being received within a community via CCTs, inputs that are then recycled through the microeconomy of that community and have a powerful indirect impact on the collective municipal welfare.

Bolsa Família's Regional Composition, 2003 to 2006

The regional composition of beneficiaries in Bolsa Família from 2003 to 2006 deserves special attention at this point. The question is whether the program was distributed successfully throughout the nation in terms of which households residing in which territories should have received it based on the explicit targeting of the program, compared to which actually did receive it. My analysis was done using state-level aggregations at a time when disaggregated program data were not available to the public. I present this analysis in order to empirically test whether the program was in fact effectively carried out nationwide via municipal enrollment efforts during the program's implementation phase. This phase of Bolsa Família began in 2003 and had to be completed according to law by 2006.

Bolsa Família is a policy of subsidization, which means that leaders cannot be certain what the territorially based political effects of transfers will be under such policies. In Brazil, where a majority party is absent, the president would appear to prefer broad national goods over geographically targeted ones because all territorial votes are equally valuable (Arretche and Rodden 2004, 557). Moreover, according to Lijphart (2002), the existence of executive power-sharing, in the form of grand coalitions, means that presidentialism is not necessarily a winner-take-all game. It is plausible to suppose that this nationally based, win-win power-sharing logic means that the federal government is not overly concerned with the political effects of transfers at other levels of government, so long as the president and the federal government can take the bulk of the credit. The existence of a consensus-like model of democracy decreases the incentive for the national government to use Bolsa Família to incorporate certain territories on the basis of a dominant partisan logic.

If we analyze the territorial distribution of Bolsa Família aggregated to the regional level (see figure 3.2) over the twelve months of

Figure 3.2. Actual Territorial Distribution of Bolsa Família in 2005

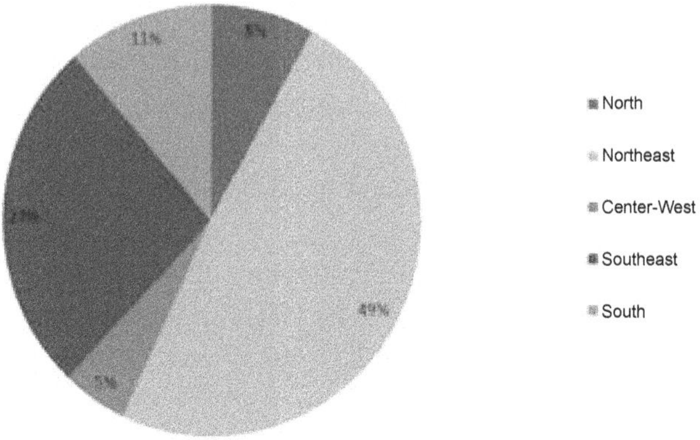

Source: Ministério do Desenvolvimento Social e Combate à Fome.
Note: Author's aggregations using distributions by state and month.

2005 prior to the presidential and gubernatorial elections in 2006, it is no surprise that many observers claimed that Bolsa Família was used as a mechanism for vote-buying in the northeast, a region composed of nine very poor states long dominated by conservative politicians and political bosses (Ames 1995). In 2002, seven of the nine northeastern governors were opposition members, one was from a swing party (PMDB-Pernambuco), and only one was a loyal member (PT-Piauí). Following the general elections of 2006, six of the nine governors were PT or coalition members, with three remaining in opposition, and no swing parties. It is also empirically true that 49 percent of the beneficiaries of Bolsa Família live in these same states.

Figure 3.2 illustrates that the northeast of Brazil benefited most from this CCT program. It does not illustrate, however, that political considerations determined the distribution of this program in the northeast. As a means-tested CCT, its selection process did not include any partisan or territorial criteria. In order to determine whether the poorer and opposition-strong northeastern region received more allocation than was proper under the program's rules for eligibility ($Y <$ R\$120), the optimal distribution of Bolsa Família is plotted regionally (based on the program's criteria) in order to compare it with the actual regional distribution shown in figure 3.2. The underlying problem of a partisan-based hypothesis (rich vs. poor—read electoral manipulation)[6] is that Bolsa Família was connected to explicit equity goals. In order to analyze the program's distribution, the equity goals of the program must be separated from the actual patterns of distribution.

By applying the methodology for measuring poverty as utilized by IBGE-IPEA-CEPAL and the data these entities produce annually, the optimal distribution, given the program's explicit targeting, should equate to all families in all regions that are classified below the poverty line (household income per capita R$120). If we compare figure 3.2 with the ideal distribution of Bolsa Família for the same year, namely, 2005, in figure 3.3, the program in the northeast is over-targeting beyond the predetermined goals by only 1 percent. This outcome offers little empirical evidence that this particular region was being overly targeted by the program or had been encouraged to carry it out for political ends, beyond the level justified by the preexisting heterogeneous socioeconomic realities in Brazil. Most importantly for this study, it shows that Bolsa Família was territorially allocated throughout Brazil during its phase of expansion as would be expected according to the program's design, that is, based on municipal identification of eligible families.

Figure 3.3. Ideal Territorial Distribution of Bolsa Família Based on Its Criteria

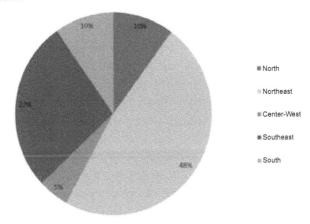

Source: Author's aggregations using IPEA data.

Eligibility for Bolsa Família is based simply on a household income below the threshold set by the national government. Sufficient evidence of electoral manipulation is not provided, based on the fact that most of the poor in Brazil live in the northeastern region. The southeast region, where Lula traditionally had his electoral strongholds before 2006, should have received 27 percent of the program's benefits based on household poverty rates, and did indeed receive precisely 27 percent in 2005. The northeast should have received 48 percent and in fact received 49 percent. Based on the propositions presented in this chapter, the most feasible explanation of the switching electoral patterns observed in the northeast in the 2006 general elections is, according to Barry Ames, that large portions of the northeast which are generally supportive of Brazil's political right survive on federal transfers funneled to local governments through state governors (2002). This is why ruling conservative northeastern elites have traditionally benefited from the malapportionment that overrepresents their interests in Congress.

Bolsa Família certainly did benefit northeastern municipalities where poverty rates are substantially higher than in the south and southeast. These federal funds, however, were not funneled through state authorities, nor could these authorities claim credit for the distribution of these funds. These states also could not use their overrepresentation in Congress to obtain greater benefits for their region from the Bolsa Família. If this were just another unfolding of the old story of using the government to build clientelistic support in the northeast, like the one told by Nunes Leal much earlier (Leal 1949), there would have to be evidence that targeting in the northeast exceeded the predetermined equity goals of this program in that region. There was a clear geographic bias in the outcomes of the most recent general elections because this region, with its high poverty rates, had a lot to gain from this highly visible national CCT. This does not, however, equate to clientelism, defined "as public or private goods distributed solely on the criterion of electoral support" (Brusco, Nazareno, and Stokes 2004).

Much of the national media's attention prior to the 2006 election included attempts to discredit Bolsa Família. Primary accusations included "buying the poor's vote," or that the original idea was not the PT's. In Cardoso's letter to the public in September 2006, he compared Lula to the former, centralizing president Gétulio Vargas, who was famed for buying the votes of the poor: "Pai-dos-pobres" and "Pai-Presidente" (*Folha de S.Paulo*, September 9, 2006). Bahian Governor Antonio Carlos Magalhães, among others, accused Lula of stealing programs invented by them during the "municipal era" and/or the PSDB under Cardoso (*Folha de S.Paulo*, August 25, 2006; October 4, 2006). Let us recall two points established here: first, the success of Cardoso's original three programs was compromised by intra-bureaucratic and intergovernmental wrangling. Second, a virtue of Brazil's unique political regime type, together with the fact that most Brazilians do not vote based on a fixed partisan identity, is that political actors can build upon and improve the policies of a previous administration without fear of electoral punishment, regardless of their formal alignment with the president who initiated the program.

It is particularly this latter political-institutional quality, the ability of a local policy innovation to be disseminated nationwide and then gradually improved upon by two alternative administrations, that allowed CCTs in Brazil to gradually "muddle through" and become an international success story. Lula's combination of the previous administration's three programs into one facilitated Bolsa Família's effective administration and widespread distribution at the municipal level. The consolidation behind the idea of using CCTs as a means to achieving social inclusion over the course of more than a decade, and its extensive polity-wide distribution, has generated Bolsa Família's stability.

FROM BOLSA FAMÍLIA TO BRASIL SEM MISÉRIA, 2010 TO 2014

In October 2010, a new PT president, Dilma Rousseff, assumed office. She had won the presidential elections in the second round of voting with 56.05 percent of the total vote against the PSDB opposition candidate, José Serra. Since she was Lula's handpicked successor, radical changes or significant expansions in Bolsa Família were not anticipated. Cardoso had implemented Brazil's first CCT, Bolsa Escola, producing important state-building effects such as the institutionalization of cash transfers as an effective policy instrument, the creation of a centralized database for beneficiaries, an electronic bankcard delivery system that included pioneering contracts with the Brazilian bank Caixa Ecônomica Federal, and the consolidation of CCTs linked to human development investments in education. By pursuing an endogenous mechanism of change, Lula's administration adopted a broader, integrated approach based on human development investments in health, education, and nutrition. Bolsa Família greatly expanded and built upon Bolsa Escola.

The policy focus from the perspective of the national government in both Bolsa Família and Bolsa Escola remained on the demand side: who gets what, how, and why. As discussed above, Lula's reforms broadened the policy objectives of Bolsa Escola by bringing in new actors and new sectors, and by overcoming the unintended consequences of a compartmentalized approach. Bolsa Família's success in obtaining its intended program goals within three years in terms of both territorial and absolute coverage generated powerful policy feedbacks on political behavior and individual-based political participation—all of which ultimately contributed to the more established policy "lock-in" effects in the welfare literature. These positive policy feedback effects make it very difficult for a newly elected official, such as Rousseff, to dismantle, replace, or transform Bolsa Família. None of the presidential candidates from any political party during the campaigning of either the 2010 or 2014 executive elections threatened to dismantle this social program.

Despite Bolsa Família's successful territorial distribution, in 2010, when Lula's successor was elected, the 2010 National Census revealed that in contrast to the 2009 Annual Household Survey (PNAD/IBGE) estimates of 5.4 percent of the total population living in a situation of extreme poverty, in reality, 8.5 percent of Brazilians continued to live in this category—more or less 16 million people (Neri 2011). Thus an opportunity presented itself early on in Rousseff's first term to justify further expanding the program and raising the value of the program's benefit. Therefore in 2011, President Rousseff announced a new strategy called Brasil Sem Miséria (Brazil without Misery) to alleviate extreme poverty in Brazil by 2014, within which Bolsa Família continued to be the benchmark program.

As a new government strategy, however, focused specifically on the extreme poor, Rousseff finally had to define a national extreme poverty line at R$70 per capita, readjusted to R$77 in 2014. Both Cardoso and Lula had been reluctant to set a threshold (Neri 2011). The additional benefit amount was raised from R$22 to R$32 per child, and the maximum number of children receiving the benefit in each family was increased from three to five. These changes were made to include larger families in lower socioeconomic situations who, according to the 2010 census, were still living in a situation of extreme poverty. By early 2014, according to MDS data, Bolsa Família had reached a record number of 14.1 million households in Brazil (MDS 2015, 6).

Bolsa Família remains the benchmark program of Rousseff's new strategy. It is clearly framed in government documents as the entry door for participation in the majority of the recently created programs. For example, the additional resources transferred to municipal preschools within the program Brasil Carinhoso are chosen in relation to how many children are beneficiaries of Bolsa Família. Likewise, the housing program Minha Casa, Minha Vida also prioritizes beneficiaries of Bolsa Família, and the same applies for all of the productive inclusion programs—Programa National de Acesso ao Ensino Técnico e Emprego (Pronatec) Economia Solidaria, and the National Microcredit program (MEI). Therefore, although the Brazilian strategy after Lula has officially moved beyond reliance on a single federal program, still, R$26.5 billion of Sem Miséria's entire 2013 executed budget of R$30 billion within the MDS continued to represent the expenditure of a single CCT program, Bolsa Família, and its associated costs (SIOP 2014). Moreover, and most importantly, the expansion of Bolsa Família remains entirely dependent on the willingness of mayors and their bureaucracies to actively seek out and document previously unidentified families who fall below the currently established line of extreme poverty within their municipalities.

This chapter has shown that CCTs evolved in Brazil in a process of "continuity with change" across multiple federal administrations. The policy developments and their critical outcomes are summarized in table 3.2.

Many social policy critics have referred to Bolsa Família and to Latin American CCTs in general as a rather narrow form of social protection (Hall 2007). Over the past decade, however, Bolsa Família (the largest CCT in the region) has contributed to reducing poverty and inequality for families living in situations of extreme poverty (income

Table 3.2.   Phases of Policy Development and Critical Outcomes in Brazil, 1988–2014

1	2	3	4	5
Subnational Experimentation	Bolsa Escola (Cardoso I and II)	Bolsa Família (Lula I)	Bolsa Família (Lula II)	Bolsa Família (Rousseff I)
1988–1995	1995–2002	2003–2006	2007–2010	2011–2014
	↓	↓	↓	↓
	Nationalization/ Compartmentalized Model	Expansion/ Integrated Model	100% Territorial Coverage/National Policy Objective Realized	Corrections/ Stability

Source: Author elaboration.

less than R$77 per capita per month as of 2014) and poverty (income less than R$154 per capita per month as of 2014). Moreover, the sheer size of Bolsa Família and the continuity in the policy development of CCTs in Brazil for over the past decade have been developed from a rights-based approach. CCTs are understood as a successful policy instrument to promote social inclusion and as a new contract between socially vulnerable citizens and the federal government that can be delivered without political intermediation. The families who were targeted by CCTs in Brazil were not framed as victims of economic upheaval; they were framed as citizens whom the Brazilian state had repeatedly failed to include—representing a failure of the state from a leftist perspective, in addition to the Cardoso era's acknowledgment of a failure of the market. In 2014, nearly 25 million families were registered in the national government's unified database, thanks to local identification efforts, and 14.1 million are currently receiving benefits throughout Brazil (MDS 2015). This is no small feat for a country that has been considered as suffering from a serious policy transmission problem (Malloy 1993). The successful territorial distribution of Bolsa Família is related to the program's reliance on voluntary municipal participation and the broader institutional and political factors that have motivated municipal cooperation within the context of a decentralized federal system.

In thinking about the politics of investing socially in Latin America, as asserted by Huber and Stephens (2012, 63), "we need to think about political organization, economic power, political institutions, and public administration." These are explanatory factors that go well beyond the existence of a single party or a single ideology ruling over the course of an entire decade, a condition that is satisfied in both federal countries under examination.

CHAPTER 4

Factors Encouraging Municipal Actors to Promote National Goals in Brazil

One must keep an equal distance from both alternatives.
Too much authority, or too little, and that is the end of freedom.
—Pierre Elliott Trudeau, *Federalism and the French Canadians*

The willingness of mayors to promote national policy objectives has gradually increased in Brazil since 1988, for a plethora of political, economic, and structural reasons. Brazil is a symmetric federal democracy where since 1988 the power to govern has been shared between three legally autonomous and constitutionally recognized levels of government. There are 5,564 municipalities, 26 state governments, and one federal district (Brasília).[1] Together, these comprise the *união* (union).

The central goal in this chapter is to confront the theoretical claims I have already put forward with the empirical evidence from Brazil. I have suggested that Bolsa Família, a widely distributed and applauded mass CCT, was successfully distributed polity-wide because of its ability to avoid the influence or control of powerful state-based governors. The unique characteristics of Brazil's most recent national constitution (1988), the gradual but successful hardening of subnational finances, and Brazil's consensual democratic model have all provided incentives for mayors to promote national policy objectives in specific social policy areas such as health, basic (primary) education, and social assistance (development). I assert that these three factors contributed to the ability of the national government to meet its explicitly stated social policy target, namely, to provide cash transfers to more than 11 million households in situations of social vulnerability federation-wide within a period of about three years (2003 to 2006). Moreover, from the perspective of federal theory, the ability of the Brazilian national government to design, implement, and sustain a program of this magnitude provides credibility to its highly decentralized three-level governing structure. It shows that, at least in this social policy area, federalism did not hinder a redistributive policy. Moreover, by analyzing the institutional and political conditions that encourage municipal actors to promote national goals, this chapter aims to continue solving what institutionally oriented scholars have labeled, with respect to Brazil, as the "anomaly of a feckless democracy with reasonably good policy performance" (Armijo, Faucher, and Dembinska 2006, 764).

BRAZILIAN FEDERALISM

Following a transition to democracy that began in 1974, Brazil's political institutions underwent two gradual transformations during the 1980s and 1990s, which are covered in depth by the literature. It is important to understand this period of Brazilian politics since it clarifies why governors needed to be avoided. On the one hand, the 1988 Constitution represented the consolidation of a process of "democratization as decentralization," leading to an institutional framework of overlapping policy authority between three autonomous levels of government. This constitutional design increased revenue and expenditure responsibilities at the subnational levels, creating *de jure* a highly decentralized system. Both states and municipalities gained an increased ability to act as significant players in the Brazilian federal game from 1988 onward, contributing to the system's strength. By establishing a system of de facto predatory federalism, subnational levels of government competed with one another within the context of a "soft budget syndrome" and in a highly fragmented political system. From 1988 to 1995, this institutional configuration enabled subnational levels of government to block the policy preferences of the national executive and created a situation that Mainwaring called "permanent minority presidentialism" (1992) or a "feckless democracy" (1995b).

On the other hand, parallel to this process of democratization, there were persistent macroeconomic instability and high inflation, which had begun prior to the democratic climax of the first free and direct presidential election of 1989. This economic situation not only remained unresolved but was exacerbated by predatory intergovernmental fiscal behavior. The political and economic factors of the soft budget syndrome from 1988 to 1995 compromised the credibility of the new, highly decentralized constitution. In essence, strong federalism, in the context of uncontrollable inflation and political fragmentation, impeded the national government from taking any reforming action in social policy areas and facilitated the ability of subnational levels to undermine, through simple inaction, any of its initiatives.

The characterization of Brazilian federalism as "strong" has led to a consensus over the idea that governors have the power to constrain the federal center.[2] The literature in this area focuses on how Brazil's weak political institutions, primarily its inchoate party system, produce incentives for legislators to articulate subnational interests and to behave in a manner that weakens the capacity of Congress to pass the executive's preferred reforms. Resolving the two dilemmas of federalism, namely, how to prevent the national government from encroaching upon its constituent units and how to prevent the units from undermining the national government, has been historically difficult in Brazil. After 1988 it became extremely difficult (Abrucio 1998; Samuels and Mainwaring 2004). According to Gibson, "federalism empowered local actors to hinder the efficacy of democratically elected governments at the center" (2004, 24). Even before the 1988 Constitution, it was long recognized that Brazilian federalism enabled local actors to act at the expense of the center.

Historically, states and municipalities have played a significant role in exacerbating Brazil's federal dilemma. The term *política dos governadores* was coined at the end of the nineteenth century to describe the way governors could use their power to control the election of deputies to Congress and their legislative agenda.[3] The dominance of gubernatorial interests in Congress was further complicated by state-municipal relations. Taken together, all these phenomena were traditionally known as "localism." The debate regarding state-local relations began as early as the Constituent Assembly of 1890. Many members of this assembly believed that the principle of decentralization inherent to federalism should be extended to the municipalities (Leal 1949, 98). Opponents both here and later argued that municipalities were fundamental to the power-generating capacity of the states. According to Leal's account, state constitutions reduced the principle of municipal autonomy in order to increase state power over the center. The imprecision of pre-1988 constitutions regarding state-local relations meant that states could de facto regulate these as they wished. By treating subnational power as aggregated, "localism" has long been used as a variable to explain the strength of Brazil's unique system of federalism that constrains the center and the *demos*.

HOW BOLSA FAMÍLIA AVOIDED GOVERNORS

The following sections examine the three explanatory factors put forward in chapter 2 in the Brazilian case. I argue that these factors provided mayors with an incentive to enable Bolsa Família's success by promoting it locally, identifying eligible families, and monitoring the compliance of each family with the program's conditions. A key point is that because Bolsa Família bypassed state-level involvement during its implementation and consolidation phase (2003 to 2006), credit for it was given almost entirely to the federal government. The political effects of this were visible both during the 2006 presidential elections and in the public opinion surveys taken around the 2010 and 2014 presidential

elections. What are the incentives, therefore, for municipalities to promote a national program when they appear to have little to gain? Why
would the national government not try to capture the support of state-
level power brokers and implement this politically strategic program
through governors?

Constitutional Recognition of Two Subnational
Levels of Government

Given the historical predominance of governors' power and their ability to constrain the center from 1988 to 1995, the successful territorial
distribution of later national poverty alleviation programs in Brazil depended on the ability of the federal center to legally bypass the involvement of its twenty-six state governors and promote direct national-local
policy collaboration. Operating as a permissive condition, the process
of disaggregating municipalities both in theory and in practice begins
with the legal recognition of municipal autonomy in the 1988 Constitution. This recognition, however, did not have an immediate impact on
intergovernmental relations because it occurred simultaneously with a
period of extensive fiscal and administrative decentralization.

Municipal autonomy was officially recognized for the first time in
Brazilian history by the Constituent Assembly of 1987–1988. The "decentralization as democracy hypothesis" has been used to explain the
extent of power given to both the states and the municipalities within
Brazil's most recently promulgated 1988 Constitution. Free and direct
elections in Brazil occurred incrementally. In 1982, direct elections were
permitted for legislators, governors, and mayors (except in capital cities and in areas considered to affect "national security"). It has been
argued that this slow and gradual transition to democracy enabled mayors and governors to dominate the Constituent Assembly that wrote
the new constitution over the course of eighteen months. Souza (1997)
paid particular attention to the new fiscal allocations given to both the
states and municipalities that were unaccompanied by policy responsibilities and thus policy results. As a consequence of both its notorious length and the overlapping policy ambiguity, the 1988 Constitution
strengthened the ability of the constituent units of the federation (now
officially both the municipalities and states) to undermine the national

government through free-riding, which could be accomplished through both deliberate action and, more likely, inaction.

Fernando Luiz Abrucio contended in his *Os Barões da Federação* (1998) that one of the main consequences of the 1988 Constitution was a return to the "politics of governors." Rejecting Souza's "democratization as decentralization hypothesis," Abrucio and Samuels later asserted that it was the failure of the military regime (1964–1985) to transform Brazil's elite organizational structure that allowed subnational elites to pursue their interests during the process of democratization (1985–1989) and to dominate potential national interests (2000, 46). Their portrayal has further contributed to an established consensus in the literature that state governors reemerged in 1988 as the prime brokers of legislative bargaining in Brazil (Ames 1995; Mainwaring and Perez Linan 1997).

The power of governors in Brazil to constrain the center is attributed to Brazil's highly fragmented and weakly institutionalized party system, as well as to the specific dynamics of executive-legislative relations (Samuels and Mainwaring 2004; Ames and Power 2006). From the viewpoint of the political theory of federalism (Bednar, Eskridge, and Ferejohn 2001), this fragmentation of party-based power at the national level makes it harder for a nonconsensual will to be formed, in the way, for example, that it has recently been formed in the Russian Federation. In some cases, therefore, party fragmentation can be positive. However, party-based fragmentation in Brazil and the dominant power of states make it extremely difficult for the president to govern according to his or her preferences or the preferences of presidential supporters. After 1988, center-constraining executive-legislative relations and a highly decentralized system of authority across three levels of government fragmented power to the point that Brazil appeared ungovernable.

This debilitating institutional configuration that had been triggered by the 1988 Constitution had severe effects on the country's macroeconomic stability. Unclear policy responsibilities, coupled with soft budget constraints, allowed the twenty-six states to shirk their responsibilities and shift them back to the national government, and both of these two levels of government encroached on, or shifted burdens onto, municipalities (as illustrated in figure 4.1).

By comparing revenue and expenditure levels before decentralization in 1974 and after 1988, it becomes apparent that the greatest

Figure 4.1. Predatory Federalism in Brazil, 1988–1995

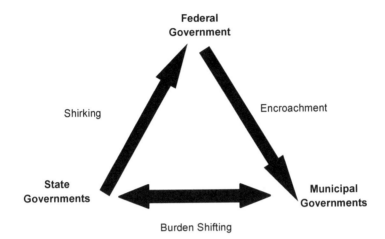

winners of de facto predatory federalism after 1988 were state governors (see table 4.1). Equally noticeable is that state revenue levels increased at a far greater rate than did their expenditure levels, indicating that increases to state finances did not follow function in 1988.

At the municipal level, it is important to note in table 4.1 that municipal expenditure responsibilities after 1988 outpaced increases to their shares of revenue, indicating that they were being overburdened by the states. From 1988 to 1995, state governors possessed guaranteed revenue in the form of taxation autonomy and transfers and the freedom to fuel money into patronage networks, and they could rely on direct market access to credit through state-owned banks (Dickovick 2003). This left mayors with no choice but to turn to the powerful governors to bail them out financially. This situation also motivated mayors to forge state-local political alliances, which contributed to the "new era of governor politics" (Abrucio and Samuels 2000).

Despite the strong findings in the earlier literature regarding Brazil's inherent institutional weaknesses, the federal government after 1995 was able to produce examples of policies whose efficiency and effectiveness can be clearly identified in objective economic and social indicators.[4] Former president Fernando Henrique Cardoso (PSDB) directly confronted the problem of strong federalism after his electoral victory in

Table 4.1. Brazil's Revenue and Expenditure by Level of Government before and after Decentralization

	Share of Total Government Revenue (%)			Share of Total Government Expenditure (%)		
	1974	*1988*	*%▲*	*1974*	*1988*	*%▲*
Central	59.8	47.1	−12.7	50.2	36.5	−13.7
State	36.9	49.4	12.5	36.2	40.7	4.5
Local	3.8	3.6	−0.2	13.6	22.8	9.2

Source: Willis, Garman, and Haggard 1999.

1994, following a campaign that prioritized macroeconomic stability by promising to alleviate economic problems, inflation, and job instability. The success of Cardoso in pursuing his social and economic agenda from 1995 demonstrated that the federal government could successfully overcome the ability of subnational actors to block executive initiatives in an institutionalized manner by using the president's tools, which include the internal rules of the decision-making process in Congress and the constitutional powers of the president. By contrast with many authors who asserted that Congress could be easily dominated by governors and state-level interest groups, the "politics of governors" (Ames 1995; Arretche and Rodden 2004), other authors argued that Brazil's electoral rules and party system features (what I classify in relative terms to Argentina as a consensual or power-sharing democratic model) institutionally render legislators' behavior extremely dependent on loyalty to a party and presidential preferences (Figueiredo and Limongi 1999; Pereira and Mueller 2004). It is increasingly accepted that this model of governance in Brazil, often referred to as "coalitional-presidentialism," enables its elected presidents "to build reasonably stable post-electoral coalitions within congress with a high level of governability by means of strong party discipline of the governing coalition" (Alston et al. 2008, 122).

From 1988 to 1995, predatory federalism hindered the implementation of policy and the ability of municipalities to exercise their constitutional autonomy. The problem of producing coordinated intergovernmental action to provide such goods goes beyond the dichotomy of decentralization and recentralization (Abrucio 2005, 42). In the area of social protection policy particularly, fragmented and uncoordinated policy initiatives cannot tackle a problem as extensive as poverty and social vulnerability given its federation-wide magnitude in Brazil. As a result, the national government's desired social and economic policy outputs were delayed until after 1995, when the economic crisis affecting all Brazilians was gradually resolved during the first term (1995 to 1998) of Cardoso of the PSDB. Therefore the ability of municipalities to exercise their autonomy and the willingness of mayors to cooperate with the national government gradually increased during these years because of a more stable national, political, and economic context, which would allow the federal government to rein in the powerful state-based veto players, decreasing their ability to undermine and free-ride on the national government, and liberating municipalities from their co-dependent relationship. This new dynamic, which has become more prevalent over time, is most often referred to as *municipalization*.

Municipalization in Brazil, defined as "the transfer of implementation responsibility and/or resources from federal and state governments to local governments" (Souza 2003, 3), was legally enshrined in Article 30 of the Constitution of 1988, which recognized municipalities as an order of government distinct from the two higher levels. The institutional norms and rules regulating this lowest level of government are the same for all 5,564 units. However, although Brazilian municipalities are institutionally homogenous, they are economically and demographically heterogeneous, which exacerbates territorially based inequality (interviews Souza 2005). For example, according to the 2010 National Census, average income per capita of the 1,668 municipalities in the southeast was R$10,128 compared to R$4,884 in the 1,792 municipalities in the northeast (IBGE 2010). In terms of population, 22 percent of Brazilian municipalities have between 2,000 and 5,000 inhabitants, whereas the municipality of São Paulo had 11.3 million inhabitants with a per capita income of R$39,450 (IBGE 2010).[5]

The obvious regional variation in technical and administrative capacity, arising out of diverse economic and demographic situations, is a challenge to the autonomous ability of municipalities to design and finance their own social policy. Many authors have observed that administrative decentralization after 1988 was implemented more successfully in states and regions that had a higher level of GDP per capita (Arretche 2000; Souza 2003) compared to states with lower levels. Both fiscal and administrative incapacity frustrated the successful management of earlier social policy decentralization to the municipal level, particularly in the context of soft budget constraints, which resulted in higher revenue transfers that were not necessarily followed by greater local policy quality. Additionally, the national government had few institutional mechanisms available to monitor municipal government performance from 1988 to 2000. Severe regional inequality in Brazil thus resulted in both low- and high-quality policy outputs. Social services that are delivered at the local level need to be designed with this inequality in mind. The diversity of social and economic indicators at the municipal level can impede the quality of purely local policy outputs, thus providing a further incentive for the federal government to create a uniform system of centrally designed and financed social policy initiatives that can be framed as expanding social citizenship.

By the recognition of the autonomy of municipalities within the Brazilian national constitution, however, municipalities are in fact provided a *de jure* choice. Either they can pursue decentralization directly at the local level, or they have the constitutional authority to autonomously *choose* to participate in a national social program. Although the separation of municipalities from the implicit power of governors took more than a decade of muddling through, the constitutional recognition of municipalities that began in 1988 has slowly enabled local leaders to have a choice over which level of government they turn to for action. Most importantly, it opened the door to extensive municipalization in Brazil.

The Muddling through of Municipalization after 1988

This shift from governor politics toward municipalization has been gradual, moving incrementally since 1988 from a two-level governing logic to a three-level governing logic. It is important to highlight the unique overlapping nature of government functions across the three levels of government in Brazil. Within the *de jure* territorial distribution of authority, municipalization is evident. In terms of political decentralization, the most significant change brought about by the Constitution of 1988 is that in Article 1, which for the first time in Brazilian history recognized municipalities as official constituent units of the federation. This gave them the same legal status as the twenty-six states and the *união*, the federal or national government. The political determinants of this change are well known to have been linked to the members of the Constituent Assembly (1987–1988), who were legislators with strong bases in both state-level and municipal-level politics (Souza 1997). The importance of municipalities in the 1988 constitution is evident in the indicators frequently used to demonstrate the extent of political decentralization between multiple levels of government (see appendix, table A.1).

The political power of governors remained stronger than that of mayors because of their strong representation in Congress and the existence of state constitutions protected by state-level courts. Additionally, the lack of a vertically integrated party system, demonstrated in table A.1, weakens the party-based incentives of subnational units to carry out initiatives emanating from other levels of government. Officially, the organic laws of municipalities cannot contradict state-level constitutions. However, the Federal Supreme Court has the power to judicially review state laws and rules. Political decentralization did not begin to liberate municipalities from governors until after 1995 because of the ability of states to continue exercising "extensive control over local finances" (Abrucio 2005, 47).

The constitutional recognition of municipalities did begin a process of democratization at the local level that enabled new actors, specifically in the areas of social policy, to both innovate and experiment. Although the heterogeneity of municipalities, in terms of size and capacity, could not be resolved through political decentralization (which in fact limited the ability of smaller municipalities to exercise their newly attributed political power), the 1988 Constitution increased the decision-making responsibility of municipalities regarding the provisioning of public services (Souza 2004).

From a political perspective, what is most important is the increase of electoral competition at the municipal level. For a political position to appear attractive to key stakeholders beyond simply the chance of electoral victory, filling the position must be meaningful. Prior to democratization in Brazil, open and direct elections were held at the municipal level in 1982, excluding state capitals and zones of national security (where direct elections were held in 1985). Although these elections were direct, party competition was still controlled through restrictive electoral laws. In the 1988 municipal elections (which were both less restrained and direct), the "effective number of parties" (ENP) elected was 4.5. By the time of the 2000 municipal elections, the ENP represented at this level had increased to 7. In 2004 it increased to 8.9, and by 2012 it had reached 10.6. The increases to the ENP elected at the municipal level indicate that electoral competition at this level has increased substantially after 1988. Notwithstanding this increase, it has long been understood that direct local elections, however competitive, do not equate to greater local power in the decision-making processes without any significant policy authority.

Social policy in Brazil provides for this authority and has generated a dynamic three-level game that is clearly visible within the distribution of social expenditure (see figure 4.2). Each level of government accounts for roughly one third of total social expenditure, excluding formal pensions (which account for a large portion of federal expenditure). Figure 4.2 illustrates that federal and state social spending seem to follow each other, as if their spending levels were interdependent, as we would expect based within a federal system that generates a "race to the top" in welfare provisioning. When Lula's administration commenced, we can see an increase in a strategy of municipalization. In 2003, municipal social expenditure was higher than both national and state spending levels. This is truly remarkable. We can see in 2004 that all three hit an equilibrium point in their spending, and that federal spending then slowly rose as municipal spending decreased. This actually occurred because in 2005 the federal government assumed a new centralized role in the area of urban development and opened a "Ministry of Cities" in an attempt to address the need for the federal government to assist with sustainable urban development. Within the disaggregate data, this new urban development role explains the decrease in municipal expenditure and the subsequent increase in central expenditure.[6]

In terms of fiscal decentralization, the 1988 Constitution increased the level of revenue transfers, primarily to the states, by 12.5 percent (as shown in table 4.1). Because expenditure levels did not increase parallel

Figure 4.2. Social Expenditure in Brazil per Level of Government, 2002–2006 (without Pensions)

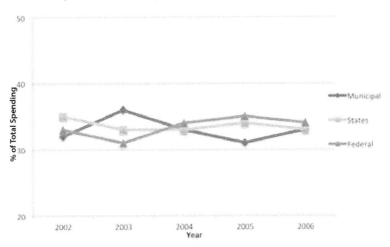

Source: Author elaboration, Ministério da Fazenda, Contabilitadade Governmental.

with the increase in revenues, the national government was in a position of fiscal weakness, with fewer resources yet still ultimately responsible for financing social policy. Fiscally irresponsible states accumulated massive deficits through engorged civil-servant payrolls and redeemable loans from state-operated banks (Fleischer 1998, 121). The fiscal stabilization plan implemented on July 1, 1994, both lowered inflation and secured Cardoso's electoral victory. When he took office in 1995, state-based debt crises were imminent. State and local governments and their representatives in the Chamber of Deputies were strongly opposed to further fiscal reforms that would effectively reduce the fiscal autonomy they had been granted in the 1988 Constitution.

Between 1995 and 1998, the federal government managed to shut down state banks and tie the hands of governors by forcing them to match their revenue and expenditure (see table 4.2). Interesting to note within the distribution of subnational revenue and expenditure before and after recentralization is that the effect of this process on municipalities was not the same as on states. The municipal level spent far more than their revenue base (calculated in table 4.2 after constitutional

Table 4.2. Brazil's Revenue and Expenditure by Level of Government after Decentralization and after Recentralization

	Share of Total Government Revenue (%)			Share of Total Government Expenditure (%)		
	1988	*2004*	*%▲*	*1988*	*2004*	*%▲*
Central	47.1	57.4	10	36.5	59	13
State	49.4	25	−24.6	40.7	26	−14.7
Local	3.6	17	13.4	22.8	15	−7.8

Source: Willis, Garman, and Haggard 1999; Afonso 2005.

transfers) permitted them after 1988. Following the recentralization implemented during Cardoso's two terms (1995–2002), municipalities' revenues increased 13.4 percent from 1988, and their expenditure decreased 7.8 percent. This facilitated their ability to match expenditure with their (constitutionally mandated) revenue shares.

This process of recentralization, following a process of decentralization, was not unique to Brazil. It was a re-equilibration of power between the center and state governments. Recentralization in Russia and Argentina was contextualized by a strong party system, where rapid but volatile partisan dynamics enabled top-down centralizing economic reforms. Most importantly for this study, beyond the expected consequences of recentralization for macroeconomic stability, recentralization in Brazil has had an impact on the quality of policy outputs delivered at the subnational levels. Intergovernmental relations became so regulated after 2000 that subnational governments had an incentive to deliver better and more efficient policy, particularly when centrally based matching grants or program-specific federal transfers were involved.

Following Cardoso's first term, which ended in 1997, the opportunistic behavior of competing units of governments changed accordingly. Fiscal regulation created new forms of cooperation. For example, under Dilma Rousseff's Brasil Sem Miséria (BSM) in 2013, if a municipality signs an agreement with the federal government under the Busca Ativa initiative, which is designed to seek out extremely poor families not yet included in the Cadastro Único database, then even though the municipality is responsible for recipient enrollments, the national government, using the "Index of Decentralization Management," will transfer federal revenues to financially assist in the administrative costs of less developed municipalities. The incentives to share power in areas of overlapping constitutional authority increased the potential for "good fiscal accounts" and thus for claiming credit at multiple levels of government. There has been a synthesis of two preexisting elements, decentralization and recentralization, resulting in a new model of "collaborative federalism" that has been distinguished, broadly speaking, by partnerships between the federal and municipal governments over the delivery of social policy (education, health, and social protection). This model has forced state governors into an unexpected federal game that pushes actors toward power-sharing arrangements that disperse power.

Moving further in this direction, the federal government developed two new subnational financing strategies. First, it de-earmarked a share of its revenues, retaining 20 percent of the constitutionally mandated transfers to states and municipalities (Arretche 2007).[7] Second, it increasingly earmarked revenue for transfers directly to the municipal level. Own-source municipal revenue collection is small. Therefore, municipalities have found themselves increasingly dependent on federal transfers to primarily fund their expenditure responsibilities, many of which are constitutionally mandated (earmarked). For example, in 2004 approximately 34.7 percent of total local expenditures, primarily in health and education, came from earmarked federal transfers (Afonso 2007, 385). Therefore as noted in table 4.3 below, the greatest vertical imbalance in Brazilian federalism (the gap between revenues collected and expenditures) is at the municipal level.

The territorial distribution of authority in a federal system is coordinated by institutional mechanisms that facilitate intergovernmental coordination and turn inputs into outputs. The distribution of governing functions across three levels of government in Brazil pushes each level of government to maximize its proportion of revenue. Fiscal recentralization after 1995 was motivated by necessity, and it successfully replaced some of the burden-shifting characteristics of the opportunistic behavior that was apparent after 1988. This coordination was further institutionalized from 1995 onward by the federal regulation of

Table 4.3. Brazil's Total Collection and Disposable Tax Revenues and
Expenditures by Level of Government in 2003

Tax Competence	Tax Revenue Total Collection	Tax Revenue as Percent of GDP	Revenues[a]	Expenditures
Central	68.4	28.8	55.4	60.1
States	25.3	10.6	26.9	25.6
Municipalities	6.4	2.7	17.7	14.4
Total	100.0	42.1	100.0	100.0

Source: Rezende 2007, 89.
[a] Disposable, including transfers. All figures percentages.

subnational spending in the areas of education, health, and personnel
and by the introduction of mandatory contributions to social funds
(Arretche 2007, 59). Additionally, the Fiscal Responsibility Law of 2000
placed limits on the expansion of both expenditure and debt by crimi-
nalizing it, with penal consequences. Within this context, mayors who
were not autonomous but did not have the ability to access "special
funds" from the Congress, as did governors, had an incentive to take
on policy execution responsibilities or adhere to the policy objectives of
higher levels of government that benefited them fiscally.

Each level of government in Brazil since 1988 has played with its
given distribution of authority and learned how to make either conflic-
tive or cooperative behavior pay off. Predatory federalism was costly
for the center and produced low-quality social policy outcomes. After
1995, the territorial distribution of authority in Brazil has paradoxically
combined high levels of political decentralization with centralized fiscal
regulations. This has left policy authority equally balanced between the
national and subnational governments. These solutions may not necessarily encourage effectiveness in another federal country, such as Argentina, whose internal circumstances are different from Brazil's.

The most striking evidence of this novel three-level relationship
within the context of strong federalism is the fact that both fiscal decentralization and the later recentralization under Cardoso privileged
municipalities over the states, especially the larger- and medium-sized

municipalities that receive a greater percentage of value-added (ICMS), property (IPTU), and service taxes (ISS). The constitutional recognition of municipalities made it possible for the federal government to pursue a strategy of multilevel governance that is based on horizontal and vertical consultation, coordination, and collaboration. Operating as (or representing, in my model) a single explanatory factor, the constitutional recognition of municipalities as distinct from the states is not an adequate explanation of either the goals and objectives of CCT expansion in Brazil, or the outcomes of Bolsa Família. Of great importance, however, constitutional recognition meant that municipalities were no longer easily captured by the state governments above them, nor did they have to negotiate with their governors when adhering to a national social initiative that would provide them with an alternate source of revenue. In both theory and in practice, this recognition allowed municipalities to be liberated from the states, even if it did not lead to greater local autonomy and instead had the unintended consequence of enhancing political capital from federal investments at the local level.

The Evolution of the Rules Regulating
Subnational Finance in Brazil, 1988–2000

It should now be evident that the factors that condition the willingness of mayors to become the prime agents of the federal government in key social policy areas are implicitly intertwined with fiscal arrangements. National-level political factors and constitutional changes do not immediately have a direct impact on the interdependent fiscal relationship existing at the subnational level between the states and the municipalities, where the latter relies on the former to finance services, and the former relies on the latter to deliver votes. Particularly for the smaller and less developed municipalities, of which there are many, their revenue-raising capacity from tax collection is low (2.7 percent of GDP out of a total 42.1 percent in 2003). The blatant lack of municipal fiscal autonomy or revenue-raising capacity after 1988 provided municipalities with an incentive to shirk their policy responsibilities and shift them back to the states (or leave them unattended), leaving subnational social programs chaotic and uncoordinated, and resulting in low-quality access to basic social services that fall within municipal jurisdiction.

As explained from a theoretical perspective in chapter 2, the rules regulating subnational finances shape the policy preferences at any given level of government. Post-1988 Brazil is a textbook example of the soft budget syndrome discussed previously. From 1988 to 1995, high levels of subnational fiscal autonomy led to continual bailouts from the national government in Brasília (Rodden 2003, 213). State-owned banks (which were also able to capture municipalities by extending credit to them) were permitted to access external market credit, thus making them precarious. Governors and mayors made use of their constitutionally allocated autonomy, but they continued to believe that if they failed to cover their expenditures they would be bailed out by the federal government (as indeed they were). Fiscal interventions by the national government arising from a fully operational bottom-up soft budget syndrome weakened overall national macroeconomic performance during these years. Moreover, the national government had many political incentives to maintain this fiscal syndrome, because of its heavy reliance at the time on the 513 subnational representatives in Congress and, to a moderate extent, on state governors. The president required the support of these deputies to pass his preferred economic policy reforms. Not only did this situation equate to a vicious policymaking cycle, but it also resulted in the new politics of governors (Abrucio and Samuels 2000).

Federalism from 1988 to 1995 was therefore also very center-constraining because of the nature of fiscal arrangements, producing territorially heterogeneous and often suboptimal social outputs. In the area of noncontributory social protection, the main national programs in place at this time were a milk program, an emergency food program in rural drought areas, a school lunch program, and an income supplement paid to elderly and disabled citizens. Pioneering subnational CCTs, however, flourished during this time because of the glaring absence of a social safety net at the local level. As mentioned previously, policy entrepreneurs who were also mayors of relatively large and developed municipalities, such as Patrus Ananias (Belo Horizonte, 1993 to 1997), Cristovam Buarque (Brasília, 1995 to 1998), and José Teixeira (Campinas, 1982 to 1990), all had a policy window open to both innovate and experiment within the context of a "soft budget syndrome."

When macroeconomic stabilization became a national priority beginning in 1993, this priority required a gradual hardening of subnational budget constraints. According to Abrucio, "the era of the *Real* marked the beginning of a crisis of state-based federalism" (2005, 50). An explanation of how Fernando Henrique Cardoso successfully pushed a prioritized economic reform agenda through Congress from 1995 to 1998 (the *real* era) within a center-constraining system of strong federalism is complex. Economic reform successes, like the success of the federal government's efforts to reduce poverty and its move toward municipalization, were achieved by gradually muddling through. Moreover, the president's success in reducing poverty, through reducing high inflation in 1994, provided him with high levels of popular support that encouraged diverse parties to join his governing coalition. The success of Cardoso's presidential-led coalition in Congress provided him with an institutional opportunity to successfully pursue his preferences and move toward a governable consensual or power-sharing democratic model. This ability to forge broad governing coalitions, coupled with the unforeseen external shocks of the mid-1990s, weakened the ability of the federal government to bail out state-level banks. According to Rodden's account, "the president [FHC] had a rare opportunity to take advantage of incentives for cooperation among some of the governors and within the legislature" (2003, 237). Achieving his reforms was costly, however, as states still tended to offload their public debts onto the national government.

Due to Cardoso's successful economic management, from 1995 onward, it became increasingly difficult for subnational levels of government to receive external market support to cover their excessive public spending, whether it was intended to finance innovative policy or not. The successful reduction of inflation, which had begun before Cardoso took office, had a positive impact on regulating intergovernmental transfers and revenues at the subnational level (Abrucio 2005). The macroeconomic stabilization achieved during the era of the Real Plan strengthened the federal government, while simultaneously weakening the fiscal situation of the states. Without inflation, states could no longer profit from high inflation by pegging their debts and expenditures to a floating and highly volatile exchange rate.

In 1997, each state agreed to a package of adjustment targets, which would place limits on personnel spending and privatize state enterprises (Rodden 2003), all measures that would decrease mechanisms that had been at their disposal to ensure state-based federal dominance. By 1998, the borrowing autonomy of states was also affected by Senate Resolution 78. This agreement enabled the national government to withhold bailouts to the states by retaining federal transfers, as had been achieved in Argentina during the crisis from 1994 to 1995 (Haggard and Webb 2004). The existence of external debt crises, however (for example, the contagion effects of the Asia crisis in 1997), had already worsened the situation of public debts in Brazil as a whole by increasing her international risk rating. This caused the federal government to float the currency in January 1999. The float rate, from R$1.21 to R$.98, raised the debt/GDP ratio considerably, reflecting the dollar-denominated and dollar-indexed federal debt (see Bogdanski et al. 2001). This being an opportune moment to pass legislation tightening subnational budget constraints, the Fiscal Responsibility Law of May 4, 2000 ("LRF") prohibited federal fiscal institutions from *ex-ante* bailing out the states. The soft budget syndrome finally had been cured. The LRF affected public policy outputs and created incentives for national-local collaboration for the following reasons: first, subnational government must establish, at the outset of each budget, annual targets for revenues and expenditures; second, personnel expenditures are set for each level of government and are enforceable through criminal law; third, the LRF prohibits state governments from lending to municipal governments (this decreases the fiscal ability of governors to make mayors beholden to them); and fourth, the LRF makes provisions for state and municipal government fiscal transparency (Dillinger 2002, 12).

The drawback of hard budget constraints is that while they induce governors and mayors (under threat of criminal sanction) to make an effort to spend within their budgets, they hold the national government ultimately responsible for tracking and regulating state and municipal policy performance. This has motivated the federal government in Brazil to set social policy targets in health, education, and social assistance, which facilitates the monitoring and evaluation of constitutionally designated subnational policy responsibilities.

Intergovernmental relations from 2000 to the present are largely conducted through legal covenants and partnerships between interested parties, and there has increasingly been a "centralization of decision-making" in key decentralized social policy areas. The ability of subnational governments in Brazil to veto social policy decisions may have decreased because of the hardening of budget constraints from 1994 onward (Arretche 2007), but, given that this power was both used and abused more frequently by state-based governors, it has arguably established a three-tiered financial structure that facilitates the ability of municipalities to become the prime agents of the federal government in the delivery of social services.

Brazil's Consensual Model of Democracy

The president's ability to govern in Brazil depends on forging broad co-alitions both within the national legislature and across levels of executive government, coalitions that may include parties outside of its ideological spectrum and even from the opposition. This characteristic disperses power among multiple interests. In a parallel fashion, it also leads to an incentive to distribute federal resources through mass social programs, such as Bolsa Família, to regions and municipalities that the ruling federal party does not control. A presidential-led coalition model such as Brazil's is noted for its lack of majoritarian imperative. These factors have been treated in the literature as contributing negatively to the performance of Brazilian democracy (Lamounier 1992; Mainwaring 1995b). More recent assessments of Brazilian democracy that focus on the post-1995 period have been less pessimistic about this governing model.

It is important to point out that the dominant debate surrounding Brazil's democratic model has not been about what it is: it is a fragmented multiparty political system that combines federalism, presidentialism, bicameralism, and proportional representation, and does not have single-party cabinet majorities (or even anything that closely resembles them). These characteristics make it feasible to classify the Brazilian model of democracy as *consensual*, or as a *power-sharing regime*, in accordance with Lijphart's theory on consensual versus majoritarian democracy (1984). This should not be a surprising classification to anyone, particularly given that many influential Brazilian political scientists have used Lijphart's criteria to describe Brazil's model, in particular, Amorim Neto (2007 and 2009). Other research by Power (2010) and Melo and Pereira (2013) prefers to call it a "coalitional-presidentialism" model but builds upon Amorim Neto's work by classifying it within power-sharing terms. All of these contributions now point in the direction of a less divisive debate about how Brazil works.[8] Nevertheless, a serious debate continues surrounding the question as to whether Brazil's model of consensual democracy is better at governing than a majoritarian-based democracy, and if this model makes a difference to what Lijphart (2008, 100) refers to as "the kinder, gentler, qualities of democracy"—which include social welfare, the protection of the environment, the nature of criminal justice, and foreign aid.

Using examples of democracies from the developed world, Lijphart was able to test his hypothesis using seventeen indicators of the quality of democracy and by running standard bivariate regressions. Given the quality of national data in many Latin American countries and the absence of many Latin American governance indicators in the datasets of international organizations, any meaningful quantitative test of this hypothesis is rather limited in scope. Therefore, it is through the strategy of a paired comparison of two similar systems, Brazil and Argentina, that we will have to draw out conclusions, using a more nuanced qualitative approach.

Brazil's consensual model, inclusive of its high levels of interparty fragmentation, is notable for lowering the importance of partisan identity in forming voter preferences, because of the large number of parties represented. For example, in 2006, the effective number of parties measured in the lower chamber was 9.3, and there were up to ten or more parties in that governing coalition.[9] Moreover, the coexistence of such a high number of veto players in Brazil's federal system lessens the use of partisanship to obtain particularistic goods (Tsebelis 1995) and encourages politicians to make personalist appeals to potential voters (see table 4.4).

Within this model, elite political actors are less concerned with office-seeking than with policy-seeking (Strom 1990). Based on electoral motives, policy success allows them to claim personal credit for increased governing performance within their territories. Through mayors' participation in the implementation of Bolsa Família (identifying vulnerable families, registering families, or assisting in documentation efforts—birth certificates, national identity number, and so on), and through their continued importance in the verification of program compliance (which includes investigation into noncompliance and

Table 4.4. Characteristics of Brazil's Consensual Democratic Model

Broad Multiparty Coalition in Congress	Single-Party Majority System	Two-Party Dominant Cabinet	Proportional Representation	Vertically Integrated Party System
Yes (ENP > 5)[a]	No (Y > 5)[b]	No	Open-List	Low

[a] Calculated by Amorim Neto (2007) for 1989 to 2006.
[b] Calculated by Amorim Neto (2007) for 1990 to 2007.

municipal social workers visiting families struggling to comply), these mayors can potentially realize some private benefit for their participation in promoting this federally led program, even if it is indirect. A fact of great importance is that the local benefits that accrue to them through greater levels of participation, such as increased economic inputs for smaller municipalities and increased improvement in and demand for local health, education, and other social services, are not linked to partisanship. This is just one of the reasons that we did not observe a massive electoral shift toward the PT at the municipal level in 2004, 2008, or 2012, regardless of Bolsa Família's popular support and its extensive territorial penetration at the local level.

In Brazil's consensual model, a subnational government does not have to belong to the incumbent president's party or even be in its governing coalition, in order for its constituents to reap the benefits of a top-down, pro-poor agenda. Additionally, in Brazil, both states and municipalities can opt out of participating in federal policy initiatives, or they can formally collaborate through topping-up the amount of the cash benefit and adding their logo to the electronic bankcard.[10] The opt-out clause provides subnational governments with a *de jure* exit option that has been used in large urban cities such as São Paulo, who fear top-down political interference in areas of municipal jurisdiction. However, when a policy solution leads to local benefits that could otherwise not be provided and has been implemented in other localities (for example, federal infrastructure investments in city-run day care centers), public pressure usually leads to municipal adherence to national social policy initiatives. In this way an albeit imperfect consensual model of democracy in Brazil constitutes a win-win game for key political actors at different levels of government, who can mutually choose to deliver policy and may not share the same party label.

The electoral success of the executive at all levels of government in Brazil rests on integrating the preferences of as many voters and as many political parties as possible. For example, based on a public opinion survey carried out by IBOPE in November 2002, Brazilians who expected Lula to fulfill his campaign promise to "combat poverty, hunger, and misery" identified with a range of political parties. Twenty-two percent were from the right-wing, opposition Liberal Front Party (PFL), 21 percent from the Social Democrat Party (PSDB), 32 percent from Lula's own party (the PT), and the rest from the centrist party the Brazilian Democratic Movement (PMDB). This means that even in a formally nonaligned municipality or state such as São Paulo and Goiás, a considerable number of voters would still expect their own government to adhere to national policy objectives they support. Moreover, Brazil's system of open-list proportional representation facilitates the ability of many diverse groups to express their interests, rather than polarizing them around a single dominant cleavage (Weaver 2002). According to the received wisdom in the literature, because politicians must win the support of an array of groups, the nature of the party system, with its open-list electoral rules, means that "the survival of most politicians depends on their ability to deliver goods to the regions they represent" (Mainwaring 1992, 682), regardless of whether this means cooperating with a party with which they are not affiliated.

Ames (1995) thus contends that the rules of Brazil's political system provide incentives to build coalitions not through ideological programs and providing national public goods, but through providing "pork." Other scholars hold that state-level power brokers make it difficult for the president to claim credit for targeted expenditures that go through the states (Arretche and Rodden 2004). From the perspective of the national government, strong federalism logically provides the center with an incentive to bypass the states and deliver national collective goods in a way for which it can claim credit. This incentive is even greater based on Arretche and Rodden's assumption that all votes matter in all territories for the president's success (2004, 557). Bolsa Família involves little participation from the states, and their formal involvement is still extremely limited in comparison to that of municipalities.[11]

Subnational representatives, on the other hand, have an incentive to carry out national policy objectives in their territories as long as it benefits their constituents, because such actions increase their own chance of political survival. Under broad coalition-based governments, the center also has an incentive to deliver basic social goods to as many groups in as much of the country as possible, in order to ensure its own political survival. A power-sharing democratic model should allow for both the "designer" and the "deliverer" of public policy outputs to mutually claim credit in different ways among their constituents. In the context of a popular redistributive policy such as poverty alleviation, everyone can benefit from participating.

The willingness of municipal actors to thus promote Bolsa Família was facilitated in Brazil by a loosely maintained coalitional logic of governance that decreases the ideological or partisan ownership of policy ideas and disperses power. Partisanship within a highly fragmented multiparty presidential system is less significant than in other countries with highly institutionalized and disciplined party systems, where voter party identification is high and interparty electoral competition is lower. Brazil's consensual model of democracy increases the de facto political autonomy of mayors because it reduces the incentive for municipalities to give up desired local benefits out of the fear of party-based punishment from the states.

MUNICIPALITIES AND CCT PERFORMANCE IN BRAZIL

In this chapter I have shown how the evolution of federalism in Brazil from 1988 onward provided the political and institutional conditions that encouraged municipal actors to promote a national policy objective, enabling the successful territorial distribution of Bolsa Família within three years. This suggests that the ability of national actors in Brazil to pursue a pro-poor agenda is due to a large degree to the political and institutional conditions that have enabled the federal government to motivate municipalities to become its primary agents in key social areas, in order to avoid the undermining constraints of what have been described by a plethora of scholars as twenty-six center-constraining states, who make it difficult to redress poverty and inequality nationwide. The three explanatory factors laid out in chapter 2 are fundamental to explaining the extent of Bolsa Família's territorial allocation and its stability. The unique configuration of institutions in Brazil that have gradually evolved since 1988 opened the door to new forms of noncontributory social policy and to new forms of intergovernmental cooperation. Because of this uniqueness, similar achievements may not be equally realizable in neighboring or other countries.

First, without the national constitutional recognition of municipalities as a distinct order of government, states cannot easily be avoided. The success of making Bolsa Família operational was dependent on the federal structure laid out in the 1988 Constitution, which officially recognized municipalities as distinct from the states. Given the known extent of gubernatorial power and its ability to constrain the center, this chapter posits that the successful implementation of CCTs in Brazil, which now cover 24 percent of Brazil's entire population, was dependent on the ability of the federal center to *legally* bypass the involvement of its twenty-six state governors in order to provide an opportunity for national-local policy-based collaboration.

These legally based agreements guarantee the program's local promotion through identifying eligible families and enabling documentation, registering families onto the national database, and monitoring their compliance with the program's rules. The provision of basic health and primary education services in Brazil falls primarily under the jurisdiction of the municipalities. Within the Bolsa Família program, municipalities are independently responsible for providing and coordinating those services within their jurisdiction upon which the cash benefits are conditional. Bolsa Família is dependent on municipal level outreach and local access to public services. As many as 689,000 new families were added to the centralized database in Rousseff's first year as president by municipal-led teams co-financed by federal revenues (MDS). All 5,564 mayors can opt out of program participation at any time; in fact, they do not even have to negotiate opting out, but may simply choose no longer to adhere to the new initiatives.

Fiscal incentives were created to facilitate municipal involvement and ensure the quality of the program's local administration. As described at the outset of the chapter, municipalities in Brazil exhibit great demographic and economic diversity. In 2006, the Ministry of Social

Development created an "Index of Decentralized Management," calculated on the basis of the quality and integrity of the information supplied to the Cadastro Único, the updating of this database, and the quality and frequency of information being sent to the federal government about the level of education and health conditions being met by recipient households within the municipality. The MDS then provided a fiscal incentive, calculated on the basis of the Index, multiplied by R$2.50, and then multiplied by the number of recipients of the program within the municipality. This incentive was created following complaints from smaller municipalities that they did not have the resources required to maintain the administrative standards expected by the MDS. This is yet another example of a kind of fiscal incentive that has become increasingly common within Brazil's multi-tiered federal system.

Although Lula had the electoral support of the national majority, his party's representation at the state and municipal executive level was low. For example, in 2002 only three states had a PT governor—meaning, counterfactually, that if states had been responsible for promoting this social program, the majority of the states would have had no incentive to enable it because they would have been unable to claim credit for it; and if this is not possible, the second best option is policy apathy. It is difficult to imagine how Bolsa Família would have been so widely distributed territorially. In the 2004 municipal elections, only 7.9 percent of municipalities shared the PT label. Yet by 2006, all 5,564 municipalities (100 percent) supported this federal program, facilitating the national government's ability to deliver benefits to its initial target of roughly 11 million families (44 million citizens). Because municipalities can opt out of participating, this result shows that shared partisanship, or vertical federal alignment, which means that there exists a vertical alliance among the levels, was not a factor in their decision to both promote and enable Bolsa Família locally.

From a functional federal perspective, the basic conclusion remains that the constitutional recognition of municipalities as a distinct order of government facilitates the ability *de jure* of a national government to seek uniformity of outcome in certain areas of social policy. Uniquely in the Brazilian case, where it has been established that governors had the ability to constrain federalism to the point of ungovernability during the period of 1988 to 1995, the increasing ability of the federal government to use municipalities as their prime agents in key areas of social policy certainly contributes both to the credibility of the national government in guaranteeing access to basic social services, and also to strengthening the "center."

Second, there is no doubt that fiscal incentives matter, and the rules regulating subnational finances are no exception. There were clearly fiscal incentives contributing to the willingness of Brazilian municipalities to carry out this national policy goal. After 2000, fiscal discipline in Brazil has been attained and enforced through the use of hard budget constraints. Uniquely to Brazil, the Law of Fiscal Responsibility enforces fiscal discipline at all levels of government, not just at the subnational levels. As already stated previously, states have a relatively strong revenue base compared to municipalities, particularly small rural municipalities. Thus, even in the context of fiscal recentralization, the states had an insufficient need for small alternative resources that would come from promoting a social program for which they would be unable to directly claim credit. Municipalities, however, did have sufficient fiscal incentives to promote a program that provided alternative resources through what Lena Lavinas refers to as the "bankization of the poor" with an end to promote mass consumption (Lavinas 2013, 37). Particularly in smaller rural localities with little access to revenue sources like the ones identified by Marques (2004), this was an incentive in itself.

Although most of the literature in this area assumes that hard budget constraints are good (Tanzi 1995; Rodden, Eskeland, and Litvack 2003), this chapter has already noted one of their negative effects, namely, the shutting down of many locally financed CCTs after 1995 and limiting further subnational policy innovation. Nevertheless, hard budget constraints do provide a mechanism to ensure subnational accountability within the context of highly decentralized social expenditure, where the federal government does not have sufficient partisan strength to enforce fiscal discipline. Stated simply, in the absence of the funds to finance local initiatives for alleviating poverty, localities with stifling levels of poverty have been forced to cooperate with national social investment schemes if they are to satisfy local demands, and if they are to attempt to reduce the intergenerational transmission of poverty through improvements in both access to basic services within their jurisdiction and the monitoring of program compliance.

Within the context of the rules regulating subnational finances in Brazil, not cooperating with the national government equates to revenue loss. However, this condition does not by itself suffice to explain why municipalities were willing to promote a national policy objective. Within a three-level federal setting, even given hard budget constraints, there is still room to maneuver in terms of whom you cooperate with, and why, and whether you shirk or shift your policy responsibilities to another level of government.

The timing and sequencing of government reforms since 1988 also appears to have mattered, but this is more a result of their unintended consequences than their expected outcomes. It is evident that municipalization and the president's ability to make municipalization work for pursuing his own policy goals required the federal center to give away a considerable amount of power, before it could slowly start reclaiming this power back through creating new intergovernmental relationships that privileged municipalities more than the states. Stated succinctly, in a more majoritarian democratic system where partisanship plays a far more divisive role, the ability of a redistributive and politically strategic social policy sector to gradually muddle through over a period of policy experimentation, which in the Brazil case spanned more or less from the early 1990s to the early 2000s, is unlikely.

The nationalization of Bolsa Família in 2001 consolidated the ideational and symbolic legacies of the two main ideas designed to alleviate poverty that had been circulating earlier in Brazilian subnational and national policy circles, and also in international ones. These ideas originated across the Brazilian political and ideological spectrum. The 2001 nationalization, which was triggered in part by the need to fiscally rein in the states and to expand the federal government's involvement in deepening social citizenship, also had the dubious challenge of creating new administrative capacities at both the national and municipal levels, which were responsible for selecting and registering eligible families. Municipal collaboration was fundamental to this evolutionary policy process. Still, many organizational difficulties surrounded the implementation of the program. One of these was the fact that the federal database for socially vulnerable families who potentially met the stipulated program criteria was not yet fully operational. Particularly difficult to resolve was the coexistence of four programs across a variety of social policy sectors, which created policy-oriented intra-ministerial conflicts. In 2003, Bolsa Família continued to build on these policy legacies, and its administrators were able to learn from the policy feedback effects of Bolsa Escola to further the institutionaliza-tion of CCTs and, in turn, produce new effects for electoral behavior and individual participation that brought rewards to the PT adminis-tration. It should be repeated that the key policy instrument to Bolsa Família's successful territorial distribution is the Cadastro Único from the Cardoso era. Without municipal actors doing the legwork, how-ever, there would be no information to store in the database. Equally important for dismissing alternative claims, it should be recalled that the original idea of providing an integrated approach to condition-ality (an idea of the World Bank and the PRI in Mexico) does not have strong links with either the Workers' Party (the PT) or its associated left-of-center progressive ideology, which adamantly supports univer-sal basic income schemes.

Within an increasingly consensual democracy driven by what are (relative to the past) policy successes, successful targeted social poli-cies in Brazil have enabled a win-win situation for key actors at various levels. The specific form of intergovernmental cooperation identified here (national-local) is a characteristic peculiar to Brazilian contempo-rary democracy. Large multiparty coalitions are recognized as lowering the importance of partisanship, which can impede, and will be shown in the Argentine case to impede, the willingness of subnational execu-tives, both provincial and municipal, to promote nationally driven so-cial policy objectives.

Democratic governance in Brazil entails that the president's ability to govern is dependent on his or her ability to forge broad coalitions. When Lula first implemented Bolsa Família, he had eight parties in his governing coalition (Figueiredo 2007, 190).[12] In January 2004, when Lula's coalition had 45.22 percent of the seats in the lower house of Con-gress, Bolsa Família was distributed to 3,615,596 eligible households. Lula's coalition's share of seats reached 69.6 percent between July 2005 and January 2007, at the beginning of which period this CCT was dis-tributed to 7,319,720 families, and at the end of which it was distributed to 10,908,542.[13] The logic of presidential-led coalitions and the Brazil-ian democratic model that creates their necessity not only provided an increased incentive for the national government to pour resources into public policy such as the one here under study, but similarly provided an incentive for mayors to distribute such benefits within their jurisdictions without fear of local electoral punishment when not formally aligned with the national governing coalition.

Brazil's institutional traits, specifically, its open-list electoral rules, which are notable for encouraging personalism, entail that for both the president and mayors alike, voters elect candidates nominally and not according to their party label. Both the president and the mayors had an incentive to deliver poverty alleviation benefits as long as it could benefit their personal constituencies. From the perspective of the states, governors reduced their participation in this social policy area because they do not depend on the delivery of such public goods to ensure their political survival. State-level political survival in Brazil remains dependent on the ability of state-based power brokers to mobilize resources for their regions through their power in Congress. For mayors, however, the offer of basic public goods, which entails small yet substantial economic inputs for some municipalities, increased their willingness to cooperate with this national policy objective that delivered national collective goods to the territories they represent. Most important, the flexibility and fluidity of the party system in Brazil meant that mayors would not be punished by governors for promoting Bolsa Família regardless of their formal alignment.

Contemporary Brazilian democratic governance within the context of post-2000 hard budget constraints, which have forced subnational budgets to contain fixed expenditures for most social policies, has contributed to liberating municipalities from being captured by state-level power brokers. This freedom provides municipalities with the willingness to cooperate with the federal government by carrying out its policy objectives, particularly when doing so brings badly needed economic resources into their territories. It provides municipalities with an institutionally derived political incentive to operate as a third level of government and not to be subsumed by the power of the states. Before 1988 this institutional configuration was inconceivable, and before the macroeconomic stabilization around 1995 it was ungovernable.

The success of Bolsa Família has contributed to reducing hunger, misery, and poverty in Brazil from 28.2 percent in 2003 to 16.3 percent in 2009 (IPEA 2010). Bolsa Família's greatest effect was on households living in absolute poverty, by reducing the severity of the poverty gap. The proportion of households living in extreme poverty in Brazil almost halved from 11.2 percent to 5.8 percent between these same years. In addition, a new rights-based approach to social protection has forged a direct relationship between citizens and the government, allowing the state to extend social citizenship rights to areas where previously there were none. The ability of this single social program to deliver benefits to more than 14 million families and sustain itself since 2003 and through two presidential, state, and legislative elections and three municipal level elections, without exhibiting volatility (see figure 4.3), shows evidence of policy stability. It is also a social policy outcome that would have been considered highly unlikely in Brazil before 1988 and even before 1995.

This sector-specific case study suggests that, within Brazil's consensual model of democracy, mayors are politically willing to promote and enable a politically powerful nationally driven and nationally financed CCT program within a robust federal system. They enabled Bolsa Família regardless of their relationship to the current federal government. The local dilemma of Brazilian federalism (governor politics) makes it difficult for the national president to claim credit for targeted

Figure 4.3. Distribution of Bolsa Família, December 2003–August 2013

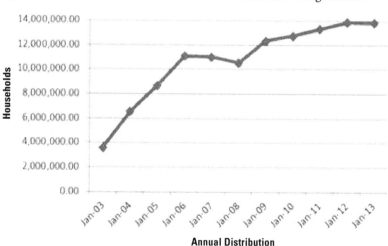

Source: Ministério de Desenvolvimento Social.

expenditures that go through the states (Arretche and Rodden 2004), or for municipalities to go it alone in providing targeted social welfare. Furthermore, given the vast territories of Brazil and the extent of its social exclusion, plus the lack of a vertically integrated political party, it was impossible for the federal government to go it alone in ensuring that targeted social welfare was widely distributed without political intermediation. This federally derived challenge provided a unique political incentive for the national government to expand its involvement through the creation of a massive social program and to rely on municipalities for its promotion. It also provided numerous new access points to local political actors who had previously remained outside of the dominant federal game played out between the national government, governors, and their representatives in Congress. Because political credit-claiming for a program of this magnitude diminishes over time, Rousseff's incentive to correct and further expand Bolsa Família in 2011, following the results of the 2010 Census, was to follow the established logic of "continuity and change" that has come to epitomize Brazilian contemporary governance.

Finally, this chapter has shown how Brazilian federalism has recently evolved, why it is different, and which political and institutional factors account for successful policy outcomes in this social policy area. This analysis offers evidence that, within poverty alleviation efforts, municipalities were able to positively affect the ability of the national government to produce and distribute an important and viable policy. By looking at the role of municipalities in enabling Bolsa Família, this book calls for a look beyond decentralization to separate the subnational level into two distinct categories: state and municipal. The unique configuration of Brazil's democratic model entails that its states can constrain the center, while its numerous municipalities can simultaneously enhance it.

CHAPTER 5

_____

CCTs in Argentina and the Politics
of Alleviating Poverty

Poverty is a recent phenomenon in Argentina, with a profoundly political background. In the political history of Argentina, the working class
has benefited from economic well-being and "political clout unprecedented in Latin America" (Manzetti 1993, 37). This "clout" described by
Manzetti was used as a collective bargaining tool, during various democratic periods, within the national government's powerful Ministry of
Labor and Welfare.[1] This ensured that the popular sectors historically
in Argentina were a powerful constituency from an electoral point of
view. Until the mid-1990s, what Oxhorn (1995) refers to as "a top-down
strategy of controlled inclusion" succeeded in keeping socioeconomic
inequality and poverty relatively low. During the 1990s, however, with
an average tenure for departmental heads of less than one year, "this
ministry . . . changed from secretariat to under-secretariat to ministry—
the position of agency head has been occupied by highly qualified tech-
nocrats, by high-profile politicians, by the spouse of one president, and

by the sister of another one" (Spiller and Tommasi 2007, 72). By the late 1990s, the level of institutionalization necessary in this increasingly important social policy area was clearly absent.

Social protection policy—the ability to protect poor, vulnerable, and marginal groups in society through the delivery of social goods—has been a fundamental part of the Justicialist Party's (Partido Justicialista—PJ) historical governing strategy. Beginning as a political movement in the 1940s, this political party, which is often referred to as Peronist because it was founded by Juan Domingo Perón himself, developed as a nationalist party that specifically represented lower-class and working-class interests. Perón's wife Evita was infamously seen as the spiritual savior of the poor. Some authors argue that this characteristic immediately creates a spurious relationship between this political party and poverty alleviation efforts (Brusco, Nazareno, and Stokes 2004). The PJ evolved politically through its alliance with the labor sector in Argentina—unions, syndicates, organized workers' movements—and through the Ministry of Labor itself. Juan Perón, having been secretary of labor (1944–1946) and having replaced it with a larger ministry after becoming president in 1947, used it as a means to create an alliance with workers.

Although this example of controlled social inclusion is similar to that which occurred under Vargas in Brazil, its impact on society was greater, given that when Perón took over the government in 1946, 62.7 percent of Argentines were already urbanized and working predominantly in industrial sectors of the economy (Torre and Pastoriza 2002). The close alliance between the Ministry of Labor and Welfare and the union movements in the 1940s was used by the PJ party as an official mechanism to distribute the proceeds of that period's rapid economic growth. In return, it created a political system grounded fundamentally in the penetrative power of a single political party, the PJ.

Argentine experience in the area of social protection, in the form of formal insurance schemes, is profound. Nevertheless, parallel to what occurred in many other countries throughout the Latin American region during the 1990s, there was a noticeable policy shift from traditional labor-oriented strategies of inclusion toward more targeted social programs within the policy area of social development—a shift, as I suggest later in the chapter, that has now reversed. Using the terms of reference of a now "global discourse," these nationally led CCTs can be classified as social investment programs that were part of a pro-poor agenda.[2] Such policy experimentation began ostensibly in 1989, following the election of President Carlos Menem (PJ), and continued under PJ presidents Eduardo Duhalde (2002–2003), Néstor Kirchner (2003–2007), and Cristina Fernández de Kirchner (2007–2015), all nominally members of the same political party.

The goal of this chapter is to trace the policy development of CCTs in Argentina and specifically to analyze the performance of Programa Familias (2003 to 2009), an internationally backed and financed integrated CCT that was intended to break the intergenerational transmission of poverty through its conditionality tied to human capital investments. Cash transfer programs have evolved in Argentina from being primarily tied to labor conditions to being tied to conditions related to education and health. The empirical evidence put forward in this chapter shows that Argentina's attempt to pursue this national policy objective from 2003 to 2009 was impeded by the ability of governors to undermine its territorial distribution.[3] Federally derived institutional and political impediments and the effects of the preceding decade of Peronist-led workfare programs are extremely important to understand and will be covered in depth in this chapter.

THE EVOLUTION AND POLITICS OF SOCIAL POLICY AS CCTS IN ARGENTINA

The Argentine story of the development and evolution of CCTs differs greatly from that of Brazil. In contrast with other countries in the region, Argentina was a late adopter of this form of social investment, which seeks to end the intergenerational transmission of poverty through promoting investments in health, education, and nutrition. It should be remembered that one of the main political intentions of CCTs is to reduce the political intermediation of collective welfare goods delivery and forge a direct relationship between the national government and its citizens. Essentially, Argentina's history with CCTs is about how domestic politics and institutions affect the development and evolution of national social investment initiatives. Policy outcomes then shape the development of future initiatives. Despite the fact that Argentine democracy has encouraged a two-party system, including "an ideal federal party"—a national party that can command the loyalties of all its members (subsets) when in power (Filippov, Ordeshook, and Shvetsova 2004)[4]—that has been dominant at the national level over most of the past thirty democratic years (Menem, 1989–1999; Duhalde, 2002–2003; Kirchner, 2003–2007; Fernández de Kirchner, 2007–present), this federal country has encountered difficulties in producing and delivering efficient and effective public policy, in particular at the local level, because of the inability of the president (the federal government) to ensure the consistent delivery of public goods nationwide.

This policy challenge faced by the national government in Argentina is extremely visible in the policy area of noncontributory social protection. This is one of the few areas of social policy for which the national government has *de jure* responsibility—food programs, workfare programs, and antipoverty initiatives. According to the municipal and provincial officials whom I interviewed during the course of my research, high poverty rates and unemployment only began to gain visibility in Argentina during President Menem's first term (1989–1995) and constituted a negative externality to the rigidly and rapidly imposed neoliberal economic reforms (interview Schmuck 2006; interview Suárez 2006; interview Cafiero 2006).

In 1989, when the PJ took over the presidency for the first time following democratization, the country was suffering from rampant hyperinflation, an inefficient economic system, and growing societal and political instability. Poverty was growing in Argentina for the first time in its history. Household poverty rates increased from 7 percent in 1980 to 38.2 percent in 1989 (INDEC 2006). In an effort to control the negative impact of increasing poverty on the PJ's political support base, between 1989 and 1999 the national government began developing targeted social investment programs to offset the effects of its radical neoliberal agenda.

Immediately upon taking office, Menem reformed existing federal social programs by replacing the previous administration's nutrition program, PAN, with the Bono National de Emergencia (BNSE). Both the old and new trademark social protection programs were administered by the Ministry of Health and Social Action. The BNSE was administered to beneficiaries at the municipal level, aided by the density of local PJ networks that existed at the neighborhood level (Lloyd-Sherlock 1997). This program was believed to have had limited effects and, amid accusations of corruption, ceased to exist in 1992 (Golbert 1996).

Although Menem's early social protection programs were superficial and part of what Weyland (1996) refers to as "neopopulism," the federal government's macroeconomic stabilization and fiscal austerity plan successfully brought about macroeconomic control and managed to alleviate poverty for all Argentines through price stability. This effect was very similar to the effect of the Brazilian Real Plan, discussed in chapter 3. Household poverty rates in Argentina fell from 42.5 percent in 1990 to 16.1 percent in 1994 because of "the inflationary effect" (INDEC 2006). This effect, however, was short-lived because of Menem's strategy of allowing the provinces to continue borrowing privately, using their federal funds as collateral, in order to wean provinces away from central bank bailouts (Treisman 2004, 413).

From 1991 to 1994, domestic demand was superficially stimulated by favorable currency conditions. This served to ease the growing social tensions caused by growing unemployment and social inequality, two factors that historically had not been common in Argentina. The long-term vulnerability of the popular classes would not become apparent until the "tequila effect," resulting from the 1994 Mexican peso devaluation that threw the Argentine economy into recession. Poverty rates began to increase again, followed by compensatory noncontributory social protection programs.[5]

After 1994, for the first time in Argentine history, targeted national programs that were intended to provide a basic social safety net would become a critical part of the national government's agenda. In this year, Menem created the Secretariat of Social Development to formally address the importance of this new policy area. As a new portfolio in the federal cabinet, however, it was marginalized by the influence of other ministries, particularly the Ministry of Labor, a traditional central bulwark of PJ governance.

Although in hindsight, weaknesses were beginning to appear in the economic system and in the national government's ability to manage them around 1994, social tolerance for medium-term hardships emanating from radical market-oriented reforms remained high. In particular, this was because of Menem's early success at controlling inflation. Menem's party, the PJ, had high credibility for having remedied the acute economic crisis that had been raging under the previous UCR government (Torre 1998).[6] This credibility, added to other key factors including a strong presidential decree power, the near decimation of the main opposition (the UCR), the emergency context provided by the preceding economic crisis, a clear PJ majority in the legislature, and the successful co-optation of the only third party (the UCEDE),[7] allowed Menem to push through a change in the constitution and win a second term in 1995 (de Riz 1996; Gerchunoff and Torre 1998). This second term was used to further consolidate the neoliberal economic and federal fiscal reforms. Negotiating these reforms, however, became more difficult for Menem after 1995 because of his declining personal popularity, his weakening political leverage over Argentina's twenty-three provincial governors, and the increasing support for the UCR and its allies (see figure 5.1).

Subsequent to Menem's reelection, urban poverty and unemployment rates began to grow steadily. By May 1995, unemployment exceeded 20 percent for the first time since democratization. High unemployment was a threat to the PJ because of its working-class identity. Menem could not afford politically to alienate this powerful traditional sector of society, even though many reforms had already divided and co-opted certain sectors in order to prevent a unified labor opposition (Gibson 1997). For this reason, the national government attempted for the second time to placate societal demands through the creation of a targeted social investment program. This new cash transfer program, created in 1996 and called Plan Trabajar, was the PJ's first workfare program that was conditional on labor contributions.[8]

This program ran for four years and was continued under the succeeding, opposition-based administration of President Fernando de la Rúa (Alianza). At its peak, it covered 20 percent of the unemployed poor, making it one of the most important programs of its time (Weitz-Shapiro 2006). The consensus in the literature on this means-tested program is that its distribution was manipulated in order to benefit certain groups, a result attributed to both partisan and protest factors (Lodola 2005; Weitz-Shapiro 2006; Giraudy 2007). It operated as a substitute for public employment and thus cannot be considered as an "active" labor

Figure 5.1. Rising Support for UCR Relative to the PJ at Gubernatorial
Level, 1989–1999

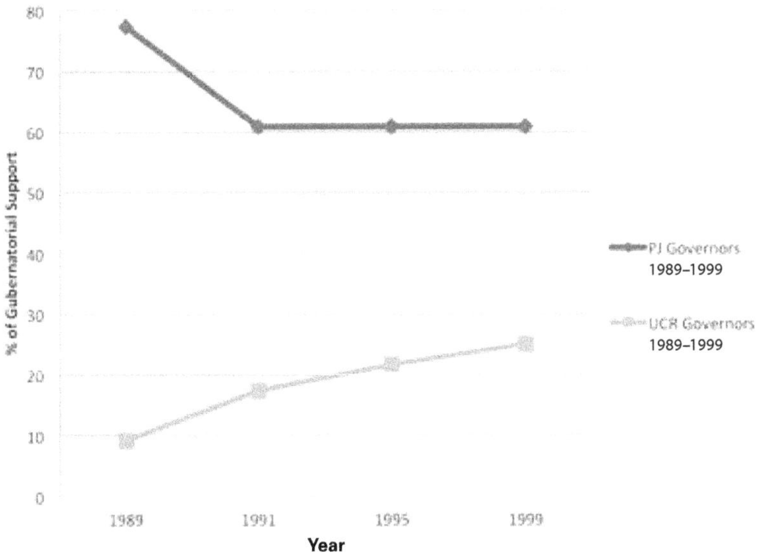

Source: Author elaboration, Ministério del Interior, Dirección Electoral.

program. Interestingly, Giraudy (2007) finds that presidential elections
are statistically insignificant to the program's allocation, and hence she
challenges the belief that there were federal motivations behind Plan
Trabajar's territorial distribution. In the next section, my analysis of the
distribution of the second major PJ workfare program that followed
Plan Trabajar and was also conditional on labor contributions, Programa Jefes y Jefas de Hogares Desocupados (the Heads of Unemployed
Households Plan, PJJHD), shows contrasting evidence.

This finding is interesting because it shows that the political dynamics of federal-provincial relations changed between these two national
workfare programs. It also shows how these largely intraparty dynamics
contributed to the volatility observed in the evolution of social programs
in Argentina from 1996 to 2003. Both CCTs are known to have been politically manipulated; however, Plan Trabajar (1996 to 2001) was federally
financed and manipulated by the provinces to increase the support base
of governors in key geographic areas—this was a federal motivation.

Plan Trabajar was implemented during a time when the national government had an incentive to court provincial governors (that is to say, Menem had no political incentive to avoid PJ governors—quite the contrary). By contrast, following the fiscal and political crisis of 2001, the political incentive of former governor Eduardo Duhalde (PJ), who was appointed president in 2002, was to directly court the popular sectors that were predominantly Peronist and were increasingly mobile. He thus largely bypassed both governors and mayors in order to forge a PJ-led national solidarity directly with key popular sectors, because he had a political incentive to claim direct credit for national social expenditures with specific groups. This is not, however, to say that party-based networks at the subnational level were not able to capture the supply-side inputs of PJJHD and use them as a power-generating resource.

According to data from the Secretariat of Social Development, during Menem's administration over fifty-six nationally financed social protection programs that involved cash transfers existed in 1995, escalating to over seventy by its end in 1999 (Ronconi 2002). Menem's CCTs were generally characterized by an unclear diagnosis of actual problems and a lack of monitoring and policy evaluation (Golbert 1996). Societal demands continued to escalate toward 1999, unappeased by various top-down policy initiatives, as did poverty rates (see figure 5.2).

Figure 5.2. Poverty Rates in Argentina, 1989–2006

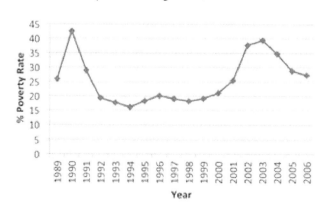

Source: Instituto Nacional de Estadística y Censos (INDEC).
Note: Years 1989 to 2000 based on GBA estimations (INDEC).

THE "EMERGENCY" PHASE OF LABOR-BASED CCTS UNDER INTERIM PRESIDENT DUHALDE (PJ), 2001–2003

On December 18 and 19, 2001, social mobilizations exploded on the streets of Buenos Aires in violent protest at the freezing of citizens' cash assets. These social movements were organized by varying factions of *piqueteros* (groups of unemployed laborers), who, armed with rocks and sticks, contributed to worsening political instability. On December 20, 2001, democratically elected President Fernando de la Rúa resigned amid rampant protests and looting on the streets of the City of Buenos Aires and its surrounding urban areas. It is well known that the power of the provinces, coupled with a weakening central bureaucracy, had complicated Argentina's attempts at achieving macroeconomic stabilization and other economic reforms, particularly after 1997. The national government's leverage over the provinces fell in tandem with President Menem's popularity and his inability to run for reelection in 1999. The public's growing fatigue with *Menemismo* (which had ruled for almost a decade) created the political environment for an alternative electoral force to win the presidency. A coalition of the center-left party FRE-PASO and the centrist UCR called Alianza (Alianza para el Trabajo, la Justicia y la Educación) duly won the national elections of 1999. According to Levitsky and Murillo (2003, 153), Menem left three legacies: a dramatic growth in public debt, an expensive privatized social security system, and widespread social exclusion.

Foreshadowing Lula's 2002 electoral campaign in Brazil, Alianza campaigned in 1999 on ending corruption, increasing government transparency, and ending the social exclusion that had been created by the rigid macroeconomic stabilization strategy.[9] Because Alianza did not have a majority in the Senate or control the majority of the twenty-three governors, de la Rúa's government was "alleged to have bribed a handful of senators in an effort to pass labor-reform legislations" (Levitsky and Murillo 2003, 154). It was not corruption that would force the president to resign, however, but a currency crisis, which wreaked social and economic havoc. The weakness of Argentina's fiscal base limited its ability to pay interest on its rapidly expanding foreign debt toward the end of 2001, triggering this crisis (Schamis 2002, 83). This situation was exacerbated by the ability of governors to undermine the president's economic reforms. The provinces continued to place greater revenue demands on the federal government even during the currency crisis.

Two successive interim presidents were selected by Congress during the last weeks of December 2001 to replace de la Rúa. All resigned within days of assuming the post. The national government finally became operational again when the former PJ governor of the Province of Buenos Aires, Eduardo Duhalde (1995–1999), was elected interim president by Congress. When Duhalde assumed the presidency on January 2, 2002, the legitimacy and credibility of the national government were at an all-time low. Duhalde's most difficult challenge was to reunite the internally fragmented PJ party under his leadership and to restore social order.

The proactive characteristics of Duhalde's leadership, which reactivated Argentina's "hyperpresidential"[10] tendencies, brought order to the country. Two social protection programs to deal with the enormous social crisis were established by executive decree in February 2002. The first was an emergency nutrition program (PEA), designed and run by Duhalde's wife, Chiche. She was also the president's first interim minister of social development and the head of the National Council of Social Policy Coordination, which was responsible for monitoring these national antipoverty programs. The second program, PJJHD, was a cash transfer program managed by President Duhalde himself, through the Ministry of Labor.[11] All previously existing workfare programs from both the national and provincial levels of government were replaced by PJJHD—under Duhalde and Chiche, there was to be no dispersion of decision-making power on the demand side (who got what, how much, and how), not even among the national-level ministries. However, the design of this new benchmark program was similar to the workfare programs of the Menem decade. It was structured around locally initiated public works projects, a characteristic that had been pushed for and supported by mayors from around the country (interview Cafiero 2006).[12] The supply-side inputs of PJJHD (community work projects) were designed to be captured by subnational power brokers. Localized control over volunteer work activities that were funded by PJJHD helped maintain the capital flow of local fiscal accounts, which had become extremely restricted because of the crisis. The registration of eligible individuals for PJJHD was open to municipal authorities only until May 17,

2002. A third CCT program based on human capital investments was also established at this time, called Plan Familias. It was supported by the Inter-American Development Bank (IDB), and it was part of the negotiations for the renewed financing of PJJHD in 2003. It remained largely dormant, however, until it was reactivated in 2004.

Duhalde's immediate new federal pact, accepted by the provinces, was meant to end the convertibility plan and offset the social costs by massively expanding PJJHD. Instead it "plunged the economy into further chaos" (Levitsky and Murillo 2003). Poverty immediately escalated throughout the country. Six months after the default, urban poverty rates climaxed at 57.5 percent (INDEC 2006). Social order was of paramount importance to the future stability of the country, and PJJHD was fundamental to the national government's ability to manage this extremely vulnerable social situation. From the supply side, PJJHD gave local PJ party brokers a powerful tool with which to reengage in the political game. It empowered local actors from the top down[13] and plugged them into a party-driven political machine (interview Rubio 2006). It gave Duhalde, like Menem, a means to forge a party-centered alliance with provincial and local power brokers and regenerate popular support for the political system, in exchange for a constant downward flow of resources, which Duhalde himself controlled (Jones and Hwang 2005). In June 2002 the economic and social chaos of Argentina reached a climax with the killing of two protesters. Duhalde was forced to step down prematurely, and elections were called (Levitsky and Murillo 2003, 155). The PJJHD, however, would play an important role in the 2003 presidential elections and in the victory of Duhalde's preferred candidate, a relatively unknown outsider candidate, Néstor Kirchner.

Within PJJHD, mayors and their employees were intended to be responsible for the registration of potential beneficiaries (individuals, not households), the electronic gathering of personal data, the communication of acceptance, the delegation of beneficiaries to work activities, and the monitoring of work conditions. In many municipalities, however, these responsibilities were co-opted by union groups, social organizations, and *piqueteros* themselves, who were able to bypass municipal authorities in order to gain access to the program. These local actors contributed to distorting the territorial allocation and targeting efficiency of this redistributive program, as did officials from higher levels of government who allocated benefits to individuals who had not officially been registered by municipal authorities. This practice also demonstrated the lame-duck status of most mayors, who chose to turn a blind eye to the program's local administration. Juan Pablo Cafiero (the former minister of public security and social development) challenges this analysis, however, claiming that beneficiaries were victimized by the belief, circulated by the media, that "there were programs given to certain groups in the Province of Buenos Aires," although according to him, "no more than 10 percent, maximum" (interview Cafiero 2006).

As previously mentioned, recent analyses have demonstrated successfully that the observed irregularities in the targeting of workfare programs in Argentina were determined by levels of protest activity and not by partisanship (Weitz-Shapiro 2006; Giraudy 2007). More nuanced qualitative research suggests, however, that the negotiations between varying groups of organized protesters and powerful government officials, at least between 2001 and 2003, were the outcome of non-institutionalized pork-barrel relations that profited Duhalde's branch of the PJ until the end of 2003. Social movements in Argentina are notoriously co-opted by state actors. The bypassing of the municipal offices that were *de jure* responsible for identifying eligible recipients, by officials from higher levels of government, was predominantly observed in key PJ localities in the surrounding urban areas of Buenos Aires Province, such as La Matanza. At the program's height in 2003, 58.5 percent of this municipality's recipients had not been registered by official local authorities. According to the responsible local office, they do not appear in the municipality's records.[14] The politically motivated manipulation of PJJHD's distribution is most visible in terms of the program's observable volatility from the latter part of 2002 until the 2003 general elections.

Figure 5.3 shows the rise in the distribution of benefits around the time of the general elections, based on an aggregation of cross-provincial data. The aggregations were calculated using the monthly distribution of benefits over twelve months, and the disaggregate data was verified through triangulation across three government offices. From the first month the graph begins, October 2002, the formal registry of the program was officially closed to further expansions. I set the amount of beneficiaries in this month at 100 to establish a baseline. However, we

Figure 5.3. Rising Distribution of PJJHD before the 2003 General Elections

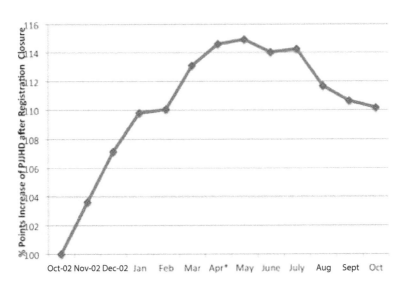

Source: Author calculations based on monthly liquidations of PJJHD per province, supplied by Ministry of Labor.
Note: October 2002 = 100%; *April 27 = date of general elections.

can observe a steady increase in the number of beneficiaries included, which peaked in May 2003. The presidential elections were held on April 27.

It is of paramount importance here that the registration for this social program was closed officially in May 2002. In figure 5.3, the program's closure was generously time-lagged by five months to allow for administrative delay until that October. Given that the program *de jure* still paid out benefits but was now closed to new recipients, there should be no observable increases in the number of recipients in the above graph, particularly since it was previously believed that there were no federal motivations behind the distribution of antipoverty programs.

President Duhalde's incentive to allow the supply-side inputs to be captured was that it contributed to his ability to bargain with provincial and local PJ bosses and to create an alliance that guaranteed that his preferred candidate, Néstor Kirchner, won on April 27, 2003. The decision-making authority over the program's subnational distribution, however, was never dispersed. In a majoritarian political regime such as Argentina's, decision-making power is concentrated in the hands of the governing party. The president had a political incentive to control the territorial distribution of this program, yet to allow subnational authorities in key localities that were purposely targeted to capture the *contrapresaciones* (workfare conditions) as a substitute for traditional patronage-based public employment, which during this period was extremely limited.

Néstor Kirchner won the presidency with 22.24 percent of the vote after Menem withdrew from the second round. Kirchner's regional dominance in these direct elections was based primarily in the Patagonian provinces, whence he originated, and, most significantly of all, in the Province of Buenos Aires (Cheresky and Pousadela 2004). The use of a cash transfer program conditional on labor inputs to win the 2003 elections was a perfect mechanism, for several reasons. First, at the time of the presidential election in April 2003 the federal government was still lacking in performance-based legitimacy, thanks to the 2001 crisis. And second, during that same year national household poverty had increased to 42.6 percent, making poverty alleviation crucial to electoral campaigning. This entrenched fiscal-political-social crisis context gave Interim President Duhalde a favorable situation within which he could engineer the presidential elections to keep out his political enemy, Menem. Additionally, Duhalde, as the former governor and PJ boss in the Province of Buenos Aires, controlled the PJ mayors of the surrounding urban areas, who appeared with Kirchner on campaign posters. Moreover, the politicized nature of the bureaucracy in Argentina entails that the staff of certain ministries have partisan affiliation. It is widely believed that the national ministry responsible for the day-to-day operation of PJJHD was very much controlled at that time by Duhalde (PJ-Buenos Aires). Together, by manipulating the distribution of the program, they were victorious.[15]

The main point of the above section has been to demonstrate that national PJ workfare programs were used to generate political support for the PJ, following a majoritarian or power-concentrating logic, but that during Menem's administrations that support was more powerful when it was widely dispersed throughout multiple programs, allowing a plethora of party-affiliated actors to claim credit for them. This dynamic also served to encourage the proliferation of social programs through-out Argentina at the time. In contrast, Duhalde needed to more tightly control the effects of his benchmark workfare program PJJHD in order to concentrate power within the presidency during a time of internal fragmentation within the PJ party.

THE TRANSFORMATION OF CCTS FROM LABOR TO HUMAN CAPITAL UNDER PRESIDENT KIRCHNER (PJ), 2003–2007

Even though the role of PJJHD had been pivotal in contributing to Néstor Kirchner's election, as a strategic political resource it remained largely controlled by Duhalde. Once elected, President Kirchner had a personal incentive to concentrate power within his own administration and restore the public's faith in the national government. The national policy objective of the new administration (2003–2007), therefore, was to create a new CCT based on cash transfers linked to investments in human capital that were free of political (that is, provincial) inter-mediation. This would also entail discontinuing PJJHD, which would weaken Duhalde's support base. In order to do so, via decree 1506/04, the president prolonged the national employment emergency legisla-tion from 2002 and promised the continued payment of PJJHD benefits until December 31, 2004. Additionally, he gave the Ministry of Labor and the Ministry of Social Development (Desarrollo Social) 180 days to coordinate their databases and reclassify the recipients of PJJHD into two categories: employable and unemployable. The employable would continue receiving PJJHD, while those who were not would be trans-ferred into a program "either created or to be created by the Desarrollo Social." This latter ministry was put under the charge of his sister, Alicia Kirchner. The official plan of the federal government was to create a new CCT that was under an appropriate ministry and that was designed to provide longer-term social protection free of political intermediation.

According to the former vice-minister of the Ministry of Social De-velopment, Daniel Arroyo, the intention was to develop a CCT that would be largely based on the Mexican model of Progresa-Opportunidades-Prospera, not on Brazil's Bolsa Família—that is, it would be tightly centralized from targeting to monitoring and not dependent on any self-reported means-testing (interview Arroyo 2006). Unlike Mexico, however, Argentina is a strong federal system where the ability of the president to govern is dependent on the president's relationship with PJ provincial bosses (Jones and Hwang 2005; Levitsky 2003), hence this intended design would be unpopular among the governors and provincial representatives in Congress.[16]

The national government therefore faced two choices: they could either design a CCT based on a centralized administration without any provincial or municipal involvement, or they could attempt to avoid governors and motivate some sort of local cooperation, as Bolsa Família had done in Brazil. Kirchner had successfully won the 2003 elections with Duhalde's backing in the largest province, Buenos Aires. His own support at the subnational level, however, was low, because he was not the PJ party's official candidate (there were three of these). Menem finished ahead of Kirchner in the first round with 24.45 percent of total votes, but he withdrew from the second round.[17] Although 66 percent of the winning governors in 2003 were formally PJ, only four of the eight provinces belonged to Kirchner's faction, called the Frente para la Victoria (FPV).[18] At the municipal level, Kirchner's base was even weaker. For example, in the Province of Buenos Aires, which represents 38 percent of the country's population, the effective number of parties represented at the municipal level was a low 1.97. Out of these two dominant parties, 56 percent of the province's elected mayors were Duhalde-aligned PJ members, and the next-largest party, the Union Cívica Radical (UCR), managed to be reelected in its stable dominant localities within the province—31.34 percent overall.[19]

In the end, Kirchner opted to design a CCT that was not wholly based on either the Mexican model or the Brazilian model, but that was adapted to Argentine circumstances. The Argentine program was far more centralized than its Brazilian equivalent, yet unlike Mexico's Progresa-Opportunidades-Prospera, it still relied on subnational acquiescence, particularly at the local level. This program feature would prove difficult, given that Kirchner's electoral strength at the municipal level in 2003 was not sufficient for him to encourage municipalities to directly promote this new policy objective without their province's backing. Based on the previous experience of social protection programs in Argentina, provincial backing meant political intermediation.

Additionally, the continued dominance of party-centered provincial power in Congress and the control of provincial power brokers aligned with Duhalde over PJJHD would be further obstacles to Kirchner's proposed reforms and the eventual success of his benchmark CCT. It was originally called Plan Familias, then renamed as Programa Familias para la Inclusion Social.

The utility of PJJHD as a political instrument would make it difficult to dismantle this program, yet its reputation with the past and its association with Duhalde would make its termination necessary for Kirchner to establish his leadership. PJJHD had been successfully used across three levels of government to pump patronage into the PJ's localized networks, many of whom were unemployed program recipients. The PJ is much more heavily supported by less-skilled constituencies than are other parties (Calvo and Murillo 2004). Moreover, the effect of generating mutually beneficial patronage across three levels of a decentralized party structure had served previously to motivate a vertical alignment within the ruling PJ.[20] Because the PJ's ability to govern is dependent on its ability to create an intraparty alliance, PJJHD had created a win-win situation for official PJ party leaders at both the provincial and national levels—the federal government could claim direct credit for the downward flow of resources, and local PJ party brokers could claim direct credit for the community-based projects that relied upon volunteer labor. At the time of its intended termination, the use of PJJHD for patronage ends was both recognized and entrenched in the public's opinion of this program and of federally financed social investment programs in general.

EXPLAINING THE UNDER-PERFORMANCE OF PROGRAMA FAMILIAS, 2003–2009

As a new ambitious president who had been elected with only 22.24 percent of the total vote, Kirchner sought an alternate strategy of delivering noncontributory social benefits designed to promote social inclusion. It involved three principal social programs: El Hambre mas Urgente, a nutritional program; Manos a la Obra, a community-based work program; and Plan, then Programa, Familias, an integrated CCT program.

Programa Familias was intended to be the government's benchmark CCT that would consolidate government action toward families in situations of social vulnerability. According to the Secretary of the Ministry of Social Development, the country's emergency situation had not yet been overcome, and therefore the country's social programs needed to be redesigned with a longer-term investment perspective (interview Arroyo 2006). The government's intended strategy was that former recipients of PJJHD who were eligible for the new CCT would be transferred by February 2005. From 2003 to 2006, however, PJJHD coverage only decreased from its peak by 33 percent. Of the households no longer receiving PJJHD, only 15 percent transferred to Programa Familias.[21] Only 27 percent of the total households receiving Familias were in fact former recipients of PJJHD. The bulk of Programa Familias beneficiaries were new recipients. Despite the government's attempt to discontinue PJJHD, over 1.2 million recipients remained within it in 2006 and at least 500,000 until 2009.[22] The Kirchner administration's goal to discontinue PJJHD and transfer recipients classified as "unemployable" to Programa Familias had been largely unsuccessful, even though it had a clear political motivation to break with the past and had been backed by international financing and technical support.

Several domestic factors impeded the territorial distribution of this CCT, which have implications for future Argentine social investment initiatives that are based on intergovernmental and cross-sector collaboration. First, the confusion surrounding both the discontinuation of previous social inclusion initiatives (primarily PJJHD) and the creation of a completely new policy strategy led to a proliferation of uncoordinated social programs with no clear national policy objective.[23] Second, the "not-completely" centralized administration of Programa Familias that limited local authorities from participating denied them any right to claim credit for the program's implementation in their territories, yet ironically the program still required their promotion efforts, given that it intended to integrate PJJHD's beneficiaries and to distinguish employable from unemployable households.

Third, the ambiguous discontinuation of PJJHD and the creation of the new Programa Familias impeded a common understanding of an explicit national policy goal by the multiple ministries involved. The technical coordinator of PJJHD in the Ministry of Labor stated that the goal of Familias was to absorb the recipients of the previous emergency program, which had been "discontinued" (interview Espinoza 2006). The former research director of Public Spending and Social Programs in the Ministry of Economy stated, "*de jure*, yes, but, de facto, nothing has occurred over three years and I cannot see that it will" (interview Bonari 2006). In the Ministry of Social Development (Desarrollo Social) the goals of the program were reported differently.

The coordinator of Programa Familias within the ministry stated that in 2004 there were three choices: first, leave each program running; second, unify them; or third, reformulate them. She stated that Desarrollo Social opted to reformulate, and that (at the time of the interview) "the transfer of eligible beneficiaries is being coordinated with all the municipalities; we meet with each mayor in order to coordinate it mutually" (interview Tedeschi 2006). This was contradicted by a senior representative from the municipality of La Matanza, who stated that "official municipal authorities have nothing to do with Programa Familias and we have never been approached; it is a centralized program" (interview Colicigno 2006). Alicia Kirchner's then right-hand official, Daniel Arroyo, stated that Programa Familias was intended in the long term to be the only CCT in Argentina for the poor, and that it would be conceived as an "entitlement" (interview Arroyo 2006). He further stated that his and Alicia Kirchner's vision was for this CCT to become an extension of the "family grants" that are part of the formal system of social security in Argentina, which did in fact come to fruition in 2009 within a completely new program, Asignación Universal por Hijo (AUH), discussed below. AUH, however, is neither a CCT nor a universal family allowance, but rather a hybrid between the two (Lo Vuolo 2013, 56). Evident during these interviews with varying senior bureaucratic and political actors across different levels of government was the lack of an explicit national policy objective during the most crucial phase of this CCT's intended transformation into a benchmark federal program.

As an integrated CCT, Programa Familias worked as follows. A conditional cash transfer (CCT) was made to the female head of the household with dependent children under the age of eighteen.[24] She received $150 pesos a month, plus $25 pesos per child, up to a total maximum benefit of $225 pesos. From 2006, the family could earn other income as long as the amount, including the CCT, did not exceed the minimum wage of $800 pesos a month per household. The conditions were based on the dependent children's education and basic health certificates, to be presented to the local program office three times a year. Originally, the money was transferred to this local office in the form of paper checks for distribution. After evidence surfaced regarding fraud between 2003 and 2005, the money was instead delivered using an electronic card issued by the Banco de la Nación. The program prioritized families with children, based on three variables: first, whether or not they had been former recipients of PJJHD; second, if they were below the poverty line; and third, an exogenous variable based on where they lived (interview Tedeschi 2006; interview Arroyo 2006). The choice of indicators used to target households demonstrates that although Familias was a new program, it tried to integrate the previous, patronage-based program, which was well known to have been designed to generate popular support for a particular political group. Therefore, a potential trade-off existed between appeasing former recipients of PJJHD and the intended transparency of Familias, a CCT with international aspirations.

The National Coordinative Council of Social Policy was responsible for the oversight of Familias and PJJHD, among all other social investment initiatives. This council was created in 2005 (decree 15/05) to give economic, logistical, and technical support to social policy implementation and its monitoring in both the Ministry of Labor and the Ministry of Social Development. The Council of Social Policy is under the authority of the Minister of Social Development, Alicia Kirchner (2006–present). Beyond providing technical support, this council is also responsible for completing a cross-check of multiple databases in order to ensure that recipients are not double-dipping and are in fact eligible based on each program's criteria.

The data cross-check was designed to provide this information using SINTYS, a national IT system that by law cross-checks in-house, inter-sector databases every three months (interview Rubio 2006; interview Espinoza 2006). The execution of this mechanism is under the authority of Minister Alicia Kirchner. Two technical sources from the Familias team and the PJJHD team responsible for aggregating consolidated social expenditure confirmed that this well-intended monitoring tool was *not* in fact used every three months (interview anonymous Ministerio de Desarrollo Social 2006; interview anonymous Ministerio de Trabajo, 2006). In 2005, there was only one reported cross-check completed, and within the first nine months of 2006 there had been none (interview Bonari 2006). The proliferation of preexisting social programs and the creation of a new CCT, each with its own database located in its separate bureaucracy, coupled with the fact that oversight was tied closely to the Casa Rosada (the Pink House—the president's office), facilitated the prevalence of executive authority within these social investment initiatives.

Within Argentine federalism, executive authority is used to control the political effects of a redistributive policy. Additionally, the centralized organizational structure of Familias was not built upon intergovernmental cooperation, reflecting the federal government's lack of trust in provincial and local authorities. It was, however, not nearly as centralized as the institutional design of the Mexican CCT model, which is considered in international policy circles as the gold standard in targeting performance, given its technocratic (and randomized) selection method that invites preselected households into this heavily federally-enforced CCT (see Levy 2006; and de la O 2013). The administration of Programa Familias was completely centralized, yet the delivery and monitoring of this CCT remained based on the willingness of mayors to cooperate with this national policy objective.

The amount of recipients to be allocated to each designated province by the national government was based on a formula that included three variables: 10 percent based on the size of the province's population, 30 percent based on the number of beneficiaries within the provinces that had received PJJHD, and 60 percent based on the number of families with dependent children under eighteen below the poverty line resident within the province. The selection of municipalities was not very clear. Officially, the municipalities were selected based on the last census (INDEC 2001), which has an index of the quality of life of each family based on a territorial location. Each family receives an individual score based on the component variables of "quality of life" designated by the annual census.

In the Province of Buenos Aires, however, according to official data received from the office administering Programa Familias within Desarrollo Social, from 2003 to the end of 2005 only ten municipalities received Programa Familias: E. Echeverria, Florencio Varela, Jose C. Paz, Ituzaingo, La Matanaza, Lomas de Zamora, Moreno, Quilmes, San Fernando, and Mar del Plata. Except for Mar del Plata, which from 2003 to 2007 was governed by one of the earliest Radicales K–aligned mayors, Daniel Katz, the remainder of the mayors were considered then (and many remain so today) the "Barons of Kirchnerismo" in the Conurbano (surrounding urban area) of the City of Buenos Aires.[25] In terms of the Province of Buenos Aires's share of Programa Familias relative to that of the nation, based on the same data source it equated to 32 percent, which is basically Buenos Aires's proportion of the nation's population.

Until 2003, each province simply selected the municipalities within the province to be allocated the program. Thereafter, however, each selected municipality had a designated team in the national program office and one within the province. The provincial team was selected by *ternas*—whereby the province short-listed three candidates for each position to be filled—and the national program office then made the final selection. Some provinces insisted on selecting their team autonomously and rejected the use of short-lists (*ternas*). In such cases, the national office either denied the program to that province or accepted the candidates selected by the province on an ad hoc basis.

The same process existed for municipalities, without provincial intermediation. All employees, office equipment, and infrastructure were paid for and supplied by the national office. The local office was accountable to a member of both the provincial and national offices, making it a hierarchical program, which actually meant that both provincial and municipal intermediation were built into each administrative team. One interviewee reported that there was frequent tension and conflict within this organizational setting (interview anonymous Ministero de Desarrollo Social 2006). All communications between the three levels were also hierarchical. The national office would contact the provincial office about a discrepancy, the provincial office then sent someone out to the local office, which then sent someone out to the family to enforce compliance. This centralized and hierarchical structure did not motivate local participation because it excluded local authorities from administrative participation in the program's implementation. Yet the system ironically continued to require municipal collaboration to monitor conditionality and provincial cooperation to both supply and guarantee the quality of the health and education services required by households in the program.

What appears most salient in the case of this CCT, however, is the inability of mayors to claim credit or benefit in any way for promoting this national program within their territories. It did not even lead to an increase in the demand for locally provided social services, because most of the education and health services required by Programa Familias are provided by the provinces, and this CCT's conditions were largely punitive, side-stepping the need for any local social assistance networks. In Argentina, mayors operate as gatekeepers between highly organized community demands and a multitude of government-funded programs and services controlled by higher levels of government. Although both federalism and decentralization have played a key role in Argentina's development path (see Saiegh and Tommasi 1998), the stability of the party-centered majority logic at the provincial level has weakened the incentives of municipalities to support national policy objectives that are not politically funneled to them through higher levels of government. Therefore, the only constituent units that had a political incentive to claim credit for this CCT were the provinces, which in turned used this "political clout" to bolster federal support for their benefit. The officially declared intended political effects of this national CCT, however (and CCTs in general), did not include bolstering the governor's popularity. In fact, it was intended to foster a direct relationship between the federal government and its citizens. Therefore, opposition provinces and territories had both the ability and the political incentive to undermine this CCT directly through impeding its territorial distribution or indirectly through policy apathy.

Programa Familias Regional Composition, 2003–2006

An important question concerns the regional composition of beneficiaries in Familias: was Programa Familias territorially distributed throughout the nation according to political variables that are salient at the provincial level? I analyzed the program's performance from 2003 to 2006 in terms of how well it was distributed, based on which provinces should have received the benefits and which provinces actually did, using the program's own criteria supplied by the Office of Programa Familias inside of the Ministry of Social Development. Because of the program's criteria, I aggregated the provinces into several groups in order to determine whether the territorial allocation of the program provided any evidence of politicized program distribution.

I divided the provinces into three territorial blocks according to their formal alignment with the president in 2006, inclusive of the five governors who declared themselves UCR-aligned supporters of the Kirchner (FPV) national electoral coalition in early 2006 (see appendix, table A.2). From 2003 to 2005, Argentina continued, on paper, to be dominated by a single party, which controlled over 60 percent of institutional power across all three levels of government.[26] In reality, it was in the midst of a crisis of party representation, which divided the country into a multiplicity of intraparty fragmentations and varying PJ-based fronts and alliances, most, but not all, of them aligned with the incumbent government.[27]

Five provinces (counting CBA) were not covered by Programa Familias during Néstor Kirchner's tenure. They were Neuquén, the Autonomous City of Buenos Aires, La Pampa, Catamarca, and Santiago del Estero. Interviewees confirmed that the opposition province of Neuquén and the Autonomous City of Buenos Aires blocked this CCT from operating in their territory (interview anonymous Ministerio de Desarrollo Social 2006; interview Puchiarelli 2006; interview Ibarra 2006). Three other provinces—La Pampa, Catamarca, and Santiago del Estero—were excluded from the program by the federal government for undisclosed reasons. Santiago del Estero was the subject of a federal intervention in 2004 and was slowly regaining its provincial credibility. The governor of Catamarca at the time of analysis was a recently declared supporter of the Radicales K (a faction of the UCR that was formally aligned with the ruling FPV). La Pampa was a PJ province that was not officially aligned with the federal government. The following analysis of which provinces, aggregated according to their formal alignment with the Kirchner government, *should* have received Programa

Familias is based on the program's criteria, including the five provinces that block, or are blocked from, the program. Both component variables have been time-lagged by one year, 2005 (see figure 5.4). Figure 5.4 clearly illustrates that the bulk of Programa Familias, based on its ideal targeting criteria, was designed to go to households living in officially PJ-aligned territories. It is important to remember that Programa Familias included the targeting of PJJHD, even though the program had been largely discredited because its distribution had been politically manipulated by PJ-party brokers. Patronage-based relationships are common in Argentina. Their effects and consequences have been documented both in national media sources and in academic circles.[28] The traditional dominance of the Peronist party meant that patronage represents deeply entrenched political networks across all three levels of government. These networks continue to allow the PJ to dominate at the subnational level.

Figure 5.5 is based on which groups actually received Familias in 2006. This analysis uses recipient data from the office responsible for the program's day-to-day operation. The opposition group received close to their intended share of the program, namely, 22 percent of benefits. Interestingly, however, the bulk of the difference between what was

Figure 5.4. Ideal Distribution of Programa Familias in 2006

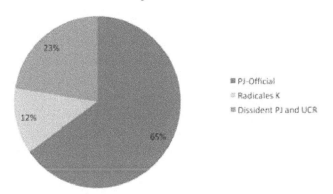

Source: Author elaboration, INDEC; Ministério del Trabajo; Ministério de Desarrollo Social.
Note: Based on estimates of Programa Familias's reported targeting criteria (including excluded provinces). See appendix, table A.3.

Figure 5.5. Actual Distribution of Programa Familias in 2006

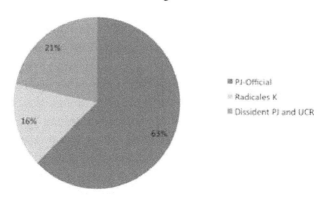

Source: Author elaboration. Based on disaggregated territorial data supplied by Ministério de Desarrollo Social.

delivered and what should have been delivered profited the Radicales K. This can best be explained by the fact that only one province, Mendoza, had all of its municipalities (total provincial coverage) included within the targeting of this federal program. Mendoza was a Radicales K province in 2006.

Additional Testing: An Ordered Counterfactual

In order to substantiate this observation further, I constructed an ordered counterfactual of who would receive the program in the future, based on 2006 spending patterns (see table 5.1). This test was constructed using an odds ratio, based on 2006 program data, 2005 PJJHD actual allocation per province, and household poverty and population statistics per province collected by the National Institute of Statistics and Census (INDEC 2006). The odds of success are particularly low because of the limited actual distribution levels of the program.

These results provide interesting insights. The only group that was found empirically to have higher odds of success in receiving benefits in the future was the officially aligned Radicales K group. In fact, households were 1.5 times more likely to receive a benefit if living in a Radicales K territory than they are if living in either a PJ-dissident

Table 5.1.   Counterfactual Order of Future Beneficiaries of Programa Familias

Group	Actual	Potential	Proportion	Total	Odds Ratio
PJ-Official	232,748	1,458,982	0.14/0.86	1,691,730	0.16
Opposition	79,967	506,787	0.13/0.87	581,754	0.15
Radicales K	58,575	262,583	0.18/0.82	321,168	0.22

or PJ-official territory. This finding was completely expected given the political context of 2006.

The potential explanation for this finding can be found in Dixit and Londregan's (1996) federal spending model. This model, based on majority voting patterns between two competing parties in the United States (with the assumption that voter's affinity is heterogeneous, as it is in post-2003 Argentina), predicted that the party with the ability to deliver more benefits will target swing voters. They proposed in their formal model that this targeting of swing voters was dependent on differences in the parties' ability to deliver such benefits. Using the dominant Peronist hypothesis in the literature, Calvo and Murillo (2004) concluded in their study that the PJ clearly had this advantage in Argentina, which would explain the results observed in the counterfactual presented above. These results can also be explained in hindsight by the fact that Cristina Fernández de Kirchner ran for the presidency in 2007 with a UCR/Radicales K vice president on her ticket, Julio Cobos, who came from the province that had been most heavily targeted by Programa Familias in 2006—Mendoza.

THE END OF FAMILIAS:
ASIGNACIÓN UNIVERSAL POR HIJO, 2009–2013

In October 2007, Argentine voters elected Cristina Fernández de Kirchner to the presidency, along with Julio Cobos as her vice president, with 45.3 percent of the total vote. Given that she was her husband's successor and that her sister-in-law remained in her post as the Minister of

Social Development, the continued expansion of CCT coverage within Familias and the discontinuation of PJJHD were to be expected. The new president was able to continue slowly reducing PJJHD, but not through transferring beneficiaries to Programa Familias, a program whose take-up remained rather slow (see figure 5.6).

With a clear majority in Congress, President Fernández de Kirchner ultimately was able to realize her late husband's goal of terminating PJJHD, a goal he had declared in 2003 when he took office. As we have seen, this "emergency" social protection initiative, created in 2002, had been left to operate "unofficially" as a parallel program to Programa Familias, a CCT also created in 2003. PJJHD, along with Programa Familias, was finally terminated in October 2009 by Fernández de Kirchner, just before the midterm legislative elections of her first term (when she lost her legislative majority) and around the same time that her vice president, Julio Cobos (Mendoza), publicly opposed her and returned to the formal opposition.

The institutional design of Familias had been compromised by its intention to integrate PJJHD's beneficiaries and because of this previous program's poor reputation, otherwise known as *malafama*. Its distribution was undermined by the politicized nature of Argentine intergovernmental relations. In a highly credible public opinion survey taken in 2007, 88 percent of Argentine respondents believed that noncontributory cash transfer programs were used for political motives (Cruces and Rovner 2008). Therefore, the Fernández de Kirchner administration opted to terminate Programa Familias once and for all, alongside PJJHD, replacing it by executive decree with a completely new and highly centralized noncontributive family allowance benefit that is specifically focused on investing in children, called Asignación Universal por Hijo (AUH). Because AUH would not be financed through the federal budget, it did not go through any executive-legislative bargaining when it was announced. AUH does not use any targeting criteria or any geographical quotas within its distribution; hence its potential for coverage is far greater than either of the two previous CCTs that existed from 2003 to 2009. Several ambiguities surround this most recent national social program, however, including its conditional elements, its formal inclusion within the formal social security system, and its financial sustainability.

Figure 5.6. Gradual Discontinuation of CCTs in Argentina, 2003–2010

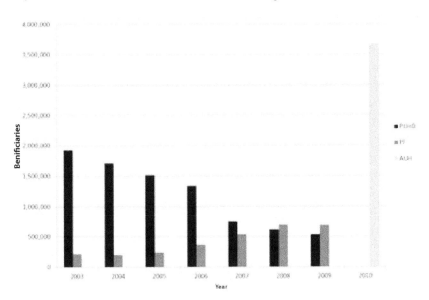

Source: Author elaboration. Data supplied by Ministério de Trabajo; Ministério de Desarrollo Social.

AUH is entirely child-centered. In 2013 it delivered a benefit of $460 pesos to each dependent child under the age of eighteen (ANSES 2013).[29] It was implemented in 2010 and soon included over three million recipients. Its coverage was then further expanded in 2011 with another family allowance benefit given to pregnant women, called Asignación Universal por Embarazo (AUE). Like the Canadian welfare model implemented in the 1940s, these "universal family allowances represent a clear step toward social policy centralization and the direct intervention of the federal government into the everyday lives of [Argentine] families" (Béland and Lecours 2008, 49). Because of the way AUH is financed and administered, directly via the already existing family allowance scheme that is a formal component of the Social Security System in Argentina and is controlled by ANSES, the National Administration of Social Security, no formal or informal bargaining with either the provinces or the municipalities was required for its implementation. This makes AUH a *hyper*-executive program.

Family allowances in Argentina (*Asignaciónes Familiares*) are universal in nature and consist of two streams: one contributory, based on formal family incomes, which cover approximately 55 percent of Argentine children under the age of eighteen, and the other noncontributory—that is, AUH, which since 2010 covers another 31 percent out of the total 12.1 million minors in the country under the age of eighteen (Curcío and Beccaria, cited in Jaime and Sabaté 2013, 7). Although still relatively new, this program stands out from other CCTs in Argentina and from the region for several reasons. First, as previously mentioned, it includes no quotas or limits on its potential distribution because it is part of the law of formal benefits for employed workers, which is universal (Lo Vuolo 2013, 54). Second, the role of conditions and their enforcement is rather ambiguous, making it extremely difficult to be classified as a CCT that can be associated to the intended goals of an "active welfare state." Without any subnational involvement to assist in the monitoring of the conditions for those of the 12.1 million children whose parents are unemployed, within the context of a highly decentralized robust federation, it is unlikely that this program had any intention of being closely monitored. As stated quite succinctly by Lo Vuolo (2013, 53), "AUH was designed to compensate for the incomplete coverage of traditional family allowances." This does not make it a social investment program that is designed to contribute to reducing the intergenerational transmission of poverty. Moreover, and of great importance, there are currently no existing intergovernmental mechanisms in Argentina between the three levels of government to share information regarding school attendance and childhood vaccinations. Even the national Ministry of Social Development has been largely excluded from this new noncontributory benefit stream. From the perspective of ANSES, many provinces and their databases are incompatible with those at the federal level, which may make program compliance extremely difficult. Therefore at the moment, proof of compliance is self-supplied by the beneficiary, unlike either Progresa-Opportunidades-Prospera in Mexico or Bolsa Família in Brazil. In fact, 80 percent of the benefit is transferred automatically to the family via ANSES's formal social security system per month, with the remaining 20 percent delivered at the end of the year after a single piece of paper, folded to form a book, is stamped by the school and health authorities and submitted directly by the mother or father to ANSES. Also, a matter of considerable debate from a moral normative perspective, children receiving this equivalent monetary benefit through the contributory scheme are not subject to any conditions.

Second, although AUH is considered noncontributory in nature and framed as "universal," Lo Vuolo (2013) and others object that it is neither, primarily because it is financed out of income tax contributions from formal employment and because it prioritizes individuals already registered in the social security system who are now classified as unemployed, based on who ANSES decides to include. Additionally of great concern, because of the public administration system that it relies on, AUH does not include families that have never been registered formally within the social security system or those whose children have never attended school. In stark contrast with CCTs in Brazil, municipalities are not involved in any sort of outreach (*busca ativa*) or documentation efforts, in order to include families and children that have fallen through the cracks of the formal social security system. How is ANSES, one of the largest and most bureaucratic arms of Argentina's formal social security system, supposed to locate a child born in the remote northwestern Quebrada de Jujuy that borders the Altiplano and the sub-Andean hills, for example, in order to include that child in this "social investment" program?

AUH fails to include many children because they are simply not registered within the national social security system. Curcío and Beccaria (cited in Jaime and Sabaté 2013, 7) calculate that 9 percent of children in Argentina are not covered by family allowances. Deeper academic analysis of this most recent program is extremely limited, however, because of the legal restrictions of sharing private information about the citizens registered in the formal security system, and given the much hypothesized contemporary unreliability of Argentine government indicators of poverty, unemployment, and inflation (see "Don't Lie to Me, Argentina," *The Economist*, February 25, 2012). There is currently no empirical evidence that AUH is anything more than a noncontributory benefit stream for families already officially registered within Argentina's formal social security system whose income temporarily, or permanently, falls below the government's set benchmark.

Third, the future sustainability of AUH is reliant on the availability of revenues made through formal, private contributions to the ANSES. In 2011, the World Bank pledged a 3.6 million dollar loan to increase the coverage of AUH, but there was no mention of either strengthening the conditional aspects of the program or ensuring the availability of monitoring mechanisms to do so, within this relatively small loan. This is hardly surprising. In response to my question "Why not just get rid of the conditions?," a high-ranking government official stated, with respect to the difficulty of ensuring subnational cooperation within the enforcement of Familias conditions, that "the IDB and the Bank needed the labor and human capital conditions there or they would never have financed these programs" (interview anonymous Ministerio de Desarrollo Social 2006). According to Jaime and Sabaté (2013), the IDB provided as much as US$700 million to Programa Familias in 2005 and as much as US$950 million to PJJHD from 2003 to 2009. Both programs were heavily framed as being conditional on labor and human capital investments.

Fourth, the lack of provincial and local participation within AUH or their implicit agreement to participate has opened the door to intergovernmental policy competition. By 2013, the media reported that there were 110 CCT-like programs in various social sectors operating within the Province of Buenos Aires alone; 58 federal and another 52 provincial ("El Gobierno Reparte $64,400 Millones en 58 Planes Sociales," *La Nación*, March 20, 2013). Such intergovernmental overlap and high fragmentation in social protection initiatives, coexisting in an uncoordinated fashion, mirrors the second term of Menem's administration prior to the Argentine crisis. President Duhalde (PJJHD) and President Kirchner (Familias) had both sought to avoid this kind of policy fragmentation, which is caused by intergovernmental policy competition over which level of government can claim credit for various cash transfer schemes. There is nothing fundamentally wrong with subnational social investment initiatives from a policy perspective, but the nature of majoritarianism in Argentine democracy, particularly at the provincial level, entails that there are currently no mechanisms for the sharing of any information regarding socially vulnerable families between the federal and provincial levels, and therefore between the federal and local levels. Moreover, if the subnational service providers do not comply with ANSES requirements, the benefits are immediately suspended, which calls into question the so-called citizenship rights of the families receiving this federal income stream.[30]

In social policy circles, AUH is widely viewed as a nearly universal cash-based child allowance that works like other federally based family allowance schemes that have existed in Anglo-American welfare states. Its goals are to provide monetary assistance to children under eighteen whose household members are unemployed or work in the informal sectors earning less than one minimum salary. For these reasons, available analyses of its preliminary results have reported no changes in variables such as school attendance and vaccination rates ("Una Asignación de Débil Efecto," *La Nación*, April 14, 2012). Moreover, the volatility in Argentina's inflation rate since the program's inception in 2010 has entailed that the benefit amounts and the eligibility criteria for this cash-based child allowance are a continually moving target, requiring month-by-month adjustments. According to the former director of INDEC, Graciela Bevacqua, inflation has risen from 2002 to 2014 by 1,060 percent, which has a detrimental effect on the purchasing power of cash transfers for the poor.[31] AUH recipients therefore cannot count on the purchasing power of their monetary transfer or on the government's continued ability to raise the benefit amount to match the current rate of inflation. Much further research is required to evaluate this program's impact and its political effects on the 2015 presidential elections; this cash-transfer program is far from transparent given the increasingly volatile economic and political context of Argentina since 2010.

This chapter has shown how CCT schemes have evolved in Argentina and provided evidence of high levels of policy volatility across multiple federal administrations since 1989. It has also shown how domestic politics made it very difficult for Argentina to replace previously established workfare programs with a new CCT model linked to human capital investments. In particular, organized unemployed workers formed a powerful interest group in Argentina that was tied to subnational party brokers, both of which facts can explain part of PJJHD "stickiness"—a

Table 5.2. Phases of Policy Development and Critical Outcomes in
Argentina, 1989–2014

1	2	3	4	5
BNSE and Plan Trabajar (Menem I and Menem II) 1989–2000	PJJHD Social and Economic Crisis (Duhalde) 2001–2002	PJJHD and Programa Familias (Kirchner I) 2003–2007	Programa Familias and PJJHD (Fernández I) 2007–2009	AUH/AUE (Fernández II) 2010–2014
↓		↓	↓	↓
Labor-Based CCTs Patronage Programs Provincial Capture		First Attempted to Terminate Workfare/ Integrated CCT Model	Limited Coverage/ Low Visibility Slow Uptake	CCTs Terminated/ New Non-contributory Family Allowance Benefits

Source: Author elaboration.
Note: BNSE = Bono National de Emergencia.

term used to explain when a policy's feedback effects impede institutional change. The policy developments and their critical outcomes are summarized in table 5.2.

Despite President Néstor Kirchner's intentions, the federal government was unable to dismantle a short-term emergency cash-transfer program tied to labor conditions and replace it with a CCT tied to human capital investments; a national social program that was designed to bypass political intermediation. The limited territorial distribution of his CCT, Programa Familias, can be seen in its slow uptake. Within Kirchner's term in office (2003 to 2007), it was delivered to less than 400,000 households in 232 municipalities, and its coverage excluded five entire provinces, even though there were over 2.3 million households living in a situation of social vulnerability throughout Argentina (INDEC). When Programa Familias was terminated in 2009, its absolute coverage had peaked at little more than 700,000 households. The inability to generate stable intergovernmental cooperation within a highly decentralized and robust federal system such as Argentina's greatly restricts the performance of CCTs that are intended to break the intergenerational transmission of poverty and expand social citizenship rights nationwide. A noncontributory family allowance scheme such as AUH does not represent the *federalization* of social policy, but rather the *centralization* of social policy, within a more traditional policy approach of a passive welfare state that has financial sustainability issues over the long term.

CHAPTER 6

Factors Impeding Municipal Actors from Promoting National Goals in Argentina

To conceive civilization and barbarism as an irreconcilable polarity
is to ignore, in "Argentine History," an interchangeable
game according to circumstances.
—Roberto Yahni, *Facundo*

Mayors are fundamental to the power-generating capacity of governors in contemporary Argentina, who remain the "kings" of public policy-making.[1] This characteristic greatly reduces the willingness of mayors to promote national policy objectives that would provide few fiscal and political benefits to the provinces. Argentina is a highly decentralized federal country, with twenty-three provinces and one autonomous city, Buenos Aires, constituted in 1994. The success of democratic federal governance in Argentina has historically been linked in the literature to the following factors: the success of a single, integrated, "adaptable" federal party (Levitsky 2003); a two-tier party system (Gibson 1996; Jones 1997; Malamud and de Luca 2005); a moderate to high level of party discipline in the literature (Jones and Hwang 2003; Jones et al. 2002); and "the nation's federal framework [that] reduced the winner-takes-all nature of politics by providing areas of subnational autonomy for opposition parties" (Jones 1997, 261). There has been very little dissent or variation in the views expressed in the literature covering the years 1983 to 2000. The majority logic inherent in Argentine democracy is not problematic in a regime/stability dimension, given that this institutional trait did in fact allow Argentina to survive its worst political and fiscal crisis in recent history. It does, however, have an impact on public policy because it creates a system of punishment-and-reward federalism played both ways between the federal and provincial levels of government, which has a deleterious effect on the quality of policy outcomes.

The central goal of this chapter is to confront the theoretical claims put forward earlier in the book with the empirical evidence from Argentina. Argentina is an interesting case to contrast with Brazil because of the relative strength of its own governor politics and the observed variation on the outcome variable—the performance of CCTs. In the previous chapter, I suggested that Programa Familias, a narrowly distributed and relatively unknown national social program, was limited by its inability to avoid provincial intermediation. As a result, it was not distributed in four of the provinces or the Autonomous City of Buenos Aires (CBA) within President Néstor Kirchner's entire term in office. Moreover, the president's inability to dismantle a previously implemented emergency social protection program and successfully replace it with an internationally supported and financed CCT that was intended to avoid governors demonstrates the way in which subnational actors in Argentina can constrain the federal government from reaching its intended national policy objectives.

Moreover, federalism in Argentina contributes to policy volatility in this socially important sector. Specifically, I assert that the configuration of power in Argentina—the lack of municipal autonomy within the National Constitution, the de facto soft budget constraints, and a majoritarian democracy, all of which allow the provinces to capture municipalities to increase their own power over the center and within their own territories—does not encourage mayors, who have few political or fiscal incentives to promote national goals that bypass governor intermediation.

The most problematic issue with the claim above is that Argentine federalism also provides few incentives for the national executive to follow its first order of preferences: to create policy-based partnerships with the provinces. This is because the governors are always seeking to undermine the federal center in order to further their own agendas. From the perspective of federal theory (primarily, Madison's Federalist paper no. 10), this situation ensures that Argentine governments are always unstable; the public good is disregarded in the conflicts of rival party factions across two levels of governments; and measures are too often decided not according to the rules of justice and the rights of minority parties, but by the superior force of an interested and overbearing majority. In the domain of CCT programs promoting human capital investments designed to reduce the intergenerational transmission of poverty and extend social citizenship rights nationwide, the inability of encouraging mayors to promote national goals compromises both the performance and the design of national CCT programs. Of great importance, it also compromises the intended long-term outcomes of CCTs.

ARGENTINE FEDERALISM

Two overlapping trends distinguished Argentina after 1983. On the one hand, from 1983 to 1995 the federal government was able to consolidate democratization by augmenting its executive authority over the twenty-three provinces thanks to the strength of its two-tiered party system, which between 1983 and 1989 generally aided democratic stability. On the other hand, the available social and economic policy options and the federal government's ability to use them seemed to weaken during this same period. The first democratic government from 1983 to 1989 was plagued by pervasive inflation, a failed stabilization plan (the Austral Plan), and growing citizen unrest. When Menem assumed the presidency, he continued to struggle against inflationary pressures. In 1991, he successfully implemented the Convertibility Plan, which pegged the national currency to the US dollar and successfully reduced inflation.

Argentina became "Washington's Poster Child" (Gibson 1996). From 1989 to 1995, Menem prioritized macroeconomic stability and low inflation, achieving high economic growth rates and maintaining his political credibility.

The federal government under Menem strengthened its hand vis-à-vis the provinces, but not without a tremendous amount of intra-party and intergovernmental bargaining, particularly in fiscal matters. This intergovernmental dynamic contributed to a weakly institutionalized national governing bureaucracy that basically had an incentive to turn a blind eye to events at the subnational level. Following re-democratization, however, the success of the PJ's strategy for governing Argentina (that is, winning elections and finishing its presidential terms in office)[2] marked the ability of this well-established party to become an institutional source of federal stability. This is most commonly attributed to the PJ's flexibility and willingness to adapt to external challenges (Levitsky 2003). The consensus in the literature, however, is that it is a "patronage-based party" (Calvo and Murillo 2004; Remmer 2007). Therefore, this party-centered strategy contributed to the ability of the national government to avoid the undermining constraints of its federal system to a large extent through its ability to finance patronage, from the top all the way down to the neighborhood level. Taking this into account and based on government performance, it is plausible to conclude that between 1989 and 1995, intergovernmental collaboration was feasible because of a more stable political and economic context that allowed the president, to use Tulia Falleti's expression (2003), "to govern the governors."

During President Néstor Kirchner's first term, the export-oriented commodity boom from 2003 to 2007 also led to a similar phenomenon (see Richardson 2009). In both periods of considerable economic growth however, from 1989 to 1995 and from 2003 to 2007, the problem of controlling governors and increasing central governing capacity was solved by circumstances, not by any formal institutional mechanism. Additionally, the ability to "govern the governors" enabled a single political party, the PJ, to become an independent force able to coerce powerful provinces into cooperating through patronage and federal payouts. It still does not imply, however, that a PJ president can achieve "an even distribution of primary public goods across different jurisdictions"

(Porto and Sanguinetti 2001, 239), chiefly because of the ability of two dominant levels of government, the federal government and the provinces, to play a game of punishment-and-reward federalism.

Strong federalism in Argentina, with no effective institutional mechanism to control its effects, hinders good governance because it creates volatility and politicizes the delivery of national collective goods, a phenomenon largely described in the previous chapter. This system creates divergent policy preferences and incentives between the federal government and the provinces, and the situation is worsened by the fact that both Congress and municipalities are captured by the preferences of the governors. This eliminates the ability of the president to pursue policy objectives through either the legislature (as occurred, for example, in the case of Mexican CCTs) or through municipalities (as occurred in the case of Brazilian CCTs), resulting in governance by executive decree ("hyperpresidentialism") and the continued ability of governors to undermine the center by inconsistently implementing national policy. Moreover, the accrual of benefits from policies attributed to the president (macroeconomic and foreign policy) and from policies attributed to the governors (public policy and local investments) is not shared between the levels, undermining any incentives for them to cooperate in both good and bad times.

Additionally, the traditional dominance of two main rival parties and the existence of electoral rules that enabled them to create legislative majorities when in office have not facilitated durable national-provincial policy-based collaboration—"as parties [and their factions] alternate in power, the content of some policies may be shifting all the time" (Spiller, Stein, and Tommasi 2008, 10). The inability of Argentina to overcome these governing challenges did not motivate mayors under President Kirchner (2003–2007) to promote a nationally designed social program, such as Programa Familias, when it would not accrue benefits to their governors to whom they are subordinate. Nor did it motivate President Fernández de Kirchner (2007 to present) to pursue a deeper redistributive social investment agenda that would largely fall outside of her policy control. According to the common theoretical wisdom of comparative politics and the key political institutions of Argentine federalism, a highly decentralized system of public spending and political power *ought* to lead to both economic efficiency and effectiveness, juxtaposed against a high level of representation for policy preferences. This is feasible in part because of the presence of an "ideal federal party": the PJ *ought* to be able to induce intergovernmental cooperation.[3]

The problem of partisan-based cooperation as a coordinating mechanism for ensuring that intergovernmental competencies are transformed into policy outputs, however, is that such cooperation creates a politicized institutional context within which policy goods framed as citizenship rights are transferred to the general public. Stated otherwise, the federal process through which targeted social goods are delivered in Argentina privileges the dominance of particular interests over the societal whole. The main challenge of Argentine federalism, therefore—the ability of subnational actors to undermine the center— has created not so much a "transmission problem," as in Brazil, but an "enforcement problem" that can be characterized by the territorially based inconsistency of national policy implementation.

HOW PROGRAMA FAMILIAS FAILED

In the following sections I examine the three explanatory factors put forward in chapter 2 for the Argentine case. I argue that these factors discouraged mayors from enabling Programa Familias's success through local promotion efforts, such as facilitating the establishment of program offices within their territories, encouraging the voluntary transfer from PJJHD to Programa Familias, or monitoring beneficiaries' compliance with the program's conditions, all of which contributed to the eventual failure of this CCT. This noncontributory social investment program was not able to bypass provincial constraint during its implementation and consolidation phase (2003 to 2007), nor was it able to replace and discontinue the previous emergency noncontributory social protection program, leaving little chance for either its nationwide distribution or its eventual institutionalization. As a consequence, this CCT was terminated in 2009, contributing to further volatility in this specific policy area.

The intention of this research is not to find a single factor that explains the complexity of intergovernmental relations in Argentina (a highly confusing and dynamic situation), but to find a plausible explanation as to why the relationships among these levels lead to what Cai and Treisman (2004, 820) identified as not just to "a race to the bottom, but a race to escape—or defraud—the top." This dynamic constrains the ability of the federal government to forge intergovernmental policy cooperation in order to pursue a deeper social investment agenda that requires both demand- and supply-side policy inputs, and a medium- to long-term political commitment in order to generate the intended future-oriented outcomes of such an agenda.

Constitutional Recognition of Subnational Levels of Government in Argentina

Argentina remains one of the most decentralized federations in the world. In contrast with Brazil, however, its third tier of federal government, namely, municipalities, are creatures of the provinces. This means that in Argentine federalism the concept of "subnational" remains, both in theory and in practice and for historical reasons, an aggregation of both provincial and municipal power. At the time of the inauguration of the Argentine Federal Republic in 1853, the country's per capita GDP was twice the average of Latin America and Brazil (Fausto and Devoto 2004). This wealth was heavily concentrated within the Province of Buenos Aires, which included the country's only international port. Once a federal regime had been established, in 1853, this geographic imbalance led to an early conflict between "federalist centralizers" versus "federalist peripheralizers." Buenos Aires preferred a decentralized regime, through which it could dominate the country, while the other provinces who had been previously "federalists" now preferred as a second best option a centralized regime that could guarantee their own territorial autonomy by checking the power of Buenos Aires. A great struggle along these lines continued until 1880, a conflict that would shape the federation significantly. The National Constitution of 1853 today still simultaneously represents, *de jure*, both the centralizer's goals of a powerful central government and the peripheralizer's ideals of significant provincial autonomy (Gibson and Falleti 2004). This constitution was not reformed until 1994, when the Pacto de Olivos granted autonomy to the City of Buenos Aires (among other measures) but left municipal autonomy ambiguous.

Neither the 1853 Constitution nor the 1994 constitutional reforms recognized municipal autonomy, although they did recognize this third tier as an integral part of Argentine federalism. The Constitution formally recognizes two levels of government, the national/federal and the provinces. Municipalities are simply mentioned in Article 5, which states the principle that provinces must create municipal regimes (Argentine National Constitution of 1853, reinstated in 1983, revised in 1994). This means de facto that municipalities are creatures of the provinces, although they have at least the constitutional right to exist. Provinces in Argentina are institutionally heterogeneous, with the independent authority to write their own constitutions, make their electoral laws, set their election dates, and design their municipal regimes. Because of the ambiguity about municipalities in the Constitution, "the degree and extent of municipal autonomy, in the end, depends on the responsibilities/obligation that each provincial constitution, starting from their own respective organic laws, delegates or confers on local entities" (author translation, Clemente and Smulovitz 2004, 42). This means that only municipalities within territories that so choose have the right to be considered as an official third tier of federal government (see table 6.1).

Nevertheless, constitutionally speaking, the federal government cannot collaborate directly with municipalities, and municipalities cannot legally bypass the provinces, even if they are recognized as autonomous within the provincial constitutions. In this sense, one of the goals of a federal system is constitutionally assured. In 1994, however, the Constituent National Assembly attempted to alter this federal configuration by officially placing municipal autonomy on the negotiating table.

The 1994 constitutional reform package was concluded through a secret, bilateral, non-institutional bargain between President Menem and the head of the principal opposition party, ex-president Raúl Alfonsín (UCR). The non-institutionalized nature of this reform package meant that, although the public was initially consulted, ordinary citizens' opinions were not part of the negotiations. According to public opinion surveys of the time, as analyzed by Jones (1996), municipal autonomy was "least favored" in the interior provinces, where municipalities already exercised a certain amount of political autonomy, and the second "most favored" in the Province of Buenos Aires, where

Table 6.1. Municipal Autonomy Recognized in Argentine Provincial
Constitutions

Institutional Autonomy	Provinces
YES	Catamarca, Chubut, Córdoba, Corrientes, Formosa, Jujuy, La Rioja, Misiones, Neuquén, Río Negro, Salta, San Juan, San Luis, Santiago del Estero, Tierra del Fuego
NO	Buenos Aires, Chaco, Entre Ríos, La Pampa, Mendoza, Santa Cruz, Santa Fe, Tucumán

Source: Clemente and Smulovitz 2004.

local autonomy is formally limited by that province's constitution. At
the same time, the "most favored" proposed reform in the eyes of the
public in the Province of Buenos Aires was greater fiscal autonomy for
the provinces, which would effectively increase the amount of money
controlled by the province for distribution downward.

The 1994 constitutional reforms reenforced strong federalism in
Argentina but made the City of Buenos Aires a potential player. The
reform reaffirmed in Article 123 (1994) that each province *should* conform to Article 5 (1853 Constitution) by assuring municipal autonomy,
although in fact this clause has never been enforced, and many municipalities remain under provincial control. Moreover, even in the provinces that did conform to Article 5, the ability of mayors to exercise this
right of autonomy is constrained by municipalities' fiscal and political
dependence on the provinces.

The power of governors in contemporary Argentina is commonly
attributed to their partisan-based control. Provinces in Argentina, like
other federal countries in the Americas, are the focal points of partisan power because of a highly decentralized party system.[4] Provincial
power has also accumulated over time out of unintended consequences.
In 1946, following the rise to power of Juan Perón, the Argentine federal
government strengthened its control over the provinces through two
key strategies: territorial overrepresentation (through legislative malapportionment) and fiscal revenue centralization. In 1949, Perón ended

proportionality in the lower chamber by granting each province a minimum of two federal deputies regardless of their population. This minimum was later increased by the military regime during 1966 to 1973 to three, and again by the military in 1983 to five (Samuels and Snyder 2004). Today, Argentina has the most malapportioned national legislature in Latin America; provinces with 31 percent of the population control 44 percent of the seats in the lower chamber.

The principle of malapportionment was manipulated by the PJ to create its first national populist coalition. The party sought specifically to capture the support of sparsely populated interior provinces, and did so through patronage that extended its partisan-based control at the local level Traditionally, the interior provinces had supported the more conservative UCR, established in 1916. Following their overrepresentation in Congress, Perón proceeded to buy them off through a revenue-sharing scheme, established during the Great Depression. This archaic fiscal system, which continues today, authorizes the federal government to use the tax base of the provinces in return for giving back a rebated share of the revenue raised. It is known as the *ley de cóparticipación federal de impuestos* and was created in 1935. According to this highly centralized revenue-sharing scheme, the federal government collects the nation's revenues and redistributes them to provinces, which, in turn, redistribute these revenues according to their own rules to municipalities.[5]

This fiscal revenue-sharing scheme creates a large vertical imbalance (a difference between collected revenues and executed expenditures) that leads to a situation of provincial fiscal dependence on the national government, and municipal fiscal dependence on the provinces. In principle, this scheme was intended to be the mechanism through which the national government could control the effects of factions at the provincial level. Perón's governing strategy gave the federal government immense leverage over the provinces in terms of fiscal revenues, and gave the provinces leverage over municipalities. However, it also permitted the smaller, overrepresented provinces to free-ride on the national government, using their overrepresentation in Congress as leverage for greater fiscal favors (or to induce the president to ignore what went on within their provinces). The interdependence created by this imbalance between centralized revenues and decentralized provincial expenditures, and the relative insignificance of municipalities' participation because of their low levels of protection/provisions in the National Constitution, impede the ability of municipalities to exercise their formal autonomy, even when such autonomy is recognized within a provincial constitution (see table 6.2).

As table 6.2 demonstrates, after re-democratization in 1983, this fiscal dependence ensured that municipalities remained dependent on the provinces, and it reinforced a two-level federal game played between the provinces and the federal government, where the distribution of power, revenue, and expenditure fluctuates back and forth between these two dominant players in a debilitating manner. It is important to note, as shown in table 6.2, that from 1983 to 1992 there was a move toward greater decentralization of expenditure to the provincial and, to a lesser extent, the municipal level, although with little variation in intergovernmental revenue authority. This was in part because the decentralizing administrative reforms undertaken at the beginning of 1992 as part of the national budget (and never negotiated in Congress) can best be characterized as the federal government "offloading expenditures to the sub-national level without transferring resources" (Falleti 2003, 114). Governors apparently agreed to these reforms at the time because of an increase in the monetary value of automatic transfers related to the 1991 currency stabilization, and because the federal government agreed to guarantee the monetary value of these transfers.

The dependence of provinces and municipalities on federal government transfers represents a constraint on the ability of these lower levels

Table 6.2. Argentina's Revenue and Expenditure by Level of Government before and after Decentralization

	Share of Total Government Revenue (%)			Share of Total Government Expenditure (%)		
	1983	1992	%▲	1983	1992	%▲
Central	79.3	80.0	.7	63.5	51.9	−11.6
Provincial	13.7	15.4	1.7	31.0	39.5	8.5
Local	7.0	4.6	−2.4	5.4	8.6	3.2

Source: Willis, Garman, and Haggard 1999.

of government to build their own political coalitions independent of national elites (Eaton 2004a, 128). In essence, Argentina has a highly complex and dynamic system of punishment-and-reward federalism that radiates from the center outward to each province, and then from the provinces likewise to the municipalities. This federal configuration of power seriously limits the ability of municipalities to exercise any constitutional autonomy they may be given independently of governors, for quite simply they are too far removed from the center.

Furthermore, the extent of provincial dependence on central revenue transfers means that the best way the provinces can undermine the federal government is through policy apathy. As observed in chapter 5, this dynamic affected Programa Familias from 2003 to 2009. Inversely, this dynamic also means that the federal government cannot regulate the quality of policy outcomes at the lowest level of government or control their effects, as was observed in PJJHD from 2002 to 2009. Both examples of how the provinces can affect the performance of national policy goals are strengthened by fact that municipalities are constitutionally creatures of the provinces, and, in conjunction with other factors, they are also dependent on the provinces for their political and fiscal survival. The lack of national constitutional recognition of municipalities, therefore, and primarily their lack of distinction from the provinces after 1994, closed the door to further decentralization in Argentina and consolidated federalism without municipalities

Federalism without Municipalities after 1994

Lacking constitutional recognition at the national level, municipalities remain institutionally weak, and they serve to strengthen provincial power. From 1994 until today, this equates to a situation of federalism without municipalities, an institutional configuration that makes it very difficult for the national president to utilize mayors as the prime agents of national policy objectives that do not align with provincial ambitions. It further reinforces the main weakness of Argentina's federal structure—the ability of politically powerful provinces to undermine the federal government through noncooperation, and the ability of the federal government to encroach upon the power of its constituent units by withholding fiscal revenues. Moreover, the fiscal dependence and constitutional subordination of municipalities to the provinces serve to reinforce provincial-municipal partisan loyalty and municipal partisan stability. From 1995 to 1999, there were only five opposition governors (UCR), not including the Autonomous City of Buenos Aires. At the municipal level during these same years, there were only five provinces where the majority of mayors were not PJ, and these were the same five provinces: Catamarca, Córdoba, Chaco, Chubut, and Río Negro.[6] Additionally, from 1983 to 1999, 78.7 percent of municipalities reelected the PJ party, and 69.6 percent reelected the UCR party. This illustrates the incredible level of partisan stability at the municipal level and its tendency to follow the logic of provincial politics. Thus, for example, if the governor of Santiago del Estero chooses not to be included in a national CCT that has potential direct electoral feedbacks for the national incumbent, there is little the federal government can do to encourage mayors within the province to promote a national social program that the province has decided to undermine. Within Argentina's federal arrangements, for a mayor, this quite simply equates to committing fiscal and political suicide.

The credibility of decentralized federalism in Argentina is compromised by a lack of robustness at the municipal level, which, I suggest, in fact strengthens the provinces.[7] There is a dichotomy between disconnectedness and subordination at the provincial and municipal level (Medina and Ratto 2006) because of the ability of provinces to threaten municipalities with punishment if they do not cooperate with key provincial stakeholders. This not only reduces the incentives of local elites to provide constituency services to their communities, but also reduces the incentives of mayors to cooperate with nationally designed social policy objectives. The lack of robustness at the municipal level in Argentine federalism is clearly evident within the territorial distribution of authority across the three levels.

In terms of political decentralization, as previously mentioned, the most significant changes to the Argentine Constitution of 1853 were the 1994 reforms. With these reforms, the UCR succeeded in gaining autonomy for the CBA (a party bastion) and a third senator for each province, all reforms intended to reduce the ability of the PJ to dominate the country's institutions. Menem (PJ) succeeded in getting constitutional permission to run for reelection and in fortifying the independence of presidential elections from the provinces by means of two rounds of voting (a second round follows when no candidate in the first round scores above 45 percent). What did not change in these reforms was the power controlled at the provincial level or the electoral rules that motivated provincial-local interdependence. The frequent indictors used to demonstrate the extent of political decentralization show the low degree of importance given to municipalities in Argentina (see appendix, table A.4).

The political power of governors is considerably stronger than that of mayors. Before 2006, governors had the freedom to set the dates for provincial and municipal elections and to decide on their own set of electoral laws. Thus they had an institutional opportunity to manipulate electoral laws and electoral calendars in order to guarantee their own continued dominance (Gibson 2004; Calvo and Micozzi 2005). Beyond the *de jure* limitations of local political autonomy, it is well known that the powerful majoritarian bias of many provincial electoral systems severely limits the political autonomy of municipalities, and thus also their agency.

From a political perspective, the lack of municipal interparty competition is eye-opening. Gibson and Cao-Suarez said of the late 1990s that "partisan realignments modified this two-party scheme somewhat" (2007, 20). At all events, it is worth noting that, for example, in 2003 the effective number of parties competing for provincial governor in the Province of Buenos Aires rose to 4.94, but at the municipal level in the same year they remained a low 1.9 (based on data from Calvo and Escolar 2005). Provincial partisan realignments did not affect the two-party scheme at the municipal level. Using interparty competition as a gauge to indicate the desire of political leaders to fill local positions, it is evident that beyond the electoral authority that can lead to political career-making within Argentina's two nationally integrated parties (PJ and the UCR), the position of mayor in and of itself does not offer many inducements to ambitious career politicians. Moreover, unlike local elections in Brazil, which use open-list voting systems for legislative positions at all levels, Argentina's party-based nomination procedures for selecting electoral candidates provide few incentives for provincial and local elites to promote constituency services to bolster their personal popularity. It is the party's interests they need to support to further or maintain their careers, not their constituents. This is in part because the ability of Argentine voters to reward individual candidates for their "good governance," particularly at the local level, is reduced by each party's candidate nomination procedures and closed-list electoral rules.

Only two national parties have had access to centralized state resources, the UCR and the PJ, thanks to their alternating monopoly of the national executive. This has contributed to the complete failure of any new national "third" party to make inroads at the municipal level (Jones and Hwang 2005). Even more significantly, many studies have suggested that when the provincial and local levels are both dominated by the Peronist PJ, the chances of municipal subordination are even higher, given the characteristics of Peronism and its dependence on localized networks (Auyero 2000; Calvo and Murillo 2004; Brusco, Nazareno, and Stokes 2004). Even though local government was assumed to be accountable by virtue of the fact that it was elected (Stoker 1988), falling out of favor with the dominant party especially during a period of economic boom can equate to political alienation at both the provincial and municipal level.[8]

Turning now to policy decentralization, the institutional ambiguity of municipalities, coupled with their limited political autonomy, has not encouraged a process of democratization at the local level that enables new actors to innovate and experiment with public policy, as was seen in Brazil after 1988.[9] Given that municipal autonomy was never seriously considered during the 1994 constitutional reform, the political decentralization that has occurred in Argentina after 1983 has not increased the decision-making responsibility of municipalities regarding the provision of social services or their quality. According to Falleti, the 1992 decentralization reforms that transferred responsibility for secondary education and national hospitals to the provinces can best be characterized as the federal government "offloading expenditures without revenues" (2003, 114). Without these social policy areas being accompanied by federal earmarked transfers, as is the case in Brazil in the areas of basic health and education (where fiscal laws not only stipulate federal contributions but also mandate state and municipal fiscal contributions), limited fiscal decentralization has created a huge discrepancy in provincial spending priorities. For example, while the Province of Buenos Aires spent 39.3 percent of its 1999 budget on health, 32.3 percent on education, and 13 percent on administration, the Province of La Rioja spent 9.2 percent on health, 23.7 percent on education, and 40.2 percent on administration (Rezk 2000). The ability of the provincial authorities to set their own budget priorities and control the amount of revenue they transfer to municipalities within their territories has impeded policy decentralization to the municipal level and led to policy heterogeneity at the provincial level. There exists no uniform mechanism to distribute financial resources to municipalities in Argentina. This means that where municipal decentralization has occurred, as in the case of the city of Rosario (interview Schmuck 2006), it does not reflect a uniform process throughout the federation. Clemente and Smulovitz confirm the limited role of municipalities in delivering services, based on 1999 figures:

> While the average of resources per capita of national origin that the provinces receive is $827, the average of resources per capita that the municipalities receive from the provinces is $159.9. The difference between these two average indicates that a significant part of the resources that the Nation transfers to the provinces is retained at a provincial level. (2004, 50)

The national director of public expenditure and social programs in the Ministry of the Economy added that "tributary per capita is calculated by each province using their own variables" (interview Bonari 2006). He claimed that in the absence of a legal responsibility of provinces to pass municipal fiscal data to the federal government, "there exists no disaggregated expenditure for the municipal level in Argentina," making it almost impossible to use either constitutional authority or fiscal expenditure at this level to measure the amount of de facto policy decentralization. The provincial allocation of policy responsibility in the National Constitution and the current system of fiscal revenue transfers to the provinces, coupled with a weakly institutionalized mechanism to distribute revenue from the provinces to municipalities, have impeded the federalization of social policy, local democratization, and citizen participation in Argentina.

The "kings" of public policymaking in Argentina remain the governors (Braun and Ardanaz 2008), who are responsible for providing the majority of social public goods. As already explained, however, the vertical fiscal imbalance created by decentralized expenditure and centralized revenue in the context of a two-level game of punishment-and-reward federalism makes decentralized social policy delivery highly politicized and problematic. This has seriously affected the consistent implementation of social policy. Although the implementation and the quality of social policy delivered by the provinces are uneven, because of the high levels of provincial autonomy in public-service provision there is little ambiguity in the Constitution as to who is responsible. The only policy area where municipalities emerged after 2003 with a new role, that of deliverer and executor, was the area of social assistance and social protection, because of the growth of noncontributory social programs and the increased need for social assistance at the community level (Clemente and Smulovitz 2004). The dynamic nature of this two-level game is clearly visible within the distribution of Argentina's social expenditure, for which I was able to obtain data from 2001 to 2006 directly from the Ministry of Economy. These figures do not include pensions, which account for a large part of federal expenditure.[10] Figure 6.1 clearly illustrates that during the Kirchner administration, the level of federal social expenditure slightly decreased and municipal social expenditure increased, but the provinces remained the prime agents of social expenditure. Moreover, provincial levels of spending seem largely unaffected by the movements occurring between the federal and municipal levels.

Policy decentralization has also been impeded in Argentina, as in Brazil, by macroeconomic instability. Social programs in both federal democracies could be advanced in a permanent fashion only when the national government could ensure stable economic policy (Alston et al. 2008). Arising out of this goal of macroeconomic stability, in 1991 the PJ administration's fiscal stabilization plan eliminated central bank financing for provincial deficits. The decentralization of national hospitals, secondary schools, and national food programs to the provinces was part of the 1992 federal budget. Although "there is no official record of what happened in the closed-door negotiations," it is commonly believed that governors agreed to the reforms because the federal government argued

Figure 6.1. Social Expenditure in Argentina per Level of Government, 2001–2006 (without Pensions)

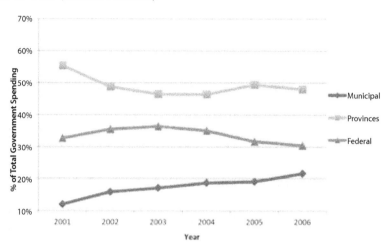

Source: Author's aggregations, Direción de Gastos Públicos y Programas Sociales, Ministério de Economía y Hacienda.

that the increase in the monetary value of automatic transfers would pay for the services provided by the provinces (Falleti 2003, 142). Inflation was eventually controlled in 1995, and this resulted in a slight increase in provincial revenue transfers from the levels before decentralization.

In terms of fiscal decentralization, controlling price inflation resulted in temporary increases during 1992 of the net revenue transfers to the provinces, although a process of recentralization that began soon thereafter with the fiscal pacts of 1992 and 1993 allowed the federal government to retain 15 percent of these revenues to fund national fiscal obligations and to eliminate some subnational taxes (Porto 2004). This effectively reduced the net transfers to the provinces. Like macroeconomic stability, however, this recentralization of subnational revenues was short-lived. Governor power reemerged after 1995, as did their revenue transfers. Table 6.3 shows that although the fiscal pacts of 1992 and 1993 recentralized some revenues, these fiscal reforms did not have an overall negative effect on revenues available to the provincial governments. The provincial share of revenues actually increased, while their expenditures were held constant. The share of municipal

Table 6.3. Argentina's Revenue and Expenditure by Level of Government after Decentralization and after Recentralization

	Share of Total Government Revenue (%)			Share of Total Government Expenditure (%)		
	1992	2000	%▲	1992	2000	%▲
Central	80	77.4	−2.6	51.9	56.30	4.4
Provincial	15.4	22.6	7.2	39.5	39.20	−0.3
Local	4.6	N/A	—	8.6	4.50	−4.1

Source: Willis, Garman, and Haggard 1999; Porto 2004.

(local) expenditure, however, decreased and shifted back to the central government.

Many explanations have been offered for how Menem managed to bring about fiscal recentralization in a country where governors are kings. Jones (1997) asserts that Menem's success was determined by a two-party dominant political system and high levels of party discipline. Gibson and Calvo posit that it was not just partisan control of Congress and the governorships that mattered, but the fact that many of the governors and deputies came from overrepresented peripheral provinces. They assert that political support for the reforms was achieved by postponing public sector unemployment cuts in peripheral provinces and increasing subsidies to "some" provincial coffers (Gibson and Calvo 2000). Beyond the subtle differences in these arguments, there is a general consensus in the literature that partisan factors and party-system characteristics facilitated Menem's ability to build a reform-supporting coalition that would pass administrative decentralization in 1991, fiscal reforms in 1992 and 1993, and constitutional reforms in 1994, all affecting the territorial distribution of power between the levels of government.

These reforms were all weakly institutionalized because of the party-centric way in which they were negotiated. This has resulted in inconsistent implementation (many of the 1994 reforms were never implemented) and low enforcement (fiscal revenues after 1995 began to flow again toward the provinces). The federal executive's intention in transferring expenditure responsibility to the provinces without additional revenues was to force them to reduce public-sector employment and use their non-earmarked transfers to pay for social services (Eaton and Dickovick 2004). In fact, this strategy led to a provincial debt crisis that gave the federal executive an unintended opportunity to privatize provincial banks (a recentralization measure). However, with Menem's decreasing popularity after 1995 in the lower chamber of Congress and a worsening fiscal situation in Argentina caused by the (now recognizable) flaws of the convertibility plan, governors successfully reemerged as the key power brokers in Argentina's federal game (Eaton 2004b). According to Spiller and Tommasi (2008, 100), provincial governors in Argentina have only a secondary interest in national public goods and in the quality of national policies; "their primary interest—on the basis of which they grant or withdraw support to national governments and their policies—is access to common-pool fiscal resources." The strategy of provinces exchanging votes for cash did not enable the federal government to ensure fiscal stability.

In 1996 (the same year Finance Minister Domingo Cavallo resigned), Congress once again moved toward fiscal decentralization, increasing the transfers from taxes to the provinces. Again in 1998, governors forced the federal government to increase the revenue guarantee from US$740 million per month to US$850 million (Eaton and Dickovick 2004). The ability of governors to punish the federal executive would increase with the election of opposition candidate Fernando de la Rúa as president in 1999. The governors eventually toppled his administration and contributed to Argentina's unprecedented economic crisis (Eaton and Dickovick 2004; Spiller and Tommasi 2007).

Neither expenditure decentralization nor revenue centralization from 1989 to 1999 altered the *productive* or *allocative* efficiency of Argentine federalism. It was simply a vicious game of policymaking between two politically interdependent levels of government. Of great significance was the national government's lack of political incentive to regulate subnational finances and to enforce fiscal reforms on the subnational public sector. United PJ governors continued to extract further revenue increases from President de la Rúa in 1999–2000, despite the decreasing levels of centralized taxation and an evident national currency crisis. De la Rúa continued hopelessly to play this game in exchange for their political cooperation.

A decentralized structure of federal government is coordinated by a given set of institutional mechanisms, which provide either incentives or deterrents to intergovernmental cooperation. Each level of government in Argentina, as in most federal countries, wants to maximize its portion of revenue. In a system of intergovernmental fiscal relations where the provincial and municipal governments are completely separated from taxing and revenue decisions, an expansionary bias is built into subnational spending (Jones et al. 2002). Such fiscal relations work as a deterrent to greater interprovincial and vertical intergovernmental cooperation. In fact, "if you raise your capacity to collect taxes, you are less likely to benefit from future bailouts" (Tommasi, Saiegh, and Sanguinetti 2001, 186).[11] The fiscal situation in Argentina is made worse by the near total discretion of the provincial governments over social policy and budget priorities, and the lame-duck status of most municipalities within this federal arrangement.

Menem had believed in 1992 that transferring policy responsibilities without financing would force lower levels of government to "mop up" their poorly used automatic transfers. It did not work: the intergovernmental fiscal scheme allowed both municipal and provincial governments to blame poor social policy performance on a lack of funds emanating from a higher level of government.

Within a context of punishment-and-reward federalism lacking any real municipal involvement, an incentive was created for provinces to compete with each other for revenues, which led to the infamous federal "race to the bottom" in local tax rates. Within this context, political, fiscal, and policy decentralization was unaccompanied by any genuine redistribution of governing capacity or improvements to public policy outputs.

In contrast to Brazilian federalism, the definition and the rules regulating municipalities in Argentina, including the extent of their autonomy, borrowing capacity, and the percentage of provincial resources that they receive, are decided by each province's constitution. Because of this institutional characteristic, it is impossible to generalize about the role of municipalities in Argentina in either theory or practice. For example, the constitutions of the provinces of Buenos Aires, Entre Ríos, Mendoza, Santa Fe, and Tucumán provide for no autonomy or organic laws for their local constituent units even though this is constitutionally encouraged, if not stipulated. These five provinces account for 36 percent of the country's total municipalities. The remaining eighteen provinces provide for local autonomy in their constitutions, but the right to be defined as a municipality is dependent on various population requirements, peculiar to each province. Some provinces, such as Buenos Aires and Mendoza, have only one level of local government (regardless of autonomy), whereas San Luis nominally has six levels, with each unit's status and level of competence decided on the basis of its population size.

Beyond institutional heterogeneity, additional factors, similar to those in Brazilian municipalities, create geographic and economic inequality. These territorial-based inequalities are exacerbated in Argentina, however, by the lack of institutional uniformity at the municipal level, which is a product of the heterogeneity in provincial constitutions that govern them. Using a classification developed by the Argentine Ministry of Economy, table 6.4 offers an idea of the number of developed versus less-developed municipalities throughout Argentina.

Both the socioeconomic and the institutional heterogeneity of Argentine municipalities limits them from becoming the prime agents of the federal government in key social policy areas, as occurred primarily in the areas of social protection and social assistance in Brazil. From 1983 to 2004, however, there was an expansion of the percentage of GDP that municipalities spent on social policy, in particular after 1995 (see figure 6.2). It is evident from this graph that education and health decentralization to the provincial level from 1991 to 1992 did have a small effect on increasing the percentage of GDP spent in these areas at the municipal level. This means that some early and primary education was effectively decentralized to the local level in the larger urban municipalities. Most evident is the expansion of municipal participation in the areas of health and social protection, which began to increase after 1991. The sharp increase in social protection spending at the municipal level after 1996 was the result of Plan Trabajar, which was dismantled in 2000. Interestingly, Programa Jefes y Jefas de Hogares Desocupados (PJJHD) did not have an effect on municipal social spending parallel to that of the earlier Plan Trabajar.

Table 6.4. Socioeconomic Diversity of Argentine Municipalities

Socioconomic Classification[a]	No. of Municipalities[b]
Advanced: City of Buenos Aires, Santa Cruz, Chubut, La Pampa, Tierra del Fuego, Neuquén, Buenos Aires, Santa Fe	280
Intermediate: Córdoba, Río Negro, Mendoza, Entre Ríos, San Luis, Catamarca, San Juan, Tucumán	518
Underdeveloped: La Rioja, Salta, Jujuy, Misiones, Corrientes, Santiago del Estero, Chaco, Formosa	362

Source: Ministry of Economy, Province of Buenos Aires, 2001, "Cuaderno de Económica 56."
[a] Indicator based on population, literacy, education, infant mortality, household characteristics, exports, electricity, GINI coefficient, poverty, and (un)employment.
[b] See methodology and typology in Porto (2004, 40), which includes only the first level of local units.

Figure 6.2. The Evolution of Municipal Social Spending, 1980–2004

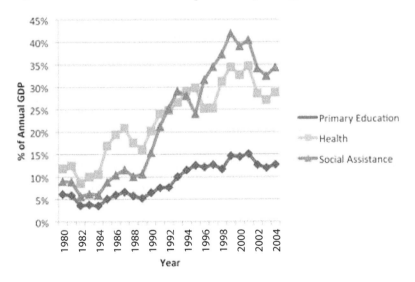

Source: Author elaboration, Direción de Gastos Públicos y Programas Sociales, Ministério de Economía y Hacienda.

Most municipalities (with the exception of those in the provinces of La Rioja and Santiago del Estero) have the right to create and sanction their own budgets and calculate revenues. The federal revenue-sharing scheme, however, does not privilege municipalities over provinces. There is no guaranteed revenue transfer from the national government to municipalities or from provinces to municipalities. Using municipal expenditure data as a measure can provide some insight into what municipalities are administering, but the use of local expenditure and revenue data in Argentina is generally considered unreliable (interview Bonari 2006). Additionally, municipalities have extremely limited tax collection, collecting only 0.04 percent of the total (Porto 2004). The lack of fiscal autonomy impedes any real distribution of governing capacity to the local level and limits the development of their organizational capacity.

The constitutional authority of provinces to regulate municipalities within their constitutions insulates local governments from the national government, and vice versa. The limited national constitutional protection provided to municipalities makes them entirely dependent on their provincial government for both financial assistance and political existence. The greatest implication of such low levels of municipal autonomy for this study is that, within the context of majoritarian democracy, mayors have few incentives to promote national social investment objectives, to provide constituency services such as the supply-side inputs that are required by CCTs, or to enforce program compliance at the local level. The importance of intraparty politics and closed-list candidate nominations reduces the incentive of mayors or local legislators to generate personal reputations among voters that are independent of an overarching party identity. Individual political careers will be furthered more by promoting the party agenda that is located at the provincial level than by generating innovative local policy. Mayors and local legislators also have no incentive to complement the policymaking of the national government in order to provide social services to their constituents if such action goes against the local party's political interests. Low levels of municipal autonomy reduce the agency of municipalities to collaborate with higher levels of government on their own terms and for the direct benefit of their individual constituents.

The Evolution of the Rules Regulating Subnational Finances and the Argentine Soft Budget Syndrome

It should now be evident that the factors that condition mayors in Argentina to undermine national policy goals through either direct action or policy apathy are implicitly intertwined with fiscal arrangements. Post-2003 changes to national political alignments, in particular the descent of the UCR as a national force to be reckoned with, did not have a direct impact on the interdependent political and fiscal relationship existing at the subnational level between the provinces and municipalities, where the latter relies on the former to finance locally controlled patronage, and the former relies on the latter to buy votes. Particularly in Argentina, where the revenue-raising capacity of municipalities is very low, as are earmarked national grants that bypass the provinces, mayors have an incentive to either support or at least not impede provincial political agendas. As already alluded to, governors themselves have few incentives to enable a national policy objective for which they cannot directly claim credit, particularly when they themselves have national aspirations. Therefore, the national government can either try to indirectly involve local governments—as they attempted but failed to do in the case of Programa Familias—or they can opt to go it alone, as they have done since 2009, leaving program-related conditions ambiguous, their enforcement/monitoring low, and inclusion rates limited to families already included in the databases of the National Administration of Social Security (ANSES).

As explained from a theoretical perspective in chapter 2, the rules regulating subnational finances shape the policy preferences at any given level of government. A federal country like Argentina that has an ideal federal party such as the PJ theoretically should not require hard budget constraints to ensure subnational fiscal discipline—provided political parties can play an integrating role. However, the extent of party decentralization in Argentina and the tendency, in particular after 2003, toward internal splits within the PJ mean that even this political party cannot ensure subnational fiscal discipline when it holds power. Therefore in practice, the Argentine case is an anomaly, because of its accumulation of political power at the provincial level. Even though the president has often exhibited the ability to centralize power, generally from 1989 to 1995 and from 2003 to 2007, the national government's ability to centralize fiscal resources or sustain subnational fiscal discipline has been relatively limited.

Argentina (like Brazil from 1988 to 1995) is a textbook example of the soft budget syndrome, like the one theoretically demonstrated in chapter 2. The effects of a soft budget syndrome in the context of a system of punishment-and-reward federalism operating at two levels of government have not only produced suboptimal economic and social policy outputs, but have also made such policy outputs politicized and volatile. Social investment strategies that are designed to have long-term outcomes require a stable fiscal context in order to be considered sustainable. Despite all the efforts of international financing institutions, the lack of political incentives for the national government to regulate subnational finances has made it extremely difficult to harden their budget constraints. Within the logic of Argentina's democratic model, the federal government requires the power to use discretionary fiscal transfers to control the provinces politically. This characteristic requires that budget constraints in Argentina remain flexible in order to ensure government stability, at the cost of entrenching a state-corroding form of federalism.

Soft Budget Constraints, 1983–2001

Argentine provinces and municipalities during the 1980s faced extremely soft budget constraints. During the late 1980s, provinces accounted for approximately 40 percent of the nation's deficit and were considered a source of national financial and macroeconomic instability. As the fiscal crisis of 2001 approached, provincial governors continued to borrow large amounts of revenue to cover their expenses through private loans that were guaranteed by their constitutional revenue transfers. Although the central bank intended to withhold a portion of the provinces' co-shared federal revenue transfers to cover their private loans, provincial loans increased when the fiscal situation deteriorated in the late 1990s, simultaneously with governors' demands for increased revenue transfers from the central government. By 1999, aggregate provincial debt accounted for 57.58 percent of total provincial income, a 40 percent increase from 1994 (Tommasi, Saiegh, and Sanguinetti 2001).

Fiscal recentralization did not in fact have a considerable effect on provincial debt accumulation and fiscal behavior during this decade.

Despite Argentina's inherent majoritarianism, which in certain circumstances leads to hyperpresidentialism, provincial governors and mayors who shared the same party label do not have a self-induced incentive to support long-term national fiscal stability—a necessary condition for future-oriented social investments. During Menem's first term, the national-level PJ had managed to create a "credible political coalition" (Treisman 2004, 411) to support early fiscal reforms. This political coalition was temporary, however, and thus did not permanently weaken the ability of governors to politically bribe the federal government for fiscal bailouts. When the presidency passed in 1999 to the opposition leader Fernando de la Rúa (UCR), he was unable to create a credible political coalition as his predecessor had done in order to harden the rules regulating subnational finance, and was thus even more vulnerable to provincial blackmail.

Like Cardoso, Menem reduced the ability of governors (who controlled municipal debt and borrowing) to use central bank bailouts to cover their deficits from 1994 to 1998, by closing twenty of the twenty-six provincial banks. However, unlike Cardoso, in order to convince governors to enforce these reforms, "Menem let them borrow privately, using their future federal transfers as collateral—this provided credit, but made default costly" (Treisman 2004, 413). Like the provinces, municipalities could borrow funds from external sources, provided the provincial legislature approved these loans (except in the Province of Santa Fe, which has no legislation regulating provincial or municipal borrowing). As already stated, under the PJ's leadership the national government had some success in regulating subnational fiscal behavior, but these informal national-provincial relationships did not stand the test of a change in executive power. When the national fiscal crisis became visible, around the same time as the 1997 legislative elections, provincial debt stocks (which include those of the municipalities) went from 61 percent of total revenue in 1997 to 75 percent by the end of 1999 (Webb 2003, 202). The de la Rúa government understood that it had to harden government budget constraints in order to maintain national fiscal stability.

In an effort to accomplish this task, in 1999 the federal government concluded the "Federal Agreement for Growth and Fiscal Discipline."

This agreement was intended to provide an incentive for lower debt financing to those provinces that agreed, *ex ante*, to fiscal reform measures. However, because of the rigidity of the 1998 Fiscal Convertibility Law (law 25.152), which prevented the central bank from financing any internal debts, international financial institutions were expected to finance assistance to the provinces. All such financial assistance was guaranteed ultimately by the national government, an arrangement that did not ultimately differ from Kornai's traditional classification of a "soft budget syndrome." In the end, the legal rigidity of Argentina's currency parity reduced its risk rating for external lending agencies. This context was accompanied by a politically driven subnational preference for market-driven budget constraints (soft constraints) that made "borrowers and lenders too bold" (Webb 2003, 207). After more than a decade of parallel cross-national efforts in Brazil and Argentina to achieve macroeconomic stabilization, it became apparent that Cardoso's payouts to the states, which Menem had avoided through effective party-based bargaining, would cost Argentina more over the long term.

Hard Budget Constraints after 2001

In 2001, currency parity with the US dollar officially ended in Argentina. What followed has been well documented as one of the largest economic, political, and social crises in Argentina's contemporary history. Immediately thereafter, a zero deficit law was passed (no. 25.156) to ensure that expenditures would only be paid using current revenues (Braun and Gadano 2006). This law entailed a drastic decrease in the payment of public salaries and public pensions, a practice declared unconstitutional in 2003 and consequently abolished. It was soon replaced, however, by the 2004 Law of Fiscal Responsibility.

This law, as in Brazil in 2000, was intended, among other measures, to limit provincial (including municipal) debt to 15 percent of their current revenues (Braun and Gadano 2006). According to the national director of public expenditure and social programs in the Ministry of Economy (2003–2007), this agreement required that disaggregate subnational fiscal information be provided to the national government; "but at present there exists no mechanism to do so, which means, de facto, only weak fiscal regulation can be enforced" (interview Bonari 2006). Braun and Gadano present similar evidence, stating that "the federal council of fiscal responsibility has no fiscal information about the national government, the provinces, or the municipalities" (2006, 16). Without an institutional body to enforce sanctions against provinces that did not conform, similar to the design of the central bank and central treasury in Brazil, ultimately the LFR existed only on paper. In spite of a strong party system with relatively high levels of party discipline in Congress, the national government in Argentina was not strong enough to either regulate or enforce a rules-based approach to subnational fiscal behavior. This inability to institutionalize a rules-based approach weakens the ability of the national government to encourage mayors to participate in national social policy objectives through using small fiscal incentives schemes such as Brazil's decentralized management index. It also weakens the fiscal incentive to promote CCTs locally, in order to increase the potential small economic inputs that flow from them to local communities. More abstractly, it contributes to the ability of provinces, together with their municipalities, to undermine the ability of the national government to realize its national policy objectives. By continuing to prolong the soft budget syndrome, the subnational levels continue to believe they can "go it alone." What is predominantly an ad hoc, two-tiered financial structure in Argentina does not encourage mayors to promote national policy objectives when the financial risk of a mayor who falls out of favor with the governor, who controls the downward flow of revenue transfers, is far greater than the political or fiscal benefit of promoting a national CCT such as Programa Familias.

Argentina's Majoritarian Model of Democracy

The governing ability of the Argentine national government depends on its capacity to maintain legislative majorities and dominate at the subnational levels—both of which, since 1983, the PJ has done more successfully than its main rival, the UCR. This characteristic concentrates power within either a single party-based faction or within a single institution that has the power to dominate over the rest. From 1983 to 2007, Argentine political institutions over all tiers remained largely controlled by these two rival parties (see figure 6.3), albeit with greater force at the subnational levels than within the National Congress over the time specified.

Figure 6.3. UCR and PJ Combined Dominance in Democratic Institutions, 1987–2007

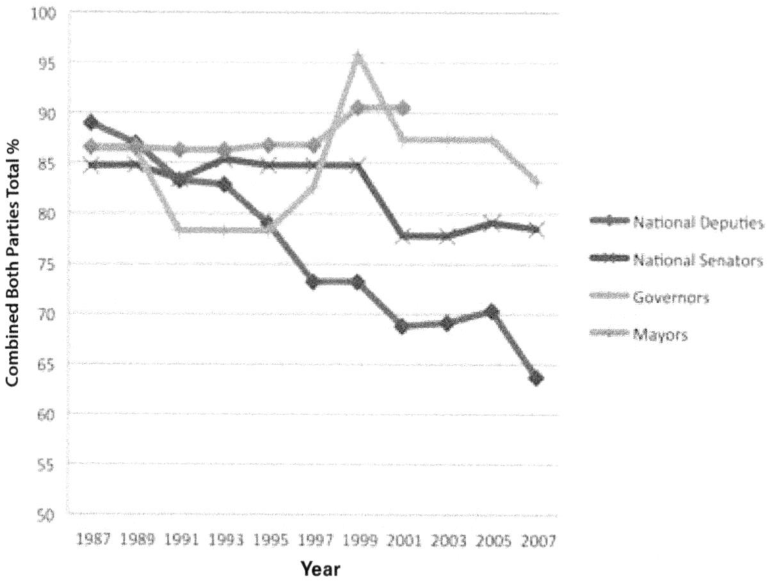

Source: Author elaboration, Ministério del Interior, Dirección Electoral.

Given the growing levels of party fragmentation that became increasingly visible in the lower chamber and in the Senate after the arrival of the Kirchners in 2003, the Kirchners' faction of Peronism, which has now governed successfully for over a decade, has done so through a strategy of concentrating power within a single political institution, the national executive. This strategy enables their faction to dominate the subnational levels—directly, through personal appeal, popular support, and a dash of good old-fashioned populism. Nevertheless, in order to be successful this governing strategy required that President Kirchner (2003 to 2007) confront the "leagues of governors and the urban mayors of Buenos Aires" (Tonelli 2011, 11). Interim president Duhalde had negotiated with this group during the fiscal crisis, primarily through the PJJHD, which Duhalde had financed but had allowed subnational party brokers to control for their own accumulation of power in return for their political support of "Duhaldismo."

This alternative governing strategy, in the context of an unstable political crisis in which few could govern, provided President Kirchner with an incentive not only to concentrate power in the hands of a select majority but also to attempt to bypass the governors—with whom he did not want to negotiate. I suggest that this was the political motive to discontinue PJJHD and replace it with a CCT that bypassed both Congress and the governors. Thus, it was an attempt to cut out the governors yet continue to garner the popular support that comes from antipoverty programs. Programa Familias, however, ideally was still designed to rely on local promotion efforts (or at least local acquiescence). Thus when its success proved limited after more than seven years, it was replaced by a completely new centralized program called AUH, which, as I argued in the previous chapter, represents not the *federalization* of social policy but rather a *centralization* of social policy. The lesson learnt is arguably that within a democratic system built on a majoritarian imperative that is particularly strong at the subnational level, without a formal vertical party alignment across the three levels that is more than nominal (there was no formal alignment between the national government and the five territories where Familias was not distributed during Kirchner's term), mayors are not encouraged to promote a national social policy objective.

In contrast with Brazil, Argentina's democratic model is what Lijphart (2008) would label relatively majoritarian and party-centered (see table 6.5). Argentina does not fit an *ideal* classification of majoritarianism, and, as Lijphart himself stated, "most countries are located somewhere between the extremes of majority rule and consensus" (2008, 118). Viewed through the lens of a paired comparison, however, the extent of majoritarianism within Argentine democracy becomes salient. Particularly from 1983 to 1995, majoritarianism was attributed positively to the performance and consolidation of Argentine democracy. Low levels of interparty competition meant that President Alfonsin's (UCR) and President Menem's (PJ) ability to govern was dependent on their ability to use partisan affinity to secure their preferences from Congress and to encourage subnational actors to carry out the government's desired reforms. Because of the strength of the PJ at the subnational level, the latter president succeeded in this more than the former.

Within a majoritarian democracy, partisan identity is intrinsic to forming voter preferences. Argentina is no exception to this rule,

Table 6.5. Characteristics of Argentina's Majoritarian Democratic Model

Broad Multiparty Coalitions in Congress	Single-Party Majority Cabinets	Two-Party Dominant System	Proportional Representation Party System	Vertically Integrated
No	Yes (See fig. 6.3)	De facto, Yes De jure, No	Closed-List Party-Centered	Contextually Determined

although the nature of its majoritarian politics follows a unique logic. In theory, political parties "should" facilitate citizen participation in forming government decisions and, through the democratic act of voting, control the quality and implementation of those decisions (Leiras 2004). Historically, in Argentina there are just two main national parties, the UCR and the PJ. Although Jones and Mainwaring (2008) have stated that party nationalization (defined as the extent to which a party receives similar levels of electoral support throughout the federation and at all levels of government) is low overall in Argentina, a single party alone, the PJ, has successfully controlled electoral majorities at all tiers and in all branches, except in the Chamber of Deputies from 1997 to 2002 and from 2009 to 2013, where opposition-based power and internal opposition toward the president prevailed. Gervasoni challenges this premise of PJ dominance, however, by asserting that the fifteen PJ-governed provinces in 2007 and the seventeen PJ-governed parties in 2011 are only "nominally" PJ (2011, 125). Nevertheless, this single political party, which has occupied the presidential office twenty-two out of the last thirty years of democracy, still fulfills the Lijphartian majoritarian principle, where a single party (or its faction) is supported by a majority in the legislature and controls the cabinet.

The logic of party-centered majority rule within the PJ makes elite political actors more concerned with office-seeking than with policy-seeking. Moreover, as we have seen, the strength of this majoritarian imperative at the provincial level makes it very difficult for mayors who carry out national policy objectives to personally claim credit for their success. For example, the urban municipality of La Matanza in the Province of Buenos Aires has one of the highest concentrations of both poverty rates and voters in the country. Its mayor from 1999 to 2005, Alberto Balestrini, had been a key figure in the municipality. He had been involved with local syndicate groups and unemployed workers and had participated in crucial negotiations with national and provincial PJ forces that had enabled a steady flow of badly needed resources into the territory he governed during the political and economic crises from 2001 to 2003, in particular resources related to PJJHD and local work projects (interview Suárez 2006). When it came time for Balestrini's race for mayoral reelection in September 2003, however, he did not campaign on the basis of what he had been able to accomplish for the municipality during the crisis or attempt to personally claim credit for any of its successes. Rather, he was "office-seeking" by aligning himself in the media with the right provincial leaders (namely, Duhalde), who controlled the internal selection process that would not only give party approval to his reelection but also place him on the party-controlled ballot ahead of his internal PJ rival. Having carried the infamous "Duhalde conducción" (Entin 2004)[12] during the internal dispute, Balestrini went on to be reelected. But once his local political battle had been won, he shifted his alliance from Duhalde to Kirchner. Therefore, office-seeking (that is, securing a local nomination and the seal of approval that supports an eventual local victory) is achieved through internal party-based cooperation and what Behrend (2007) calls the "closed game" of subnational politics.[13] In practice, this has made the vote an insufficient mechanism in Argentina for compelling candidates and their organizations to follow a certain course of action (Leiras 2004).

The electoral success of the president in Argentina depends on taking on board the preferences of as many provincial actors as possible, as long as they are part of the incumbent national leader's internal faction. The partisan stability of the PJ at the subnational level has facilitated its ability to continue dominating at the national level, even though national competition has undeniably increased since 1999, particularly within the National Chamber of Deputies. However, the highly decentralized organization of the two dominant political parties (particularly, in more recent years, the PJ's de-nationalization) impedes the ability of national party representatives and national political elites to integrate, challenge, and directly influence policymaking or policy outputs at the municipal level that are not conducted via provincial-level party brokers. For example, from 1983 to 2007, fourteen provinces can be classified as exhibiting a predominant party system, because only one or none of their last eight gubernatorial elections resulted in an alternation of power. Four provinces feature a two-party system, and six (the more urban and less represented in Congress) have a limited plural system.[14] Since 2007, only two provinces, Santa Fe and Río Negro, can no longer be classified as exhibiting a predominant party system; the rest remain unchanged. Because of the evident partisan stability at the provincial level over more than two decades, as demonstrated in figure 6.4, provincial electoral patterns since 1989 have nearly always led to a PJ majority at all electoral tiers, contributing to the majoritarian principle.[15]

I have already alluded to the fact that Argentina's majoritarian model of democracy is further enabled by its unique electoral rules. Each province is allowed to choose its own type of provincial voting system, electoral calendar (including for national office until 2007), and municipal electoral system. The voting systems include nearly every possible setup: single and multi-member districts, d'Hondt and Hare formulas, majority-PR, or varying electoral thresholds. Seventeen out of twenty-three provinces (twenty-four counting the CBA) allow multiple reelections (seven indefinitely), and some provinces allow *lemas* (the ability of a candidate to compete on multiple lists). According to Calvo and Micozzi's study (2005), thirty-two constitutional reforms and thirty-four electoral reforms have reshaped the subnational electoral map of Argentina since 1983. They show that "reforming the subnational electoral system allowed the incumbent to minimize the risk of electoral defeat, improve their control over provincial legislatures, and escape the negative consequences of what was emerging as a more competitive national level race" (Calvo and Micozzi 2005, 1052). The ability of provincial power brokers to constantly shape the rules of the game at the provincial level resulted in more than a majoritarian bias; it resulted in an incumbent bias (Calvo and Micozzi 2005; Malamud and de Luca 2005).

Subnational competition should be greater given that provincially based parties need the signatures of only 2 percent of registered voters in the given province in order to nominate candidates to national, provincial, or municipal office. However, closed-list proportional representation, coupled with varying district sizes set by provincial power

Figure 6.4. PJ Dominance in Argentine Democracy, 1989–2011

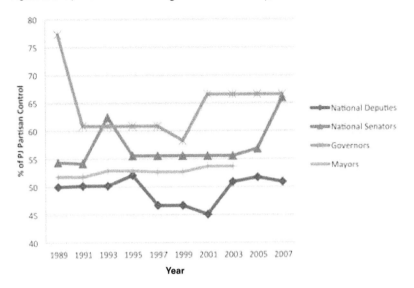

Source: Author elaboration, Ministério del Interior, Dirección General Electoral.

brokers, has limited the ability of third and fourth parties to enter Congress. To date, the only significant third parties to win at the provincial level have been the PRO in the City of Buenos Aires, the Socialist Party in Santa Fe, and the ARI in Tierra del Fuego. Alternative parties are generally elected in highly urban and nationally underrepresented provinces, such as Buenos Aires, the CBA, and Santa Fe. Provincial parties emerging in these territories have had limited capacity for spreading nationally and gaining access to official resources, a problem that is also related to the territorial bias in the Chamber of Deputies. Moreover, the failure of alternate parties to influence national policy, mainly because of the PJ's constant majority in the Senate and its persistently large block in the Chamber of Deputies, means that even when subnational voters do support a third-party provincial candidate, they are stimulated to vote strategically for one of the traditional parties to represent them nationally (Malamud and de Luca 2005).

Mayors are an additional feature of provincial party system stability, and they help to further decrease interparty competition at the municipal level. The internal rules of provincially based parties and their high level of electoral regime autonomy lead to strategic manipulation, and rarely allow opposition parties to build electoral support on the basis of experience in municipal government. This party-centered context motivates ambitious local leaders to utilize the dominant party label of a given province in order to advance their careers beyond local horizons. These local leaders prioritize the creation of what Remmer calls "political reward networks," based on the distribution of patronage-based public goods. By creating these networks, they can then offer them to party-based affiliates at higher levels of government to further their own careers and those of their co-partisans (Remmer 2007). With few incentives to provide constituency services at the municipal level because of closed-list electoral rules and low interparty competition, the incentive of a mayor to provide services for senior party affiliates is powerful.

The obvious implication of what can be classified as a majoritarian democracy, which thrives on the intrinsic value of partisan-based patronage networks for building one's political career, is that voter responsiveness does not revolve around mass programmatic appeals, such as social policy efforts, participatory budgeting, and poverty alleviation efforts. Rather, it revolves around the ability of local officials to deliver resources to a small but politically powerful segment of local society. Moreover, the majority-rule principle that extends all the way down to lower levels of government has ensured stability at the subnational level, but it has not encouraged local democratization, extensive policy innovations, or greater citizen participation within policymaking. This has led numerous influential researchers on Argentina to conclude that political patronage is, in fact, compatible with democracy (see Medina and Stokes 2002; Levitsky 2003; Jones and Hwang 2003; Calvo and Murillo 2004; Brusco, Nazareno, and Stokes 2004; Remmer 2007).

It is in this sense that majoritarianism in Argentina extends all the way down to the voters, who understand that they will pay a penalty if they defect from trading with a party monopolist and turn instead to the competition. The underdevelopment of municipalities in Argentina has contributed to the political monopoly of Peronism since 1983 and to the low level of importance given to this level of government. Most important for the argument being made here, it is the majoritarian imperative at the subnational level that discourages mayors from enabling a national policy objective that may benefit their constituents, yet decrease their own chances of political survival, if such national welfare goods are unaccompanied by the provincial *conducción*.

The chosen governing strategy of the two Kirchners gave them an incentive to provide collective welfare goods to as many territories as possible, provided that these policies directly contributed to their personal concentration of power. PJJHD had the seal of approval from provincial power brokers, which made it possible for these brokers to control the PJJHD at the subnational level and use it as a subnational political resource. It also made it very difficult to discontinue. Programa Familias did not go through this provincial rite of passage, and thus it was met with inconsistent implementation, local apathy, low levels of promotion, and lower levels of territorial penetration. The result was its eventual extinction. In contrast, AUH requires no provincial rite of passage and no subnational monitoring, promotion, or enforcement, because it is part of a centralized formal insurance scheme that is designed to generate popular support for the national executive. As such, this program was not designed to produce local externalities, such as improved local administrative capacity, increased demand for locally provided basic social services, or increased national monitoring of access to local services and their quality—all of which calls into question its long-term intention to reduce the intergenerational transmission of poverty, which within a decentralized federal framework is dependent on subnational participation.

SUBNATIONAL POLITICS AND CCT PERFORMANCE IN ARGENTINA

The purpose of this chapter has been to show how domestic structural, political, and fiscal factors shaped Argentina's poverty alleviation agenda and undermined the policy objectives of both Kirchners to implement and expand an internationally backed and financed CCT, which dated back to 2002. Given the severe rise in poverty rates in 2001, the distribution of noncontributory social protection goods to alleviate poverty and reduce the risks of social vulnerability was clearly on the federal agenda because of public demand. Although the Kirchner administrations tried to deliver such goods by ending the emergency workfare program PJJHD and replacing it with a new CCT, Programa Familias, they were unable either to immediately discontinue the older program or to generate political or popular interest in the new one—in particular at the subnational level. The three political-institutional factors highlighted in chapter 2 are fundamental to understanding why the PJJHD was politically very difficult to terminate, and why mayors had little interest in promoting Familias to socially vulnerable families. Of the three explanatory factors, I stress the fact that municipalities, which were intended to be the agents of the federal government within Familias, lacked sufficient political and fiscal incentives or the required institutional capacity to play this complementary role.

First, the nature of the party system in Argentina and the extent of majoritarianism it generates have a clear impact on both federalism and its policy outcomes. The president, when he or she is of the PJ,[16] does not have to negotiate with smaller opposition parties to win approval for policy initiatives, but, once these are approved, is then forced to negotiate with powerful provincially based factions of his or her own party when it comes to making them operational. Federalism in Argentina involves a concentration of power in the national executive, juxtaposed with strong provincial governors and subordinate municipalities. Although several reforms of the 1990s attempted to change the logic of this democratic model, powerful governors retain significant political leverage and indeed exercise more control over the national executive than does Congress (Novaro 2004; Medina and Ratto 2006; Spiller and Tommasi 2007), which makes it extremely difficult to bypass them or to ignore their policy preferences.

Based on this established governing logic and in order to secure the concentration of power in the hands of a single political party label, Menem and Duhalde allowed their benchmark social programs to be captured and used by local and provincial PJ party brokers to generate their own power. It was this quality that guaranteed the success and the continuity of labor-based CCTs over more than a decade in conjunction with other important policy feedback effects. For example, the "idea" of labor-based CCTs was firmly embedded in national policy circles. They were clearly identifiable as "Peronist," and they were nearly always associated with the symbolic status of the Ministry of Labor. Moreover, labor-based CCTs affected interest group politics, primarily organized groups of unemployed workers in and around the urban areas of the city of Buenos Aires. All of these policy feedback effects created the much hypothesized "lock-in" effects that constrain future policy development and can be observed in the difficulties of terminating PJJHD. However, the most important feedback effect of CCTs, to be underscored, is their potential ability to affect "the electoral and political participation of *individuals* directly affected by concrete public policies" (Béland 2010a, 578). None of the experts interviewed for this research doubted that the electoral and political participation of recipients of PJJHD contributed to Néstor Kirchner's slim 2003 electoral victory, similar to the effects of Bolsa Família in Brazil's 2006 general elections. The difference, however, which is also well known, is that the targeting of PJJHD had been politically manipulated by allowing subnational capture—the "*malafama*" of labor-based CCTs in Argentina.

After his election, President Kirchner attempted to launch a new CCT that bypassed provincial intermediation and to terminate PJJHD. The extent of majoritarianism in Argentina, however, impeded this new national policy objective in several ways. Of great importance, mayors had little incentive to promote a national redistributive program that was not directly supported by their provincial governments and that was designed to reduce subnational capture. Whether through explicit action or policy apathy, at the end of Kirchner's term in office Programa Familias had not been implemented in any municipality in four provinces and in the City of Buenos Aires. Following an established electoral logic, it would be irrational for local officials to enable a federal social program based on a fixed targeting formula if they were not formally aligned, through partisanship, with the ruling national Kirchner PJ-FPV faction. Additionally, in the context of Argentina's unique model of majoritarianism within a strong federal system, mayors are more concerned with office-seeking, which means being aligned with provincial power brokers.

Based on the context, the mere fact that Programa Familias was intended to directly strengthen the president and the center, not via the provinces or their party brokers, meant that this social investment program actually undermined the power-generating capacity of local officials on which mayors depended to forward their own careers within their province. Moreover, mayors could not easily claim credit for the indirect benefits from the successful promotion of Programa Familias within their territory because the implementation process also largely bypassed their direct involvement. As a municipal secretary of La Matanza once complained, "within Familias, municipalities just sit back and watch" (interview Colicigno 2006).

In the absence of subnational promotion efforts and because of its inability to replace and transform PJJHD, Programa Familias gained very little public attention and acknowledgment. The registration of PJJHD had been closed by law since 2002, before Kirchner took office. In reality, however, the continuation of this social protection program was important to provincial-level PJ party brokers (particularly in the Province of Buenos Aires), enabling them to continue controlling certain organized groups and local protests. This fact, together with President Kirchner's need for the support of as many provinces as he could muster, made it almost impossible for him to either close or replace PJJHD during his term of office.

Second, the political intention of Familias to bypass provinces goes against the logic of Argentine federalism—*punto final.* Municipalities are creatures of the provinces, and they play an important role in the stability of provincial politics. They have little power to behave without either the approval or the involvement of the province to which they are institutionally, politically, and fiscally subordinate. Provinces have not uniformly provided constitutional autonomy to municipalities within their territory, as stipulated in the National Constitution, and even when they have done so, the political, fiscal, and administrative benefits of municipal autonomy remain unclear. The lack of constitutional recognition of municipalities as distinct from the provinces, coupled with decreased political incentives for mayors to promote national policy objectives, impeded the success of Programa Familias and, more broadly, impedes the ability of a president in Argentina to distribute collective welfare goods territory-wide.

As described in chapter 5, although Programa Familias was designed to bypass the provinces, the administrative team responsible for implementing this CCT within the municipalities of each province was selected from a short list of officials chosen by the province, not the federal government, because of the absence of national recognition of municipalities as distinct from the provinces (a permissive condition). The province was denied the program or else entered into "negotiations" with the national office, if it was not willing to accept the candidates selected by the province to implement and monitor the program at the municipal level. In practice, municipalities had little direct participation.

Low levels of municipal autonomy and organizational capacity prevented the federal government from distributing CCTs to vulnerable households within municipalities of a given province, if the province was not willing to play by the rules of the CCT set by Desarollo Social. Article 5 of the 1853 Constitution, reformed in 1994, clearly states that municipalities, though autonomous, are under the authority of the provinces. Article 123 guarantees municipal autonomy, but this autonomy is left to be interpreted by the heterogeneous provincial constitutions. Sixteen of the twenty-three provinces recognize varying degrees of *de jure* municipal autonomy within their provincial constitutions. For example, the provinces of Buenos Aires and Santa Fe do not grant formal authority to their municipalities. These two provinces alone account for 47 percent of the entire population of the country (INDEC 1991). Therefore, this CCT did not in fact bypass provincial (that is, political) intermediation.

Provincially based political parties control the municipal level, and party leaders (normally the governor) provide resources for municipal leaders to engage in clientelism to maintain a solid base of supporters (Jones 2008). The constitutional inability of the national government to bypass provincial intermediation politicizes the territorial distribution of redistributive social goods. A de facto two-level federal structure set within a majoritarian model of democracy provides governors with the ability to constrain simultaneously the power of mayors and the power of the president. It compromises the ability of the federal government to guarantee both the rights of social citizenship and citizens' access to them polity-wide.

Third, because of the rules that regulate subnational finances, municipalities do not have a fiscal incentive to encourage a national policy objective. Revenue-sharing in Argentina is based on the *coparticipación*, a tax-sharing agreement between the federal and provincial governments. Municipalities are dependent on the provinces for the secondary distribution of the *coparticipación* designated to them. Additionally, the borrowing capacity of municipalities is determined ad hoc by provincial legislatures. At the subnational level, between the provinces and their municipalities is another soft budget syndrome.

Municipalities are neither dependent on the federal government for resources, nor is their social expenditure hardwired to either the provincial or national budget, as is the case in Brazil. Governors have considerable influence over the execution of public policy (Jones 2008, 49) and of its financing. Therefore, municipalities that are formally aligned with the provincial incumbent are delivered resources to fuel local patronage and clientelism and public policy projects that bring more resources and jobs to that municipality; resources flow from the province downward. The small economic inputs that come from a CCT do not provide sufficient fiscal incentives to entice a municipality to give up the potential fiscal benefits it gains by directly cooperating with particularized provincial interests, which often undermine the federal government and generate power for provincial party elites. As noted above, the threat of fiscal punishment from a strong governor to a municipality that attempts to bypass the province's political interests and to promote a national policy objective with which they are not formally aligned equates, quite simply, to "fiscal suicide" (interview Pereyra 2006; interview Cafiero 2006).

President Kirchner won the first round of the 2003 elections with only 22.4 percent of the total vote. Contrary to expectations surrounding the elections, voter turnout was high, at 78 percent, which "is on par with previous elections" (Levitsky and Murillo 2003, 157). Kirchner's personal electoral strength did not provide him with a clear mandate to improve *government* performance. However, following the high levels of public protest and the public's demand "que se vayan todos" (that they should all go), Kirchner had a considerable challenge ahead of him to improve upon from his weak position as the president in 2003.

In terms of economic performance, as noted earlier, Kirchner did extremely well because of rapidly increasing commodity prices on the world markets, particularly the price of soya, of which Argentina produces a considerable amount. During his administration, annual growth rates averaged 7.85 percent from 2003 to 2006 (World Bank Annual Growth Rate Index). Such high GDP rates also enabled the federal government to boast relatively high fiscal surpluses and central bank reserves. To a certain extent, positive economic performance reduces poverty for certain sectors of the population. Trickle-down logic, which maintains that growth is causally linked to poverty reduction, however, has long been dismissed, particularly in countries with substantial economic inequality. When Kirchner left office in 2007, Argentina had a Gini coefficient of 0.48, up from 0.38 in 1980 (World Bank GINI Index). In reality, this positive economic performance did not solve the intergenerational transmission of poverty or lessen inequality over either the medium term or the long term, but it did ensure the continuity of "Kirchnerismo" in the short term.

By the end of President Néstor Kirchner's term in office, his benchmark social inclusion program delivered monetary benefits to 372,000 households in 232 municipalities. Simultaneously, the previous politicized program PJJHD still existed. By 2006, only 21 percent of Argentine municipalities were included in his CCT. Former interim president Duhalde's emergency workfare program, however, continued to make over 1.3 million payments per month. In August 2006, the last month for which disaggregated program data is available, 36 percent of the monthly payments of PJJHD were allocated within the Province of Buenos Aires (data supplied by the Ministry of Labor, 2006). As suggested in chapter 5, the expansion of Familias relative to the discontinuation of PJJHD was difficult, with AUH effectively replacing both of them in 2010.

The previously mentioned policy feedback effects from PJJHD certainly contributed to the low performance of Programa Familias. In terms of direct policy feedbacks from Programa Familias itself, it is unclear if there are any real winners given the inability of the president to use it to replace PJJHD and the institutional constraints to its territorial distribution. It therefore cannot be asserted that this CCT contributed to the popular support of the Kirchner government, which was taken over by Cristina Fernández de Kirchner in 2007. According to a credible public survey conducted by CEDLAS in collaboration with the World Bank, the best-known CCT at the end of Néstor Kirchner's term (2007) remained PJJHD (Duhalde), followed by Plan Trabajar (Menem), with Programa Familias (Kirchner) last. This is in great contrast to a similar opinion poll taken in Brazil in May 2006 (IPSOS), which reported that 99 percent of respondents had some knowledge of Brazil's Bolsa Família, compared to lower program recall for earlier social programs

in Brazil (see Lindert and Vincensini 2010).[17] Moreover, over 97 percent
of randomly selected Brazilian interviewees in 2004 assessed CCT programs positively; around half cited concerns over implementation; and
46 percent specifically cited delays in electronic payment and inclusion/
exclusion errors (Pesquisa Vox Populi, in Lindert and Vincensini 2010,
33). By contrast, table 6.6 provides further insights gathered from similar Argentine surveys regarding the public's perception of CCTs.

The findings of a large and credible survey conducted by Cruces
and Rovner (2008), presented in table 6.6, show the high number of
respondents in 2007 (88 percent) who believed that CCTs were manipulated according to political motives. I have referred to this earlier as their
malafama, emanating from the practices of PJJHD. However, 61 percent
believed that as a policy prescription, CCTs are still required. This survey, at least, demonstrates a public demand not only for CCTs but also
for their improvement. Interestingly, in another subset of questions in
the same survey, 33 percent believed CCTs should be implemented and
monitored by municipalities, and 32 percent by the national government, but only 24 percent by the provinces (Cruces and Rovner 2008).

This sector-specific case study suggests that within Argentina's majoritarian democracy, mayors have few incentives to promote a national
policy objective within what is considered in the traditional literature
to be a *strong* federal system. Although from a veto-players perspective, this system is considered to be less strong in practice than Brazil's
(see Stepan 2004), municipalities in Argentina could not easily participate within Programa Familias without provincial agreement, and some
provinces in fact acted as direct veto players within this national policy
objective. The ability of governors to control the majority of mayors in
Argentina increases the strength of not only federalism in Argentina but

Table 6.6. Public Perceptions of CCTS in Argentina in 2007

Do you feel CCTs should be eliminated?	28% Yes
Should CCTS continue to exist as they are currently designed?	58% Yes
Ratio of respondents who thought current CCTs were good	2/10
Respondents who believed normatively CCTs were required	61%
% of respondents who felt plans were used for political motives	88%

Source: Cruces and Rovner 2008.

also the veto potential of governors. It is theoretically true that President Néstor Kirchner could have opted to deliver his CCT through the provinces. However, this would have made it very difficult for him to claim that there was no political intermediation in his CCT, although the political intention of this and most internationally financed CCTs was to deliver social citizenship rights polity-wide without political intermediation. Furthermore, working with the provinces was not within the president's set of preferences at the time.

Social investment programs designed to alleviate the intergenerational transmission of poverty are necessary in a country reporting over 3.4 million persons living in extreme poverty and over 10.6 million living in moderate poverty, according to official government poverty figures at the time President Fernández de Kirchner took office (INDEC). Moreover, in a strong federal system where the national government does not have the authority to unilaterally implement a targeted social investment strategy polity-wide that is conditional on human capital investments outside its jurisidiction, intergovernmental collaboration is essential. However, although both the public in the 2007 survey and the government officials interviewed in this study at the end of Néstor Kirchner's term believed that CCTs should be implemented and monitored by municipalities and that they needed to be structurally improved, the ability of the first Kirchner government to achieve these ends was limited, and this situation has continued.

As the nation's new president, Cristina Kirchner had few options left, given the policy feedback effects of PJJHD and Programa Familias, except to implement a narrower, heavily centralized, child-centered, cash-based, noncontributory family allowance linked to the formal family allowance system under ANSES (AUH). The disadvantages of AUH emanate from both the way it is financed and the ambiguity surrounding its conditionality. The ability of a mammoth and politically charged federal agency, ANSES, to enforce user compliance in AUH, as is the case in Mexico's CCT model, or to assist and accompany socially vulnerable families to meet program requirements, as is the case in Brazil's CCT model, is extremely unrealistic. The major challenge confronting AUH is an enforcement problem rather than a transmission problem.

CHAPTER 7

Federalism and the Territorial Distribution of Targeted Social Welfare

In Comparative Perspective

This book has explored the understudied relationship between the federal government and municipalities using the strategy of paired-comparison. It suggests that under certain conditions, municipalities can facilitate the performance of national CCTs designed to reduce the intergenerational transmission of poverty without political intermediation. By 2006, Brazil had successfully implemented Bolsa Família in all of its 5,564 municipalities. It had reached its target, set in 2004, of delivering monetary benefits to 11 million households, allocated on the basis of explicit program criteria. Several authors have suggested that various electoral motives were behind the program's success (Hunter and Power 2007; Nicolau and Peixoto 2007; Soares and Terron 2008; Castro, Licio, and Renno 2009; Zucco 2013; Power and Zucco 2013). Although electoral theory can suggest why a president such as Lula might be motivated to deliver poverty alleviation goods at particular times, it cannot explain why Lula's attempt succeeded while other presidential attempts, such as Néstor Kirchner's in neighboring Argentina, were more limited. Moreover, there exists no empirical evidence that Bolsa Família was not distributed in accordance with its explicit targeting criteria. In the evolution of social protection policy in the context of Brazilian federalism from 1988 onward, multiple institutional mechanisms have contributed to the resolution of its federally derived policy challenge of protecting and delivering basic collective social goods to all of its citizens. In this specific social area, municipalities, operating as the prime agents of the federal government, have been the dominant mechanism used by the national government to overcome the main factor hindering the credibility of a highly decentralized system of federal government in Brazil (namely, the strength embedded in its state governors). According to the prevailing wisdom in the literature, and also in accordance with the observations in this book on the predatory federal game functioning from 1988 to 1995, presidents in Brazil had to overcome the ability of state-based actors to constrain national social policy objectives. The key explanatory factors are the constitutional recognition of municipalities as distinct from the states, hard budget constraints regulating subnational spending at all levels, and a consensual democratic regime. All of these uniquely Brazilian political and institutional factors encouraged municipalities to promote this national social policy objective. They facilitated the successful territorial distribution of CCTs in Brazil and as a consequence have also contributed to this policy's continuity for now over more than a decade.

In Argentina, only 232 municipalities out of 1,100 were receiving Programa Familias in 2006, and among the members of the public surveyed by Cruces and Rovner in 2007, this CCT was not a widely recognized program. By the end of Kirchner's term in office, only 232,000 households were receiving benefits from this national program, even though over 1.9 million households were below the poverty line in Argentina, or 19.2 percent of the total population (INDEC 2006). The program's performance measured in terms of its absolute and territorial distribution, along with the national government's preferred intention to discontinue the previous administration's highly politicized workfare program PJJHD, was limited by Argentina's majoritarian democratic system, the lame duck status of its municipalities, and a de facto soft budget syndrome that holds local governments hostage to provincial agendas.

Evident in the evolution of poverty alleviation initiatives within the context of Argentine federalism from the 1990s onward are multiple institutional mechanisms that have discouraged broad intergovernmental cooperation in this social policy area. Non-institutionalized, national-provincial bargaining in this policy area appears to have been the dominant strategy used by the national government to overcome the main factor hindering the credibility of a highly decentralized system of government. Although two federal administrations (2003–2009) tried to bring municipalities into the nationally established goals to promote poverty alleviation and social inclusion, the political willingness of mayors to promote this goal was compromised by their dependence on provincial governors for both their financial and political existence. A competitive two-level game of federalism is dominant in Argentina, and it limits the ability of the national executive to decrease the undermining effects of strong federalism by avoiding governors.

Both countries implemented CCTs that delivered important benefits to households living in situations of social vulnerability. Compared to Argentina, however, Brazil achieved a more even territorial distribution of targeted social welfare, distributed according to explicit means-tested targeting, producing a large-scale CCT program that has been sustained over a longer period of time and a changeover in presidential power. It was not so much Brazil's high government performance that dictated the research strategy of the current book, but rather the fact that a country typically characterized as having difficulties in institutionalizing an effective capacity to govern actually performed reasonably well (and continues to do so) in promoting targeted social welfare in the form of CCTs over three different presidencies. It was only through a pair-comparison strategy built upon a specific policy sector that certain institutional differences became relevant across these two rather similar federal systems. By generating a new explanatory factor for understanding how strong federalism works in practice, *the strength of municipalities as distinct from the states/provinces*, this book's conclusions have implications for other research questions.[1]

Argentina and Brazil are both examples of strong federal systems where subnational levels of government can constrain national policy objectives. In these multi-tiered democracies, targeted social programs were set at the center, but they were to be promoted and monitored at the municipal level. The success of each government's distribution strategy, however, depended on the constitutional, political, and fiscal conditions that link all three levels of government. The center, in each of these strong and decentralized federations, sought uniformity of outcome by trying to "bypass the governors," thus avoiding the "undermining constraints" of federalism.

This final chapter aims to draw comparative conclusions from the period of nearly two decades under examination in both countries and to reflect on the implications overall. A key lesson that emerges is that institutionalizing an effective national social protection system designed to alleviate poverty depends less on the technical design and merits of the programs (as international policy prescriptions would have us believe) and more on the broader institutional, structural, and political contexts in which the programs operate. Contrary to the traditional wisdom of comparative political science, Brazil's "coalitional-presidentialism," which I labeled in this study as a consensual democracy, outperformed Argentina's more majoritarian democracy. Nevertheless, no social policy area is immune to retrenchment, regardless of its popularity or successful feedback effects.

I have suggested that the Brazilian success with Bolsa Família, a social program currently being exported and emulated throughout the developing world, was dependent on municipal willingness, and that, by contrast, Argentina's experiment with an internationally prescribed CCT was less successful because mayors could not be sufficiently motivated to enable this social program, which represents a nationally strategic area of social policy from a more rational political perspective. The book's findings have broad implications for future research about federalism and the territorial distribution of targeted social welfare in Latin America, as well as for development practitioners involved in CCT programs in federal countries elsewhere, such as India, Nigeria, and the federalized countries of the Asia Pacific. It will be useful to revisit the three original theoretical propositions.

THREE FACTORS THAT ENCOURAGE MAYORS TO PROMOTE NATIONAL POLICY OBJECTIVES

In chapter 2, I proposed that three factors determined whether or not mayors would promote a national social policy objective, and that municipal promotion was fundamental to the successful distribution and stability of Brazil's Bolsa Família. These claims deserve review in light of the empirical evidence and analysis presented in the last four chapters.

National Recognition of Subnational Levels of Government

The previous chapters established empirically that when municipalities are treated as a separate institutional category from the states and provinces, municipalities are *de jure* permitted to directly promote a national policy objective without the formal consent of governors. This is not to say, however, that they cannot have the same effect in the absence of this legal status. An excellent recent example comes from Venezuela in 2009: an opposition governor resisted a certain national policy objective, but mayors in his state who were aligned with President Hugo Chávez declared that they would enable it even if their governor opted to resist the president's policy (see Eaton 2014, 1146). In practice and in theory, both levels of subnational government within a federal system can constrain and undermine the center (either unified or separately) by not carrying out its policy goals through deliberate action or inaction. The national recognition of municipalities and their distinction from the core federal units, however, facilitates a president's ability to avoid governors and the willingness of mayors to promote national goals. Their constitutional distinction further enables fiscal, administrative, and political power to be formally dispersed between the two subnational levels and contributes to their ability to exercise power independently. Comparative federalism has often avoided an analytical treatment of state-municipal relations and of national-local relations in order to make theoretical generalizations.

The effect of municipalities on the strength of federalism is a priori dependent on the strength of the four institutional variables set out by Samuels and Mainwaring (2004): the resource base of subnational governments, the power of governors, the articulation of state-based interests in the national Congress, and the distribution of functions across levels of government. I argue in this book that municipalities can counter the ability of governors to use this strength to undermine national policy objectives (though not the strength of the variables themselves) if a particular combination of variables (regime type and the rules regulating subnational finances) can further encourage municipalities to promote national goals. Certain institutional configurations can lead to positive policy results (results that are politically viable and socially desirable), which would not be anticipated on the basis of the main effects of Samuels and Mainwaring's (2004) four variables, which, they contend, have a constraining effect on the federal governments in both Brazil and Argentina. In this study, I have demonstrated how the frequent practice of aggregating the subnational levels has limited the scope of our explanations. Municipalities, when recognized as a distinct level of government, can have an important effect on the ability of national government to avoid the undermining constraints of an otherwise strong federal system.

In the case of Argentina, municipalities are constitutionally recognized, but not explicitly as a distinct level of government from the provinces. Rather, it is the responsibility of the provinces, as stated within the national constitution, to protect their autonomy. Not all provinces have exercised their constitutional responsibility to do so, which has led to high levels of institutional heterogeneity at the municipal level across the nation. In contrast, a distinction between states and municipalities was adopted as a constitutional principle in Brazil in 1988. The institutional norms and rules regulating the lowest level of federal government are uniform throughout all 5,564 municipalities. Although some Brazilian municipalities continued to be captured by state-based power brokers after 1988, as was traditional, the state-local relationship was weakened after 1995 by fiscal recentralization from the federal government, which privileged municipalities over the states. (See table 7.1.)

The quality of municipal governance and the extent of top-down municipalization set these two countries apart. The capacity of municipalities to collaborate with CCT enrollment efforts, to promote CCTs through local access, and to provide the required social services in basic health and education as well as to monitor and accompany

Table 7.1. Constitutional Recognition of Subnational Level of Government in Comparative Perspective

Institutional Qualities	Brazilian States	Brazilian Municipalities	Argentine Provinces	Argentine Municipalities
Recognized as a distinct order in the National Constitution	Yes	Yes	Yes	No
Institutional Uniformity	Yes	Yes	No	No
Own Constitutions	Yes	Yes	Yes	Varies per Province
Revenue Capacity	Medium	Low	Low	Low
Social Policy Authority	Medium	High	High	Low
National Political Relevance	High	High	High	Low

welfare conditionality is fundamental to the performance of CCTs in each country. Prior to the implementation of Bolsa Família in Brazil, the extent of policy decentralization to municipalities had provided local governments with experience in administering social services in the areas of health care and primary education. In contrast, Argentine municipalities have been largely captured by provincial-level bureaucracies and actors and thus have had limited opportunities to develop their own administrative capacity. Furthermore, bureaucracies at the municipal level in Argentina are not known for a high degree of institutional formality or a rules-based culture.

Argentina's politicized and weak municipal institutions (limiting both their capacity and their accountability) did not provide an adequate framework through which a national CCT designed to avoid political intermediation could easily perform. Moreover, mayors often lacked the educational and health facilities required for recipients to meet the conditions set by the national center, and which the local team was responsible for monitoring by reporting noncompliance back to the central office. As a consequence of municipalities providing an inadequate local framework, there was a kind of rigidity built into Programa Familia's top-down administrative procedures. A hierarchical governing bureaucracy that is built on paranoia and mistrust becomes a vicious circle in Argentina, leading to ransacked local program offices and missing computers and equipment. High levels of local polarization meant, in addition, that the "boutique office" inside Desarrollo Social attempted to control those who were hired in the local team, which undermined municipalities and often invited provincial involvement.

Alternatively, in considering the performance of CCTs from the bottom up, the local officials whom I interviewed in the Province of Buenos Aires in 2006 did not have a positive evaluation of Programa Familias. This was in contrast to Brazil, where the state-level actors in the State of São Paulo whom I interviewed were most critical of Bolsa Família. In both cases, however, their criticisms were due to their perceived lack of importance in the operationalization of CCTs. The lack of willingness of local officials to promote CCTs in Argentina and to encourage those eligible to voluntarily transfer over from PJJHD evidently contributed to the low levels of program recall by the respondents surveyed, as cited in chapter 6, whereas the lack of willingness of the states in Brazil to promote Bolsa Família does not seem to have affected citizens' program recall, which was reported at 99 percent (Lindert and Vincensini 2010, 33).

Provincial meddling hampered the implementation process of Programa Familias in Argentina, a situation that did not delight municipal officials working in local offices of social development and that contributed to its uneven territorial distribution and absolute uptake. The Autonomous City of Buenos Aires (CBA) rejected outright the program's operation within its jurisdiction, while four other provinces (some with very high levels of poverty), not including the CBA, did not adhere to the program from 2003 to 2007 for undisclosed reasons. When the province did not adhere to the national program, local territories within the province were wholly excluded from participating in it. Undermining the governor from the perspective of an Argentine mayor is very politically and fiscally risky and was thus not a viable option. In contrast, mayors in Brazil, particularly mayors of large and medium-sized cities, had little to lose from participating in Bolsa Família. High levels of municipal autonomy, including extensive governing responsibilities in basic social areas and in the social protection of vulnerable families, particularly women and children, meant that enabling Bolsa Família in their locality and promoting its uptake entailed greater benefits than costs. As the former secretary of social development in the City of São Paulo of the PT opposition party Democratas shouted, on a particularly bad day as far as local media reports on how he was doing his job were concerned: "I don't care where it comes from, if it contributes to solving the problem [child poverty and school attendance], I'll promote anything" (interview Pesaro 2006).[2]

Rules Regulating Subnational Finances

The second explanatory factor suggested in chapters 4 and 6 as having an effect on the degree of mayors' willingness to promote national policy objectives within their territories was that of the rules regulating subnational finances. Such rules are in fact difficult to separate from the other two explanatory factors because both the national recognition of subnational levels within a national constitution and the degree of majoritarianism within a democracy dictate the need for soft versus hard subnational budget constraints. A point to be underscored, however, is that they also determine whether the national government can credibly use fiscal incentives to encourage municipalities to promote their policy objectives and avoid governors. Brazil and Argentina have taken very different paths to eliminate the deleterious effect of excessive subnational spending, a chipping-away effect that Tanzi refers to throughout his work as "fiscal termites in the basement" (see Tanzi 1995).

The new politics of governors that emerged in Brazil after 1988 were based on the fiscal dependence of mayors on governors. By means of the increased ability to enforce fiscal discipline at all levels of government after 2000 through the Fiscal Responsibility Law, the central bank and treasury, and the Congress, the Brazilian president has been able to credibly use fiscal incentives to motivate mayors to become the prime agents of the federal government in key social policy areas. In contrast to Argentina, where the president has always relied on a party-based mechanism to create temporary political coalitions to regulate subna tional fiscal discipline, the Brazilian president lacks this option because he or she governs through large multiparty coalitions. With the absence of a party-based mechanism to enforce subnational fiscal discipline, the second-best option for the Brazilian government was to hardwire its fiscal rules. Following the logic of incrementalism, the governing elite in Brazil tried numerous economic, social, and political experiments from 1988 to 1995 in order to correct the major fiscal imbalances created by the 1988 Constitution. After 1995, the governing elite managed to get it right, following many years of "muddling through." Following Brazil's established governing logic of "change and continuity," the majority of these fiscal reforms have been sustained since then under the rule of two opposing political parties, the PSDB and the PT. This result shows that the rules regulating subnational finances are an important part of the president's toolbox for governance in Brazil. Morever, subnational fiscal stability and the rules that regulate it have been just as useful to the PT's ability to govern as they were to the PSDB.

The same cannot be said of the rules that regulate subnational finances in Argentina. Shortly after the Argentine financial crisis in 2002, US President George W. Bush was reported by the *Financial Times* as stating that in order for international financial institutions to regain their confidence, Argentina would have to make some tough calls, "starting with reforming the relationship between the provinces and their budgets and the central government" (March 21, 2002, p. 1) Although many scholars believed Argentina had successfully hardened its budget constraints (Webb 2003), President Bush and his advisors recognized that they had not done so. The rationale for continuing soft budget constraints is political, and provinces continue to believe that they will be bailed out by the national government. The negative consequences of such predatory fiscal behavior have been well documented in the literature for their contributions to national macroeconomic instability. The rationale behind the extension of fiscal grants to the provinces from the federal government is to maximize its fiscal leverage over the provinces. Although the Argentine president has exercised varying degrees of power over the provinces from 1983 to 2013, the unique characteristics of Argentine federalism entail that the president cannot easily govern without leverage over the provinces.

Brazil, in contrast, is characterized by Anwar Shah as a system of "fend-for-yourself federalism." Shah further claims that "Brazil's success with fiscal rules from 2001–2007 is particularly remarkable" (2007, 386). Thus, Brazil's fiscal success has affected the behavior of its governors and mayors and has strengthened the center's ability to provide national public goods—correcting Brazil's notorious policy transmission problem. The ability of governors and mayors to fend for themselves under Brazil's current system of fiscal rules often implies cooperating with the federal government, because of the large amount of expenditure matching-grants and fiscal regulations. Within a system of hard budget constraints such as Brazil's, unless the threat of political or fiscal punishment from the state power above or from the electorate below is sufficiently substantial, there are few reasons why a municipality would not promote a poverty alleviation program that distributes monetary benefits within its local territory as well as providing fiscal incentives for good administrative performance within the program.

A majoritarian democracy such as Argentina's should in theory be able to manage soft budget constraints through party discipline. President Menem's early successes were achieved thanks to his ability to create "a credible political coalition [requiring] the weakening of some groups and the cooptation of others" (Treisman 2004, 411). The problem, however, is that such political coalitions cannot be maintained over the long term, as became evident under the opposition-based government of de la Rúa from 1999 to 2001. As Stepan (2004) asserts, from the veto-players approach, "Argentina shows how a system that has effectively one partisan political veto player (PJ) and one institutional veto player (Menem) can return to a system in which all four potential institutional veto players are actualized" (344). This situation greatly undermines future-oriented state action such as is required to end the intergenerational transmission of poverty.

Under de facto soft budget constraints, the costs of not being able to create a durable political coalition to enforce subnational fiscal discipline are extremely high. Within the current system of fiscal regulations in Argentina, the ability of governors to fiscally and politically punish and reward both the president and the mayors they dominate leads to governor politics, which are particularly voracious when the governors are not in the incumbent president's internal faction.[3] In both

Argentina and Brazil, governor politics have been used to restrict the territorial distribution of national collective welfare goods and impede national policy objectives—a situation that Dickovick (2006) and Fenwick (2009) each suggest has been overcome in at least two areas of Brazilian policy, fiscal and social, through municipalization. In Argentina, however, what Dickovick (2006) refers to as a "second-best option" developed from a more rational perspective does not seem like a viable option—even though it was certainly attempted by both Kirchner presidents.

As table 7.2 illustrates from a comparative perspective, national-provincial fiscal-political co-dependence is a dominant trait in Argentine federalism. Ironically, in Brazil, because most state expenditures are paid out of state revenues, state autonomy is equally protected. This means, however, that Brazilian governors must fend for themselves. Both countries have controlled debt accumulation by reining in the ability of subnational governments to borrow from domestic banks. However, Argentina, unlike Brazil, continues to allow subnational governments to borrow from foreign banks. Most important for this study is the extent of fiscal decentralization to the local level in Brazil, which continues to be financed through both state and federal government transfers. It is not particularly easy for municipalities in Brazil to shirk their policy responsibilities within a context of hard budget constraints when the funds that finance local responsibilities are earmarked and motivated through matching grants and performance incentives.

Nevertheless, unsolved fiscal issues remain pertinent for the quality of policy outputs in Brazil. Particularly, municipal inequality in Brazil remains a concern, and there is currently a need for the equalization of municipal revenues (Shah 2007, 374). What is most glaring in the cross-case comparison, however, is how difficult it is for the Argentine federal government to regulate, control, and even monitor how provinces and municipalities spend their resources, even though ironically almost all of their resources come from central government transfers. The Argentine federal government must guarantee financial support to these subnational levels in order to keep its governing system functional. Since this political system is highly clientelist, the incentive at the provincial and municipal levels is to ensure that political supporters are "looked after." This comes at a considerable cost to the overall effectiveness of

Table 7.2. Fiscal Decentralization and Subnational Budget Constraints from Brazil and Argentina in Comparative Perspective

	Brazil	Argentina
Governors' Influence over National Policies/Local Policies	Fair/Low	High/High
Amount of Provincial/State Own Collected Revenues over Majority of Expenditure	High	Low
Conditional vs. Unconditional Emphasis on Central Government Grants	Yes	No
Ability to borrow from Domestic Banks or Higher Levels of Bank	No	No
Ability of Center to Enforce Fiscal Discipline at Both Levels	Yes	No
Overall Fiscal Decentralization to Local Level	High	Low

Source: Shah 2007 for Brazil.

federalism in Argentina and the quality of its policy outputs. It would seem from Brazil's example, however, that in order to enforce fend-for-yourself federalism, the president must first decentralize fiscally to the subnational levels, ending the dynamic of punishment-and-reward federalism that is perpetuated by a large vertical fiscal imbalance between what provinces spend and collect. Clearly, in Brazil from 1988 to 1995 such extensive fiscal decentralization did not perform well. However, it certainly altered the rules of the game from this period onward.

Political Regime Type

The last and perhaps most counter-intuitive explanatory factor presented at the beginning of this book was the importance of a country's political regime type, which was broadly conceived within a Lijphart-inspired dichotomous framework of majoritarian versus consensual democracy. Lijphart (2008, 89) argued that a consensual democracy produced "kinder and gentler qualities" when compared to a majoritarian democracy. Among the indicators he listed with these qualities was the welfare state, the kind inspired by European experience. This study has uniquely tested this premise by examining the effects of a more nuanced consensual versus majoritarian argument within two strong federal systems in Latin America. Strong federalism within Brazil's consensual model of democracy over the past two decades has been able to produce a "race to the top" in targeted welfare provisioning that has enabled a "pro-poor" agenda to dominate electoral politics at all levels, across all parties and all ideologies.

In contrast with Brazil, where a highly fragmented party system traditionally created a distinct policy transmission problem (which has slowly improved over the past decade), nominal party dominance in Argentina within the context of a decentralized majoritarian democracy has maintained its policy enforcement problem, in particular when governors are not aligned with the president's ruling coalition. Although I purposively have avoided delving into the complexity of intraparty politics in Argentina, it is essential to grasp that more often than not, the power of majoritarianism at the provincial level has impeded intergovernmental cooperation. Majoritarian political dynamics in Argentina do not suffice as an institutional mechanism to guarantee that intergovernmental competencies will be transformed into policy outputs that are beneficial to the societal whole.

Brazil and Argentina both have presidential systems of government with proportional representation. Each has a bicameral legislature that allows the representation of subnational interests within the national legislature. Moreover, both countries have malapportionment in the lower chamber that is above the world average (Samuels and Snyder 2004, 144). In each case, this characteristic provides less developed and sparsely populated provinces and states with a veto over national reforms that would affect their interests negatively. It also provides the governors of these territories with increased bargaining power over the national executive.

However, Brazil, relative to Argentina, has greater pluralism in its party system and broad coalition cabinets at all three levels of government. In President Lula's first administration, between seven and nine different parties were represented in his cabinet (Amorim Neto 2007). By contrast, in Argentina under President Néstor Kirchner's administration, only one minister in the entire cabinet did not bear the PJ label.[4]

Presidential cabinets in Argentina tend to share the same party label but be split internally; only 25 percent of Kirchner's cabinet belonged to his faction, compared to 47 percent under Menem, even though 95 percent used the PJ label (Leiras 2008).

Contrary to earlier arguments made in the literature, Argentina's successful party system from 1983 on has been considerably challenged and was weakened after 1999. Although it is no longer limited to two parties, it remains today a federal system dominated by internal factions of the PJ at all levels. For example, in 2003, when the PJ assumed control of the federal center after a series of failed presidents, this party alone controlled over 63.14 percent of total institutional power calculated across all three levels at both the executive and legislative level (Medina and Ratto 2006). The stability of democracy in the context of Argentine federalism has arguably come at a price, which has become more salient over time.

Within the PJ, the only party to have produced successful governments since 1983, governability in Argentina can be abstractly conceived as being dependent on the ability of the federal government to increase the interdependence of both itself and the provinces, ensuring that each has leverage over the other. Evidently, Argentina is a strong federal system as defined by Samuels and Mainwaring (2004). High levels of subnational expenditure and a provincially organized party system ensure this characteristic. However, the importance of governors within this system impedes the ability of the federal government to either provide or regulate the quality of public goods. Instead, it produces an inefficient system of federalism, generating policy apathy over national goals at both the provincial and the municipal levels. Moreover, within this federal structure there is little political or electoral incentive for voters to vote out provincial incumbents or to turn their attention to the municipality and do likewise. The fear of punishment operates from both the national government to the provinces (and vice versa) and from the provinces to the municipalities. The implications of this federal game have not facilitated the kind of intergovernmental cooperation that is required to enable an even territorial distribution of targeted social welfare.

The empirical evidence presented here suggests that the degree of majoritarianism present in a federal system affects the willingness of mayors to promote national social investment programs such as CCTs. The lack of a majoritarian imperative within a coalitional-presidential system such as Brazil's needs to be considered when explaining the compliance of municipalities and their political willingness to collaborate with Bolsa Família. Mayors in Brazil, like the president, are motivated to distribute CCTs to their constituents as widely as is permitted within the rules of the program. Disciplined, traditional political parties and political alignments did not matter for the success of Bolsa Família in Brazil.

Because political parties in Argentina are more institutionalized as well as more vertically integrated than parties in Brazil, the willingness of Argentine mayors to promote Programa Familias and assist in terminating PJJHD, knowing that the new program's intention was to bypass the provinces and fortify a direct relationship between the center and its citizens, was lowered. Intergovernmental policy exchanges in Argentina are pervaded by political clienteles and a tit-for-tat mentality that does not foster executives at any level to promote the distribution of targeted social welfare goods when they cannot control their effects.

In the case of Brazil, this book has suggested that the existence of a consensual democracy has facilitated intergovernmental cooperation and the willingness of municipalities to promote the distribution of a national CCT that has now been firmly established in the literature as representing a strategic political resource to the national incumbent (see Zucco 2013). The importance of delivering constituency services and facilitating the distribution of targeted social welfare, however, matters to the incumbent executives at both the national and municipal level. This win-win mentality is greatly improved by the lesser importance of partisanship in Brazilian democracy and opens the door toward cooperative federalism.

By contrast, in Argentina, extensive majoritarianism did not encourage widespread adherence to Programa Familias. There are few incentives for a local official to promote a national CCT if either the mayor or the governor of the mayor's province is not formally aligned with the president's faction. The logic of punishment-and-reward federalism between two dominant levels leads to inconsistent program implementation, policy volatility, and the political allocation of social goods such as occurred in Radicales K provinces, particularly Mendoza. Mendoza was a province that was formally aligned with Kirchner's Frente Para la

Victoria (FPV) in 2006, when it received 43.9 percent of Programa Familia's total allocation and included all eighteen of its municipalities. It received a disproportionate share of this program relative to its poverty line in comparison to other provinces.

In terms of policy volatility, CCTs gradually evolved in Brazil from Cardoso to Lula, and they have been sustained now for over a decade with few changes. Argentina's CCTs, on the other hand, equated to rapid policy developments under Duhalde, which were politically unsustainable; and then to new ideas under Néstor Kirchner, which were politically and institutionally constrained; and then, most recently under Cristina Kirchner, with wholesale policy departures within a new centralized formal insurance-like scheme. There is evidently a trade-off between response time and regime type, which has been well documented by scholars of executive-legislative relations and by Lijphart himself. However, in this social policy area and more generally within a social investment agenda that is based on future-oriented outcomes, rapid policy reforms do not equate to high performance.

BROAD IMPLICATIONS

In addition to the theoretical propositions outlined in chapter 2, this book has broad implications for how federalism and the welfare state should be studied and understood. By reflecting on the discussions surrounding federalism in Latin America, which generally apply a power-distributional approach to understanding the implementation of centralization and decentralization processes and their consequences in the region, this study contributes to two important theoretical debates. Based on a specific research methodology in comparative politics, the performances of two poverty alleviation programs have been highlighted in order to uncover subtle differences between federalism in Brazil and in Argentina, despite their institutional similarities and the strength of their governors. Additionally, the two empirical cases have produced evidence that the federal government cannot "go it alone" when attempting to build a "social investment welfare state" based on future-oriented outcomes. The willingness of mayors to promote policy goals that are nationally desirable may not be politically and fiscally encouraged in all federal systems, particularly those that are "robust" and exhibit high levels of majoritarianism along the executive-parties dimension. This observation points to the need to further validate Lijphart's assertion that more consensual federal democracies exhibit "kinder and gentler qualities," but using contemporary indicators that are part of current global predicaments: these include the ability to create a "social investment welfare state," an "environmentally sustainable state," or "a state where every citizen's security is guaranteed," which is qualitatively different from a traditional "universal" welfare state and requires different kinds of consensus, cooperation, and political commitment—which may not be as readily available in a more majoritarian-based democracy, whether federal or unitary.

FEDERALISM

Each of the two countries under study in this book chose to adopt CCTs in order to promote social inclusion. These were national programs that required local collaboration. Initially, following the relatively parallel regime transitions in Brazil and Argentina during the mid-1980s, new opportunities arose in both countries for social policy experimentation at all levels of government. Both federations struggled to achieve the intended social and economic benefits of democratization and decentralization for a variety of reasons. Particularly evident, however, is the emerging capacity of Brazilian federalism to avoid governors (Dickovick 2006; Borges 2007; Fenwick 2009; Cheibub, Figueiredo, and Limongi 2009) and the lack of opportunity to do likewise in Argentina. What Dickovick (2006) argues is a second-best option to achieve recentralization in Brazil was not available to the national government in neighboring Argentina, regardless of what Stepan (2004, 341) identified as "a partisan-based political party" that is supposed to decrease the robustness of her institutional veto players. Mayors in Argentina are therefore caught between increasing governance challenges in the local and urban areas (such as decaying infrastructures, environmental challenges, poverty, citizen insecurity, informality, unemployment, and inadequate resources) and the reality of a dominant political game that does not encourage them to privilege public policies that benefit the societal whole. Given their dependence on provincial level politics and fiscal resources for their own political survival, bypassing governors is practically impossible. Argentine presidents cannot easily "avoid governors" either. This is the "anomaly" of Argentine democracy.

Of particular interest for scholars of Brazilian and Argentine politics, disaggregating the *subnational* into two distinct players provided a more accurate description of the Brazilian case and challenged the conventional view in the literature that governors can undermine national social policy objectives (Malloy 1993). The Brazilian case within many policy sectors has recently become what Lijphart called a "deviant case" (2008). This is not to say that Brazilian federalism is not "robust," since its strength has been firmly established in the common wisdom of the traditional literature (Abrucio 1998; Samuels and Mainwaring 2004; Stepan 2004; Ames and Power 2006); but it does mean that a modified proposition that includes the strength of municipalities, as distinct from the states, may be better for understanding contemporary Brazil. What I am proposing, in the words of Richard Synder (2001, 95), is a "potentially confounding omitted variable" that requires independent consideration within our analyses.

This research finding has implications for federal theory because it demonstrates that the effect of strong federalism is not constant over all federal cases. Within a multilevel federation, municipalities can reinforce or detract from the ability of governors to constrain the center. Strong federalism will continue to have the ability to undermine the center, and the ability to impede the territorial distribution of citizenship rights. However, this argument assumes that municipalities will *always* behave as creatures of the states or provinces. The ability of the provinces or states to undermine national goals is conditional on the ability of governors to capture the municipalities within their territories.

GLOBAL SOCIAL POLICY

The findings of this study also have policy implications. The territorial expansion of social policy initiatives, particularly when tied to civil, social, and political rights, is important because poverty, social vulnerability, and inequality pose considerable threats to the quality of democracy in developing countries. When individual citizens are cut off from allies and resources already present in the national polity, it means not only a lack of economic resources but also a loss of political voice (Rueschemeyer 2004, 83). The ability of all citizens to use their political voice is of fundamental importance to the practice of democracy. Increasingly, within the new generation of targeted social policy programs framed within a global social investment perspective (basic health, education, productive inclusion, and social protection), the provision of social services is uncomfortably attached to both a "rights-based" agenda and conditionality. The conditions that are attached to CCTs should not be seen as punitive if they are in fact tied to citizenship rights. The only way in which the punitive nature of welfare conditions can be relaxed and the conditions can be viewed instead as a development tool, however, is if local service providers have the power to monitor and investigate why families are struggling the meet the stipulated conditions. If the desired outcome of CCTs is genuinely to increase human investments for future benefit, intergovernmental and bipartisan support is required to ensure both change and continuity. Such support however, is not easily attainable in all democratic governing systems.

APPROACHES TO FUTURE RESEARCH

CCT research has flourished across the social sciences in recent years. Three key research questions surrounding CCTs have been explored, producing important findings. These questions are where CCTs originated and how they were diffused; how they are designed and what is their impact; and whether it can be quantitatively established that they affect electoral outcomes and/or have been politically manipulated. More academic analysis is needed, however, in relation to what Béland and Lecours call the "three major approaches to social policy development" (2008, 219–20): the culturalist model, the power resource approach, and historical institutionalism.

The "Culturalist" and "Power Resource" Approaches

Sugiyama (2013) has importantly touched on the culturalist perspective in her study of CCTs and subnational diffusion during the municipal era in Brazil, where she concluded that subnational diffusion was driven by "principled and other-regarding reasons," not rational (that is, electoral) motivations. Other recent research by Hunter and Sugiyama (2013) on the local meanings of clientelism and citizenship also importantly fit into this approach. Alternatively, the power resource approach is based on class mobilizations. Important scholarly analyses surrounding the question of whether Bolsa Família bought the votes of the poor are cognizant of class divisions (Hunter and Power 2007; Zucco 2008; Power and Zucco 2013). However, these authors were not analyzing how class mobilizations affected the development and sustainability of CCTs per se, and how class mobilizations will affect their sustainability, but rather whether Bolsa Família's success had created an electoral/participation feedback effect for the 2006 and more recently the 2010 general elections. This research stream has demonstrated a socioeconomic cleavage not frequently observed in Brazilian elections. Further research needs to examine both the causes and consequences of this newly visible cleavage for Brazilian democracy.

Historical Institutionalism

The results of my research, which has drawn from a historical approach, are meant to contribute to an understanding of how institutions impact social policy development. Future research may identify earlier trajectories or, as Huber and Stephens (2012) have done, develop the power resources approach from a deeper historical understanding. I have shown that the development of social protection policy in Brazil was shaped by Brazilian federalism itself. Formal political institutions had already affected the way interest groups and territorial entities accessed political resources and influenced "pro-poor" policymaking in Brazil, even before, as Zucco says, "scholars and pundits noticed this program" (2013, 811). Argentine federalism also shaped the development of this country's social investment initiatives; their underperformance is not a consequence of either poor design or the roles played by international organizations, but rather of the structural, fiscal, and political constraints that affect the territorial distribution of targeted social policy goods.

Beyond the role of formal political institutions, I have also referred to the idea of policy feedbacks to describe how previously enacted policies in both countries impacted the development and design of both programs and, subsequently, how the feedbacks of these programs themselves have recently contributed to their "change and continuity" or their termination. It was evident in chapters 3 and 5 that key decision makers in the governments of both Lula and Néstor Kirchner took into account the vested interests created by Bolsa Escola and PJJHD, contributing to the performance of Bolsa Família and the eventual termination of Programa Familias. Quite simply, Lula wanted to expand and entrench Bolsa Escola's interests within his CCT, while Kirchner wanted to maintain PJJHD's interest groups but minimize their uncontrolled expansion. Municipalities had a key role to play in each case. Bolsa Família not only created a powerful constituency (the program's 44 million beneficiaries) that will continue to consolidate CCTs into the future, but the extent of its territorial penetration also helped consolidate the role of municipalities within Brazilian federalism. Scholars of global social policy and international development practitioners should take "going local" much more seriously. This does not signify a return to the bottom-up democratization strand of comparative politics of the post-transition period. Rather, it implies the need for a revised literature that recognizes the ability of municipalities to collaborate with higher levels of government in order to regulate and provide access to the public goods that are most needed in their territory.

Today, there are an increasing number of examples of successful city-based governments and local policy experimentation (for instance, participatory budgeting, urban food programs, noncontributory conditional cash transfers, and early childhood education and primary care health programs) in Brazil and, to a lesser extent, in Argentina and Mexico. In these instances, medium- to large-sized municipalities have been able to dislodge the electoral dominance of hegemonic regional elites through a *policy*-led path, which, like the *party*-led path described by Gibson (2008), takes place within the local institutional status quo. Particularly interesting is that many of these local policy innovations were later nationalized, yet continued to rely on local governments for their promotion. Writing considerably before the economic boom, Jonathan Fox called such social initiatives "the new generation of demand-driven partnership programs" (1994, 115). After nationalization (or diffusion, for those who prefer that concept), these initiatives became both supply-driven and demand-driven intergovernmental partnerships. These partnerships, however, whether bottom-up or top-down, should be national-local strategies because ultimately (and constitutionally) the federal government is responsible for guaranteeing the social rights of citizenship, and spatially, only groups and individuals at the local level really know what goods and services will end the intergenerational transmission of poverty in their areas. Mayors can most certainly empower and facilitate local actors access points to national resources that have already been selected to achieve this end.

Evidence from Latin America on the use of CCTs to achieve social inclusion and extend territorially the social rights of citizenship has great potential both in the region and beyond, but significant attention must be given to domestic constraints. In relation to questions about the value of subnational CCTs, a former Brazilian minister of social development and former mayor commented: "The states and municipalities cannot replace the national government" (interview Ananias 2006). By the same token, the Argentine national government (or any other federal government) also cannot replace the states and municipalities.

CASES FOR FUTURE RESEARCH:
CCT EMULATION AND DIFFUSION

In addition to the two case studies in this book, other cases throughout the region and beyond allow us to explore the links between regime type, local government participation, and CCTs. Following the "municipal era" of CCT development in Brazil discussed in this book (1995–2001), other countries in the region created national-level CCTs based on the idea of alleviating poverty through investing in human capital development. Presently, more than thirty countries throughout the developing world now have active CCT programs. In 2009, for example, the World

Bank provided US$2.4 billion to scale up and start CCT operations.[5] From an international development perspective, the idea of CCTs as an effective policy instrument for alleviating poverty, tied to human capital and social development goals, enjoys a broad consensus of support from international organizations and national governments throughout the developing world, a consensus that was originally based on the experience of countries in Latin America.

This consensus and the rate of emulation and spread of CCTs linked to human development are largely to be attributed to the early and rapid successes of national-level CCTs in Mexico (1997) and Brazil (2001) and their established positive impact—which, beyond providing high promise, garnered international support for this policy instrument. Even though Mexico's national experience predated that of Brazil's by three and half years, in the eyes of the world the fame, success, and sheer size of Brazil's most recent CCT program, Bolsa Família, have largely promoted this model for emulation in particular throughout Africa. Brazil's successful domestic performance and international promotion of its CCT experience has prompted other countries to adopt similar policy innovations. These new experiments, however, can also overestimate the success of these innovations on a very limited base of experience.

There is no doubt that both the Brazilian and Mexican CCTs, each implemented in large federal countries, have produced positive outcomes. Both programs roughly touch one in every four citizens in large populations—198 million in Brazil, 112 million in Mexico—and each program has been sustained through changes in executive power, inclusive of a change in the governing political party. Rigorous program impact evaluations have also been compiled. Each pioneering program was shaped by domestic context; the Brazilian model is far more decentralized than Mexico's Progresa-Opportunidades-Prospera, and Brazilian federalism is far more decentralized than Mexico's. However, from a social investment perspective, local promotion and monitoring, particularly in terms of the rate of inclusion and the supply side, are fundamental to the successful territorial distribution and future-oriented goals of such social programs. CCTs should not be thought of, as Santiago Levy suggests, "as a kind of social security program" (2006, 97). That description would approximate the current goals of Argentina's AUH, although ironically even Mexico's centralized program is not run by the equivalent formal arm of the national executive branch, that is, the IMSS (Mexico's public health and social security agency), like the current Argentine program under ANSES.[6]

For international supporters of targeted social investments, such as the OECD, the World Bank, the Inter-American Development Bank, and a host of UN agencies, particularly UNICEF, the value of CCTs is intrinsically linked to their ability to shape the future (by breaking the intergenerational transmission of poverty), to invest in children (who embody the future society and its economy), and to invest in so-called human capital (health and education). Therefore, the role of municipalities in promoting CCTs to families not registered on already existing central databases, and the benefits of local monitoring of the ability of recipients to fulfill the program's stipulated conditions (as is now common practice in Brazil) should be an internationally supported priority over the more punitive (centralized) conceptions of welfare conditionality.

As Levy, the designer of the first national integrated CCT, admits, "A potential trade-off exists between centralized program administration and the quality of services received by program beneficiaries" (2006, 100). He further asserts that this trade-off can be minimized by intergovernmental cooperation across agencies and ministries, but that this result depends on the extent to which central representatives pursue quality control as part of their agenda with state governments, and also on the commitment of governors (and/or mayors) to poverty alleviation (2006, 100). CCTs will thus place different demands on intergovernmental relationships, with the onus on presidents to achieve the policy collaboration required not only for efficient CCT performance but also for effective CCT performance.

In highlighting the role of municipalities and their ability to promote national policy objectives in the present study, my hope is that this book will contribute to future scholarship on the politics of alleviating poverty in highly decentralized federal and unitary democracies. Most of the research surrounding federalism has been quite skeptical regarding its effect on producing development, democracy, and the welfare state. There are, however, nuanced yet important differences across federal systems. Weak governors can become stronger when they unite with mayors, weak presidents can become stronger united with mayors, and strong governors can become weaker when mayors are supported by the central government. By distinguishing municipalities as a separate actor in a federal political system, a dynamic intergovernmental relationship is represented; indeed, we observe power struggles between multiple levels of government and their electorates, not merely a dichotomously framed game of the national level versus the subnational. As the case studies here demonstrate, this dynamic has important implications for both social and political outcomes.

APPENDIX

Table A.1. Characteristics of Brazilian Political Decentralization after 1988

Brazil	Federal Level	State Level (27)	Municipal (5,564)
Constitutional Autonomy	Yes	Yes	Yes
Autonomous Courts	Yes	Yes	No
Direct Elections	Yes	Yes	Yes
Reelection	Once consecutively	Once consecutively	Once consecutively
Bicameral	Yes	Yes	Yes
Representation in Congress	Yes	de facto: Lower de jure: Upper	No
Requirement for Amending National Constitution	3/5 both houses plus two rounds of roll-call voting	de jure: none de facto: governor power over legislators	None
Institutional Uniformity	Yes	Yes (except Brasilía)	Yes
Timing of Elections	Simultaneous; every 4 yrs	Simultaneous; every 4 yrs	Staggered two years after federal/state elections; every 4 yrs
Vertical Integration with Incumbent President's Party	Lower/Upper		
PT 2010	17/17 (%)	19%	17% - 2012[a]
PT 2006	16/15 (%)	19%	7% - 2004[a]
PSDB 1998	19/16 (%)	26%	18% - 2000[a]

[a] Municipal election dates do not coincide with presidential/gubernatorial election dates.

Table A.2. Aggregating Argentine Provinces According to Partisanship
Based on Electoral Results, 2003–2005

Province	Governor	Legislative 2003 (% PJ-Official)	Presidential 2003 (highest vote per candidate)	Legislative 2005 (% FPV/PJ)	Partisan Grouping for Program Analysis
SE	UCR[a]	53%	Menem	73%	**No/Rad-K**
Mendoza	UCR	35%	Sáa	21%	Rad-K
Corrientes	UCR	34%	Menem	28%	Rad-K
Rio Negro	UCR	30%	Kirchner	43%	Rad-K
Catamarca	UCR	53%	Menem	54%	**No/Rad-K**
CBA	Independent	0%	Murphy	20%	**No Adhesion**
Chaco	UCR-Official	43%	Menem	30%	Opposition
La Pampa	PJ-D	18%	Menem	50%	**No Adhesion**
Neuquén	MPN-D	13%	Menem	35%	**No Adhesion**
Salta	PJ-D	49%	Menem	47%	PJ-Dissident
San Luis	PJ-D	0%	Sáa (88%)	20%	PJ-Dissident
Santa Fe	PJ	0%	Menem	33%	Opposition
Tierra Fuego	UCR	0%	Kirchner	33%	Opposition
Buenos Aires	PJ	41%	Kirchner	43%	FPV
Chubut	PJ	46%	Kirchner	52%	FPV
Cordoba	PJ	33%	Menem	63%	FPV
Entre Rios	PJ	45%	Menem	60%	FPV
Formosa	PJ	72%	Kirchner	61%	FPV
Jujuy	PJ	57%	Kirchner	48%	FPV
La Rioja	PJ	66%	Menem	55%	FPV
Misiones	PJ	46%	Menem	47%	FPV
San Juan	PJ	40%	Menem	59%	FPV
Santa Cruz	PJ	75%	Kirchner	51%	FPV
Tucuman	PJ	18%	Menem	64%	FPV

Source: Author elaboration based on data from Cheresky and Blanquer 2004; Medina and
Ratto 2006.
Notes: These groupings were based on intergovernmental party-based alignments when the
analysis was completed in late 2006. This is a very fast-moving target.
Excluded groups in table are in bold.
[a] Post-intervention.

Table A.3. Actual Targeting of Provinces for Programa Familias (PF) 2006 and Estimates of Ideal Based on Program Criteria

Province	Municipalities	PJJHD 2005	# of H poverty line	# of households	10% pop	60% PJJHD	30% poverty	Ideal #	2006 PF	Actual
Buenos Aires	10	532,808	823,407	3,920,985	392,099	319,685	247,022	958,805	111,414.00	11.6%
Catamarca	0	27,799	32,113	77,755	7,776	16,679	9,634	34,089	–	0.0%
CBA	0	34,003	74,769	1,024,231	102,423	20,402	22,431	145,256	–	0.0%
Chaco	32	101,529	102,621	238,100	23,810	60,917	30,786	115,514	17,402.00	15.1%
Chubut	5	8,114	34,763	238,100	23,810	4,868	10,429	39,107	3,658.00	9.4%
Córdoba	24	84,414	197,340	877,065	87,707	50,648	59,202	197,557	33,873.00	17.1%
Corrientes	1	56,026	99,386	225,878	22,588	33,616	29,816	86,019	10,873.00	12.6%
Entre Ríos	18	37,192	102,595	316,651	31,665	22,315	30,778	84,759	5,818.00	6.9%
Formosa	1	46,683	44,939	114,349	11,435	28,010	13,482	52,926	4,580.00	8.7%
Jujuy	2	49,841	16,421	141,559	14,156	29,905	4,926	48,987	6,541.00	13.4%
La Pampa	0	8,283	19,431	91,656	9,166	4,970	5,829	19,965	–	0.0%
La Rioja	4	16,548	18,531	68,379	6,838	9,929	5,559	22,326	3,460.00	15.5%
Mendoza	18	38,498	99,711	410,332	41,033	23,099	29,913	94,045	41,275.00	43.9%
Misiones	19	30,472	93,490	234,899	23,490	18,283	28,047	69,820	19,906.00	28.5%
Neuquén	0	14,501	33,105	128,313	12,831	8,701	9,931	31,463	–	0.0%
Río Negro	9	17,227	32,734	154,405	15,441	10,336	9,820	35,597	6,427.00	18.1%
Santiago del Estero	0	56,377	65,919	178,160	17,816	33,826	19,776	71,418	–	0.0%
Salta	15	28,766	94,099	241,279	24,128	17,260	28,230	69,617	24,858.00	35.7%
San Juan	12	13,910	2,829	148,869	14,887	8,346	849	24,081	8,632.00	35.8%
San Luis	1	1,768	26,524	101,623	10,162	1,061	7,957	19,180	3,179.00	16.6%
Santa Cruz	2	134,950	3,606	53,825	5,383	80,970	1,082	87,434	167.00	0.2%
Santa Fe	39	45,598	206,695	872,132	87,213	27,359	62,009	176,581	33,652.00	19.1%
Tierra del Fuego	2	1,326	2,002	27,812	2,781	796	601	4,178	876.00	21.0%
Tucumán	18	66,050	117,435	310,674	31,067	39,630	35,230	105,928	34,699.00	32.8%
Total	232	1,452,683	2,344,463	10,197,031				2,594,652	371,290.00	14.3%

Table A.4. Characteristics of Argentine Political Decentralization

	Federal Level	Provincial Level 23 + 1	Municipal 1,178 + 977[a]
Constitutional Autonomy	Yes	Yes	No[b]
Autonomous	Yes	Yes	No
Autonomous Courts	Yes	Yes	No
Direct Elections	Yes	Yes	Yes
Reelection	Yes (once)	Yes	Yes
Bicameral	Yes	Mixed	No
Representation in Congress	Yes	Yes	No
Institutional Uniformity	Yes	No	No
Timing of Elections	Mixed[c]	Governors set until 2007[d]	Dependent on provincial constitution
Partisan Harmony	1987–2007	1987–2007[e]	1983–1999
PJ Average (%)	49.3/55.3[f]	66	51.1
UCR Average (%)	26.3/26.2[f]	19	36

[a] Municipalities plus local units with other names.
[b] Some municipalities have autonomy sanctioned by provincial constitutions.
[c] Mixed electoral cycle (1/3 of National Congress renewed every two years); presidential and legislative elections held concurrently in 2006.
[d] Electoral calendar for national legislative and provincial governorships set by provinces until 2007.
[e] 1999 calculated as "Alianza."
[f] Upper House on left, Lower House on right.

NOTES

CHAPTER 1. THE POLITICS OF ALLEVIATING POVERTY AND WHY FEDERALISM MATTERS

1. The fourth large federation, Venezuela, is not studied in this book.

2. Data supplied directly by the Office of Program Familias, Subsecretaría de Organización de Ingresos Sociales, Ministerio de Desarrollo Social. Data corresponds to December 2006. In the "Resumen Ejectutivo" (see Ministerio de Desarrollo Social 2007), final reported territorial inclusion for 2006 was reported as slightly higher, at 389,000 beneficiaries in 258 municipalities.

3. Thanks to Lena Lavinas (private consultation 2014) for stressing that I clarify this point at the beginning of the book.

4. An extended discussion of labeling Brazil as a "consensual democracy" and the history of this classification is included in chapter 4. A more acceptable alternative for some readers would have been to label it as a "coalitional-presidential" model (see Power 2010). However, the focus here is not on executive-legislative relations per se but, more broadly, on defining the logic of Brazilian federal democracy.

5. See Power (2010) for a thorough discussion of this debate.

6. This was motivated by earlier criticisms received from Anthony Hall for not having explored sufficiently the international perspective.

7. Local governments have different names in certain Argentine provinces, such as *communas* or departments.

8. There has never been a formal partisan alignment among these three highly competitive levels of government.

9. This subnational CCT has been under the leadership of the same director since 2006 and has survived an alternation of three administrations, the last one being a complete change from the PJ to the right of center opposition PRO. This is an example of a CCT in Argentina that represents both "change" and "continuity"—the City of Buenos Aires is also governed by a multiparty coalition government.

10. Latinobarometro measures public opinion and attitudes toward democracy throughout the Latin American region. See http://www.latinobaro metro.org/lat.jsp.

CHAPTER 2. FEDERALISM, THE WELFARE STATE, AND THE RISE OF CCTS IN LATIN AMERICA

1. See, for example, Hall 2007.
2. See, for example, Obinger, Leibfried, and Castles 2005.
3. See, for example, Rice and Prince 2013.
4. This term was developed by Giddens (1998) and Esping-Andersen et al. (2002) to describe a contemporary welfare state where social investments in education and training, with a particular focus on children (the life-cycle approach), could create an "active" welfare state that required individual contributions. It has normally been applied to Europe.
5. This methodological approach to studying the politics of policies in Latin America was developed by Stein et al. (2005).
6. This is not an exhaustive list.
7. Institute of Development Studies (IDS), in *Focus*, Issue 1, May 2006, www.ids.ac.uk.
8. Briggs defines a "social service state" as a state "narrowing the extent of personal insecurity through guaranteeing families a minimum income" and "protecting citizens from individual and family crises through enabling them to meet certain social contingencies (food shortages, sickness, unemployment)" (Briggs 2006, 16–17).
9. Thanks to Kênia Parsons and Elaine Licio for sharing their research insights and information on this issue.
10. See, for example, the article "Economic Sense: A Model for Evaluating the Use of Development Dollars South of the Border" by Alan Krueger in the *New York Times*, May 2, 2002.
11. Dates for CCT adoption are taken from Sugiyama (2011, 256), except for Argentina, where our dates do not concur.
12. For an excellent study of the mechanisms that fuelled CCT diffusion throughout Brazil, see Sugiyama 2013.
13. See part 11 of FHC's *Veja* interviews by Augusto Nunes, "Programa Sociais o Bolsa Familia," November 11, 2009, at https://www.youtube.com/user /vejapontocom/videos.
14. PRONASOL was heavily influenced by Salinas 1978.
15. In 1982 Mexico defaulted on its foreign debt payments due to economic difficulties arising out of both rising US interest rates and globally falling commodity prices. This event marked the start of what would be more than a decade of macroeconomic catastrophes throughout Latin America.
16. This quotation, originally by Richard Simeon in his "The Political Context for Renegotiating Fiscal Federalism," p. 136, is given by Rodden (2001, 5).
17. Besides Mexico, Venezuela, Argentina, and Brazil, the Bolivian Constitution is considered to be essentially federal in character, while

post-democratization Chile is also divided between three *de jure* (central, regional, and local) political-territorial divisions.

18. Falleti (2003) focuses on this in her research about the timing and sequencing of reforms.

19. I am referring here to the excellent case studies of Santiago del Estero in Argentina and Oaxaca in Mexico documented by Edward Gibson (2004) and Fox's pioneering work on Mexico's transition from clientelism to citizenship (1994).

20. See Gibson 2012.

21. James Malloy (1993) asserted that the real issue in Latin America was not one of "political will" but of government capacity to define, implement, and sustain policies.

22. Subnational party stability is not a bad thing in itself, but it can lead to what Gibson called the "federalization of party politics," which results, more often than not, in a two-level, zero-sum federal game. On "boundary control," see Gibson 2012.

23. The 1994 reform to the Argentine Constitution granted autonomy to the City of Buenos Aires and reorganized the territorial division of powers.

24. An attempt to reform the territorial division of powers in Canada, known as the Charlottetown Accord, failed in 1992, ten years after negotiations had begun.

25. Venezuela, the remaining federal country in the Americas, is omitted from this list because of its currently void sense of constitutionalism.

26. According to World Bank sources, subnational debt in the late 1990s in Mexico equalled only 2 percent of GDP, compared to 7 percent in Argentina, 20 percent in Brazil, and 23 percent in Canada (Guigale, Trillo, and Oliveira 2000).

27. Kornai's theory of soft budget constraints is not restricted to governments; it is developed more broadly to apply to organizations and enterprises. I have relied on this theory in developing my own understanding of how a soft budget syndrome applies to the Latin American federal context.

28. "Uninstitutionalized bargaining" is a term developed by Filippov, Ordeshook, and Shvetsova. They define it as "a situation in which there is no such sustainable system of constraints, and in the limit, when nearly every rule and institution becomes subject to negotiation and change" (2004, 78).

CHAPTER 3. AVOIDING GOVERNORS AND THE SUCCESS OF CCTS IN BRAZIL

1. This problem identified by Camargo and Barros is the same as that identified by Salinas in his 1978 Harvard dissertation. Camargo went on to become a "PT economist" and participated in various PT conferences during the

early 1990s, and Salinas went on to develop PRONASOL and become president of Mexico (1988–1994).

2. In this light, it is also important to note, within the historical evolution of such programs, that the foundations of Bolsa Escola did not have a partisan-based ownership. This policy idea was neither Cardoso's nor that of his party, the PSDB.

3. Figures are based on IBGE data for the number of people living in permanent houses/number of permanent households in Brazil (2000). http://www.ibge.gov.br/home/estatistica/populacao/censo2000/tabelabrasil131.shtm.

4. These percentages are extremely high when compared to other campaign promises that were surveyed at the same time by IBOPE on November 12, 2002.

5. Confirmed informally in numerous interviews with state-level bureaucrats in social development sectors and in policy groups at the Pontifícia Universidade Católica de São Paulo.

6. This hypothesis was prevalent in Brazilian media circles prior to the 2006 presidential election; see, for instance, "Dividir Para Governar," *Veja*, September 6, 2006.

CHAPTER 4. FACTORS ENCOURAGING MUNICIPAL ACTORS TO PROMOTE NATIONAL GOALS IN BRAZIL

1. Brazil is institutionally uniform and symmetric, although Brasília, the national capital, does not have the same characteristics of either the states or the municipalities.

2. For example, see Abrucío 1998 and Samuels 2003.

3. The term *política dos governadores* means literally "the politics of governors" and was coined by President Campos Salles in 1900 (Fausto and Devoto 2004, 524).

4. The 2005 IDB report *The Politics of Policies* by Stein et al. ranked Brazil as "high" in its overall index of quality of public policies in Latin America (second only to Chile).

5. See http://www.ibge.gov.br/home/estatistica/populacao/censo2010/indicadores_sociais_municipais/tabelas_pdf/tab15.pdf. "Indicadores Sociais Municipais: Uma análise dos resultados do universo do Censo Demográfico 2010." This is a synthesis of the 2010 Census under the authority and authorship of the IBGE.

6. A discussion of the role of government in urban development would go beyond the scope of this study.

7. This retention of federal revenues was reestablished in 1999 (Arretche 2007).

8. For more research putting forward the consensual classification, see Anastasia, Melo, and Santos 2004; Anastasia and Nunes 2006.

9. Measured according to Laakso and Taagepera (1979).

10. Few states have opted to do this, and for those that had signed agreements, the agreements were often not carried out or remained active for only a few months.

11. See additionally Licio 2012.

12. From January 1, 2003, to January 22, 2004, the governing coalition included the PT (Workers' Party), PL (Liberal Party), PCdoB (Communist Party), PSB (Brazilian Socialitst Party), PTB (Brazilian Labour Party), PDT (Democratic Labour Party), PPS (Popular Syndicalist Party), and PV (Green Party).

13. Coalition data taken from A. Figueiredo 2007.

CHAPTER 5. CCTS IN ARGENTINA AND THE POLITICS OF ALLEVIATING POVERTY

1. The Ministry of Labor and Welfare was created in 1944 (Ministerio de Trabajo y Prevision, 1944 until 1971). Its name was changed to Ministerio de Trabajo y Seguridad Social in 1971, until 1999, when the Ministry of Social Development was created. Thereafter it became known simply as the Ministry of Labor and Employment (Ministerio de Trabajo y Empleo).

2. On the "global discourse," see Jenson 2010 and Morel, Palier, and Palme 2012.

3. When the bulk of this research was undertaken and the interviews occurred, Programa Familias was still in operation.

4. Argentine political scientist Ana-María Mustapic argues that the PJ can only command the loyalties of its members when it is in a position of strength (interview Mustapic 2006).

5. This is also the predominant explanation offered for such programs in Central America; see Dresser 1991.

6. As with Itamar Franco and his then finance minister, Fernando Henrique Cardoso, Menem's reforms were given to him in 1991 by his minister of finance, Domingo Cavallo. The continuity of political parties before and after the military period, however, meant that Cavallo had no way to ascend through the PJ ranks and take credit for his plan in 1995. Cavallo started his own party, called "Action for the Republic," in 1996 after being fired by Menem. He ran under this label against de la Rúa in 1999 and lost.

7. The UCEDE, or Union of the Democratic Center, was a center-right third party, which Menem was able ingeniously to co-opt by fusing neo-populism and neoliberalism into the political identity of the PJ party.

8. This workfare program provided $160 pesos a month to families below the poverty line in exchange for six hours of daily labor in official community projects.

9. Social exclusion is more directly related to neoliberal reforms in Argentina than in Brazil, where its causes are more structural.

10. "Hyperpresidentialism" refers to a political system where the role of legislators in shaping policy outcomes is limited because their preferences are superseded by those of the president.

11. PJJHD, like Plan Trabajar, was intended to guarantee every family a right to a basic income of $150 pesos a month in exchange for community-based labor.

12. As a former minister of social development at both the national and provincial level (Buenos Aires), Cafiero asserted that the locally based *contrapresaciones* (localized workfare conditions) were pursued by local leaders, not Duhalde, in 2002.

13. I am referring here not only to elected authorities but also to union leaders, syndicates, and political actors with electoral aspirations.

14. The official list closed in La Matanza at the level of 36,253 and peaked during the month of the election at 87,252. The 51,000 recipients of PJJHD are not registered in the municipal records (interview Colicigno 2006).

15. Both current and former senior staff from Desarrollo Social in 2006 (plus anonymous sources in the Ministry of Labor) all confirmed in interviews conducted in Buenos Aires that the distribution of PJJHD had been manipulated for political ends.

16. According to Levy, this design was likewise unpopular with state-level representatives, who initially complained about their lack of involvement (interview 2013). National legislators in Mexico, however, do not answer to governors to the extent they do in Argentina. In fact, the greatest difference between the Mexican CCTs and others in the region is that the Mexican CCTs are financed out of the annual federal budget, so they are the product of executive-legislative bargaining.

17. Electoral data obtained from the Ministry of Interior.

18. FPV is the name of the national electoral alliance of the PJ aligned with the president.

19. Data calculated from the Ministry of Governance, Buenos Aires.

20. Thanks are due to Ana-María Mustapic, Di Tella University, Buenos Aires, for this discussion.

21. Figures are based on information supplied by the national office of Familias in September 2006.

22. It had peaked in June 2003 at 1,978,149 beneficiaries (Ministry of Labor).

23. These same deficiencies are highlighted in Spiller and Tommasi 2007.

24. The issue of children and of whether families without children eventually would be eligible for the base amount has not been a key issue discussed in Argentine policy circles. Arroyo stated that the program was conceived as a right, and was not linked conceptually to the development of children in particular (interview 2006).

25. The Radicales K were composed of members of the traditional opposition party, the UCR, who aligned themselves with the Kirchners' PJ alliance, the FPV.

26. Data used for the Institutional Composition of Power were calculated by Medina and Ratto (2006).

27. The table using electoral results (appendix, table A.2) can mainly justify why provinces are in the given groups, although a few outliers existed that were intuitive. I thank Marcelo Leiras for helping me codify the provinces. Any errors are, of course, my own.

28. The following is only a partial list of studies that primarily use patronage to understand contemporary Argentine politics: Auyero 2000; Gordin 2002; Brusco, Nazareno, and Stokes 2004; Calvo and Murillo 2004; Calvo and Micozzi 2005; Remmer 2007.

29. ANSES, the National Administration of Social Security, is the national government bureaucracy that runs AUH.

30. This is parallel to what also occurs in Mexico, given that the "punitive" nature of conditions is controlled exclusively from the center (see Yanes 2013).

31. See, for example, *El Clarín*, January 13, 2015, "La Inflación llegó al 38.7% en 2014," and January 31, 2015, "Una Medida que es Consequencia de la Inflación."

CHAPTER 6. FACTORS IMPEDING MUNICIPAL ACTORS FROM PROMOTING NATIONAL GOALS IN ARGENTINA

1. Braun and Ardanaz (2008) describe Argentine governors as the "kings" of public policymaking.

2. This is Malamud and de Luca's definition of success, which makes no reference to the quality of the implemented policies (2005, 4).

3. Filippov, Ordeshook, and Shvetsova define an "ideal federal party" as one in which the party's organization exists at all levels, and where its electoral success at the national level facilitates the electoral success of candidates at the local and provincial level, yet where regional and local branches and candidates of the party retain significant autonomy (2004, 192).

4. Jones and Mainwaring (2008) assert that Argentina, Brazil, and Canada empirically have the least nationalized party system in the Americas, calculated until 2000.

5. Only in Córdoba and Jujuy do municipalities have taxing authority (Clemente and Smulovitz 2004).

6. This is based on data from the Direción Electoral National (Minstry of Interior) and the Jefatura de Gabienete (1999) supplied by Medina (interview 2006).

7. My hypothesis here was tested further by Gibson and subsequently confirmed (see Gibson 2012, 154).

8. This was asserted by the president of the Argentine Federation of Municipalities (and mayor of Florencio Varela) when asked why municipalities did not horizontally coordinate to push for greater autonomy (interview Pereyra 2006).

9. The only two plausible exceptions to this generalization are the major urban cities of Buenos Aires and Rosario. Buenos Aires City, however, is entirely autonomous.

10. The comparative graph for Brazil is available in chapter 4, as figure 4.2. I took great care to examine what was actually included in the disaggregated social spending, and aggregated it individually in order to ensure that the same policy areas were included in "social expenditure" across the two countries.

11. This was equally confirmed in an interview with Maria-Eugenia Schmuck (2006).

12. In his detailed case study, Entin (2004, 142) uses the "Duhalde conducción" to explain how Balestrini was able to defeat his rival Ledesma in the heated PJ interna in La Matanza in 2003. He defines it according to the work of Argentine political scientist Juan Carlos Torre as the situation where a candidate for office appeared on campaign posters throughout the province during the 1990s with images of Eva Perón and Juan Perón and the PJ official stamp, as a way for the provincial PJ, controlled by Duhalde, to signal to voters which candidates were loyal to them so that those voters could identify with the party's choice.

13. Balestrini continued his political trajectory upward, which culminated in his election as vice governor of the Province of Buenos Aires from 2007 to 2011, after which he was forced to retire from politics.

14. Based on Malamud and de Luca's (2005) classification, but updated to include the 2007 general elections.

15. There is limited aggregate electoral data available for the municipal level.

16. All presidents since 1983 have been from the PJ, except Raúl Alfonsín from 1983 to 1989 and de la Rúa from 1999 to 2001. These two were from the UCR. Both were unable to finish their term of office.

17. It is important to recall that both of the national CCTs that reformed and replaced earlier social programs occurred at similar times, and that both of these opinion surveys occurred at parallel end dates, making them highly comparable.

CHAPTER 7. FEDERALISM AND THE TERRITORIAL DISTRIBUTION OF TARGETED SOCIAL WELFARE

1. See an alternate use of these conclusions in Gibson (2012, 154), where my observations are confirmed.

2. The interview took place on a morning when city police officers had been photographed giving out drugs to children for consumption, in order to alleviate their hunger. As a consequence, Pesaro's efforts to assist vulnerable children within the city were being heavily criticized in the media as insufficient.

3. Thanks again to Ana-María Mustapic for explaining this characteristic (interview 2006).

4. Information on cabinet composition provided by Marcelo Leiras, University of San Andres.

5. Data available at http://web.worldbank.org.

6. When I asked Levy why Mexico's program was not run by the IMSS, he responded, "The IMSS is hardly politically neutral" (interview Levy 2013).

REFERENCES

INTERVIEWS

Ananias, Patrus. 2006. Ministro do Desenvolvimento Social e Combate à Fome. February 2. São Paulo.

Anonymous MDS. 2006. Ministério de Desenvolvimento Social, Brazil, Gabineto do Ministro. February 2. São Paulo.

Anonymous Ministerio de Desarrollo Social. 2006. Asesor Técnico por Programa Familias por la Inclusión Social, Subsecretraría de Organización de Ingresos Sociales. August 30. Buenos Aires.

Anonymous Ministerio de Trabajo, Empleo, y Securidad Social. 2006. Asesor Técnico por Programa Jefes y Jefas de Hogares Desocupados. October 5. Buenos Aires.

Anonymous Secretaria de Assistência Social, Prefeitura de São Paulo. 2006. February 11. São Paulo.

Arretche, Marta. 2006. Research Associate, CEBRAP (Centro Brasileiro Análise Planejamento Cebrap). February 4. São Paulo.

Arroyo, Daniel. 2006. Secretario de Desarrollo Social de la Nación, Ministerio de Desarrollo Social. October 12. Buenos Aires.

Bonari, Damien. 2006. Dirección de Análisis de Gasto Público y Programas Sociales, Ministério de Economía y Hacienda. September 19/October 3. Buenos Aires.

Cafiero, Juan Pablo. 2006. United Nations Development Program, Resident Coordinator Argentina. (Former Minister of Social Development, Province of Buenos Aires). October 12. Buenos Aires.

Castro Guimarães de, Maria Helena. 2006. Secretária do Estado de São Paulo, Secretária Estadual do Desenvolvimento Social São Paulo. February 2. São Paulo.

Colicigno, Antonio. 2006. Presidente de la Unidad de Desarrollo Socio-Sanitario del Municipio de La Matanza. September 30. San Justo.

Espinoza, Adriana. 2006. Coordinadora Técnica y de Planeamiento de Promoción del Sector Social de la Economía, Ministerio de Trabajo, Empleo, y Seguros Sociales de la Nación. September 21. Buenos Aires.

Figueiredo, Argelina. 2005. Professora do Instituto de Estudos Sociais e Políticos de Universidade Estadual do Rio de Janeiro. Consulted November 17. Salvador, Bahia.

Fonseca Ana. 2006. Secretária Adjunta da Bolsa Família, Ministério do Desenvolimento Social. February 25. Telephone. Brasília.

Ibarra, Aníbal. 2006. Ex-Jefe del Gobierno, Ciudad Autónoma de Buenos Aires. October 11. Buenos Aires.

Lavinas, Lena. 2014. Professora do Instituto de Economias, Universidade Federal de Rio de Janeiro. Consulted July 17. Yokohama.

Leiras, Marcelo. 2006. Profesor de Ciencia Política y Relaciones Internationales, Universidad de San Andrés. Consulted August 28. Buenos Aires.

Levy, Santiago. 2013. Vice-President for Sector and Knowledge, Inter-American Development Bank, and former general director of Instituto Mexicano de Seguros Sociales Mexico. May 31. Washington, DC.

Lindert, Kathy, Ana Fruttero, and Joana Silva. 2013. World Bank Human Development Department (Joint Meeeting). May 30. Washington, DC.

Marques, Rosa. 2006. Research Associate, Pontificia Universidade Católica de São Paulo. Focus Group PUC-SP. February 16. São Paulo.

Medina, Juan Abal. 2006. Secretario de Gestión Pública de Jefatura de Ministros de la Nación Argentina. September 15. Buenos Aires.

Mustapic, Ana-María. 2006. Professora de Ciencia Política, Universidad Torcuato di Tella. August 17. Buenos Aires.

Pereyra, Julio. 2006. Presidente de la Federación Argnetina de Municipios (FAM) and Intendente de Florencio Varela, Buenos Aires. October 4. Buenos Aires.

Pesaro, Floriano. 2006. Secretário do Desenvolvimento Social da Cidade de São Paulo. February 11. São Paulo.

Pochmann, Marcio. 2006. Ex-Secretário de Trabalho e Solidariedade de São Paulo (2001–2004). February 23. Campinas.

Pucciarelli, Pablo. 2006. Dirección General de Ciudadanía Porteña, Autonomous City of Buenos Aires. September 29. Buenos Aires.

Rubio, María Elena. 2006. Secretaria del Consejo Nacional de Administración, Ministerio de Trabajo, Empleo, y Seguros Sociales de la Nación. October 10. Buenos Aires.

Schmuck, Maria-Eugenia. 2006. Concejal de la Ciudad de Rosario, Santa Fé. September 28. Buenos Aires.

Souza, Celina. 2005. Professora de Ciencia Politica, Universidade Federal da Bahia. November (various). Salvador.

Sposati, Aldaísa. 2006. Ex-Secretária de Assistência Social da Cidade de São Paulo (2001–2004), Pesquisadora, Pontifícia Universidade Católica de São Paul. February 16. São Paulo.

Suárez, Alberto. 2006. Former Secretary of Alberto Balestrini (La Matanza). Administrative Secretary of the Camera of Deputies. September 26. Buenos Aires.

Suplicy, Eduardo. 2006. Senador por São Paulo (Congresso Nacional). February 23. São Paulo.

Tedeschi, Virginia. 2006. Coordinadora Programa Familias, Ministério de Desarrollo Social. September 20. Buenos Aires.

SOURCES

Abrucio, Fernando. 1998. *Os Barões da Federacão: Os Governadores e a Redemocratização Brasileira*. São Paulo: Universidade de São Paulo.

———. 2005. "A Coordenação Federativa no Brasil: A Experiência do Período FHC e os Desafios do Governo Lula." *Revista de Sociologia Política* 24: 41–67.

Abrucio, Fernando, and David Samuels. 2000. "The New Politics of Governors." *Publius: The Journal of Federalism* 30(2): 43–61.

Afonso, José Roberto Rodrigues. 2005. "Novos Desafios à Descentralização Fiscal no Brasil." Paper presented at the World Forum of Fiscal Federalism, December 14–15, Costa do Sauipe.

———. 2007. "Local Government Organization and Finance: Brazil" (January 11, 2007). The World Bank, Public Sector Governance and Accountability Series, Local Governance in Developing Countries, 2007. Available at SSRN: http://ssrn.com/abstract=2548199.

Aguiar, Marcelo, and Carlos Henrique Araújo. 2002. *Bolsa Escola: Education to Confront Poverty*. Brasilia: UNESCO.

Alston, Lee J., Marcus André Melo, Bernardo Mueller, and Carlos Pereira. 2008. "On the Road to Good Governance: Recovering from Economic and Political Shocks in Brazil." In *Policymaking in Latin America: How Politics Shapes Policies*, edited by Ernesto Stein and Mariano Tommasi, with Pablo T. Spiller and Carlos Scartascini, 111–53. New York: Inter-American Development Bank; Cambridge, MA: David Rockefeller Center for Latin American Studies, Harvard University.

Ames, Barry. 1995. "Electoral Strategy under Open-List Proportional Representation." *American Journal of Political Science* 39(2): 406–33.

———. 2002. *The Deadlock of Democracy in Brazil. Interests, Identities, and Institutions in Comparative Politics*. Ann Arbor: University of Michigan Press.

Ames, Barry, Fabiana Machado, Lucio Rennó, David Samuels, Amy Erica Smith, and Cesar Zucco. 2013. "The Brazilian Electoral Panel Studies: Brazilian Public Opinion in the 2010 Presidential Elections." Inter-American Development Bank Working Paper, no. IDB-TN-508 (April).

Ames, Barry, and Timothy Power. 2006. "Party Systems and Ungovernability in Brazil." In *Political Parties in Transitional Democracies*, edited by Paul Webb and Stephen White, 179–213. Oxford: Oxford University Press.

Amorim Neto, Octavio. 2007. "Algumas Conseqüências Políticas de Lula." In *Instituições Representativas no Brasil*, edited by Jairo Nicolau and Timothy Power, 55–75. Rio de Janeiro: Universidade Federal de Minas Gerais

———. 2009. "O Brasil, Lijphart e o Modelo Consensual de Democracia." Unpublished paper.

Anastasia, Fatima, Carlos R. Melo, and Fabiano Santos. 2004. *Governabilidade e Representação Política nas América do Sul*. Rio de Janeiro: Fundação Konrad Adenauer.

Anastasia, Fátima, and Felipe Nunes. 2006. "A Reforma da Representação." In *Reforma Política no Brasil*, edited by Leonardo Avritzer and Fátima Anastasia, 17–35. Belo Horizonte: Editora Universidade Federal de Minas Gerais.

ANSES. 2013. Administración Nacional de Seguridad Social. Buenos Aires: Government of Argentina. http://www.anses.gob.ar/prestacion/asignacion-universal-por-hijo-92.

Armijo, Leslie Elliott, Philippe Faucher, and Magdalena Dembinska. 2006. "Compared to What: Assessing Brazil's Political Institutions." *Comparative Political Studies* 39(6): 759–86.

Arretche, Marta. 2000. *Estado Federativo e Políticas Sociais: Determinantes da Descentralização*. São Paulo: Revan.

———. 2007. "The Veto Power of Subnational Governments in Brazil." *Brazilian Political Science Review* 1(2): 40–73.

———. 2012. *Democracia, Federalismo e Centralização no Brasil*. São Paulo: Editora Fundação Getulio Vargas.

Arretche, Marta, and Jonathan Rodden. 2004. "Política Distributiva na Federação: Estratégias Eleitorais, Barganhas Legislativas e Coalizões de Governo." *Dados: Revista de Ciências Sociais* 47(3): 549–76.

Auyero, Javier. 2000. "The Logic of Clientelism in Argentina." *Latin American Research Review* 35(3): 55–81.

Ball, Terrance, ed. 2006. *Hamilton, Madison, and Jay: The Federalist Papers*. Cambridge: Cambridge University Press.

Banting, Keith G. 1995. "The Welfare State as Statecraft: Territorial Politics and Canadian Social Policy." In *European Social Policy: Between Fragmentation and Integration*, edited by Stephan Leibfried and Paul Pierson, 269–300. Washington, DC: Brookings Institute.

Barrientos, Armando. 2004. "Latin America: Towards a Liberal-Informal Welfare Regime." In *Insecurity and Welfare Regimes in Asia, Africa, and Latin America*, edited by Ian Gough and Geof Wood, 121–69. Cambridge: Cambridge University Press.

Barrientos, Armando, and Peter Lloyd-Sherlock. 2002. "Non-Contributory Pensions and Social Protection." Issues in Social Protection, Discussion Paper 12. Manchester: International Labour Organization.

Bednar, Jenna. 2004. "Authority Migration in Federations: A Framework for Analysis." *PS: Political Science and Politics* 37(3): 403–8.

Bednar, Jenna, William N. Eskridge, and John A. Ferejohn. 2001. "A Political Theory of Federalism." In *Constitutional Culture and Democratic Rules*, edited by John A. Ferejohn, Jack N. Rakove, and Jonathan Riley, 223–45. Cambridge: Cambridge University Press.

Beer, Caroline. 2004. "Electoral Competition and Fiscal Decentralization in Mexico." In *Decentralization and Democracy in Latin America*, edited by Alfred Montero and David Samuels, 180–200. Notre Dame: University of Notre Dame Press.

Behrend, Jacqueline. 2007. "Democratic Argentina and the 'Closed Game' of Provincial Politics: Protest and Persistence." DPhil thesis, University of Oxford.

Béland, Daniel. 2010a. "Reconsidering Policy Feedback: How Policies Affect Politics." *Administration and Society* 42(5): 568–90.

———. 2010b. *What Is Social Policy? Understanding the Welfare State.* Cambridge: Polity Press.

Béland, Daniel, and André Lecours. 2008. *Nationalism and Social Policy: The Politics of Territorial Solidarity.* Oxford: Oxford University Press.

Béland, Daniel, and Mitchell A. Orenstein. 2013. "International Organizations as Policy Actors: An Ideational Approach." *Global Social Policy* 13(2): 125–43.

Benton, Allyson, L. 2009. "What Makes Strong Federalism Seem Weak? Fiscal Resources and Presidential, Provincial Relations in Argentina." *Publius: The Journal of Federalism* 39(4): 651–76.

Bermeo, Nancy. 2002. "The Import of Institutions." *Journal of Democracy* 13(2): 96–110.

Bethell, Leslie. 2000. "Politics in Brazil: From Elections without Democracy to Democracy without Citizenship." *Daedalus* 129(2): 1–27.

Bird, Richard, and Francois Vaillancourt. 1998. *Fiscal Decentralization in Developing Countries.* Cambridge: Cambridge University Press.

Bogdanski, Joel, Paulo Springer de Freitas, Ilan Goldfajn, and Alexandre Antonio Tombini. 2001. "Inflation Targeting in Brazil: Shocks, Backward-Looking Prices, and IMF Conditionality." Working Paper no. 24 (August). Brasília: Banco do Brasil. Available at https://www.bcb.gov.br/pec/wps/ingl/wps24.pdf.

Bonvecchi, Alejandro, and Germán Lodola. 2011. "The Dual Logic of Intergovernmental Transfers: Presidents, Governors, and the Politics of Coalition-Building in Argentina." *Publius: The Journal of Federalism* (41)2: 179–206.

Borges, André. 2007. "Rethinking State Politics: The Withering of State Dominant Machines in Brazil." *Brazilian Political Science Review* (Online) 2, no. se, Rio de Janeiro (December).

Braun, Miguel, and Martin Ardanaz. 2008. "Kirchners Swap Keys for Presidential Sweep." *Forum of Federations* (Fall): 29–31.

Braun, Miguel, and Nicolas Gadano. 2006. "¿Para Que Sirven las Reglas Fiscales?" 1–19. Buenos Aires: Centro de Implementación de Políticas Públicas para la Equidad y el Crecimiento.

Briggs, Asa. 2006. "The Welfare State in Historical Perspective." In *The Welfare State*, edited by Francis Castles and Christopher Pierson, 16–30. Cambridge: Polity Press.

Bruhn, Kathleen. 1996. "Social Spending and Political Support." *Comparative Politics* 28(2): 151–77.

Brusco, Valeria, Marcelo Nazareno, and Susan Stokes. 2004. "Vote Buying in Argentina." *Latin American Research Review* 39(2): 66–88.

Cai, Hongbin, and Daniel Treisman. 2004. "State Corroding Federalism." *Journal of Public Economics* 88: 819–43.

Calvo, Ernesto, and Marcelo Escolar. 2005. *La Nueva Política de Partidos en la Argentina*. Buenos Aires: Prometeo.

Calvo, Ernesto, and Juan Abal Medina, eds. 2001. *El Federalismo Electoral Argentino*. Buenos Aires: Instituto Nacional de la Administración Publica.

Calvo, Ernesto, and Juan Micozzi. 2005. "The Governor's Backyard." *Journal of Politics* 67(4): 1050–74.

Calvo, Ernesto, and Victoria Murillo. 2004. "Who Delivers? Partisan Clients in the Argentine Electoral Market." *Journal of Political Science* 48(4): 1–42.

Camargo, José Márcio, and Ricardo Barros. 1993. "Poverty in Brazil: A Challenge for the Future." In *Brazil: The Challenges of the 1990s*, edited by Maria D'Alva Kinzo, 60–78. London: British Academy Press.

Campbell, Andrea. 2002. "Self-Interest, Social Security, and the Distinctive Participation Patterns of Senior Citizens." *American Political Science Review* 96: 565–74.

Carroll, R., and Matthew Shugart. 2007. "Neo-Madisonian Theory and Latin American Institutions." In *Regimes and Democracy in Latin America: Theories and Methods*, edited by Gerardo L. Munck, 51–101. Oxford: Oxford University Press.

Castro, Henrique, Elaine C. Licio, and Lucio Renno. 2009. "Bolsa Família e Voto nas Eleições Presidenciais de 2006: Em Busca do Elo Perdido." *Opinião Pública* 15(1): 29–58.

Castro Guimarães de, Maria Helena. 1993. "Democratic Transition and Social Policy in Brazil." In *Brazil: The Challenges of the 1990s*, edited by Maria D'Alva Kinzo, 78–94. London: British Academic Press.

Cheibub, José Antônio, Argelina Figueiredo, and Fernando Limongi. 2009. "Political Parties and Governors as Determinants of Legislative Behavior in Brazil's Chamber of Deputies, 1988–2006." *Latin American Politics and Society* 51(1): 1–30.

Cheresky, Isidoro, and Jean-Michel Blanquer, eds. 2004. *¿Qué Cambió en la Política Argentina?* Buenos Aires: University of Buenos Aires Press.

Cheresky, Isidoro, and Inés Pousadela, eds. 2004. *El Voto Liberado: Elecciones 2003.* Buenos Aires: Editorial Biblos.

El Clarín. Buenos Aires. Various issues.

Clemente, Adriana, and Catalina Smulovitz. 2004. "Descentralización, Sociedad Civil, y Gobernabilidad Democrática en Argentina." In *Descentralización, Políticas Sociales, y Participación Democrática en Argentina*, edited by Adriana Clemente and Catalina Smulovitz, 39–93. Buenos Aires: Woodrow Wilson International Centre for Scholars.

Collier, David, Henry Brady, and Jason Seawright. 2004. "Claiming Too Much: Warnings about Selection Bias." In *Rethinking Social Inquiry*, edited by David Collier and David Brady, 85–103. Oxford: Rowman and Littlefield.

Collier, David, and Ruth Collier. 1991. *Shaping the Political Arena: Critical Junctures, Labour Movements, and Regime Dynamics in Latin America.* Princeton: Princeton University Press.

Cruces, Guillermo, and Helena Rovner. 2008. "Los Programas Sociales en la Opinión Pública: Resultados de la Encuesta de Percepción de Planes Sociales en la Argentina." In *Los Programas Sociales en Argentina hacia el Bicentenari*, edited by Guillermo Cruces, Juan Martín Moreno, Dena Ringold, and Rafael Rofman, 49–121. Washington, DC: World Bank.

de Andrade Baltar, Paulo Eduardo, Anselmo Luis Dos Santos, José Dari Krein, Eugenia Leone, Marcelo Weishaupt Proni, Amilton Moretto, Alexandre Gori Maia, and Carlos Salas. 2010. "Moving Towards Decent Work, Labour in the Lula Government: Reflections on Recent Brazilian Experience." Working Paper. Institute for Research on Labour and Employment, University of California, Los Angeles.

de la O, Ana. 2013. "Do Conditional Cash Transfers Affect Electoral Behavior? Evidence from a Randomized Experiment in Mexico." *American Journal of Political Science* 57(1): 1–14.

de Riz, Liliana. 1996. "Argentina: Democracy in Turmoil." In *Constructing Democratic Governance: South America in the 1990s*, edited by Abraham F. Lowenthal and Jorge Domínguez, 149–57. Baltimore: Johns Hopkins University Press.

Devereux, Steven, and Clare Gorman. 2006. "Looking at Social Protection." *International Development Studies in Focus* 1(1).

Diaz, Mercedes, and Mark Payne. 2007. "Trends in Electoral Participation." In *Democracies in Development: Politics and Reform in Latin America*, 2nd ed., edited by J. Mark Payne, Daniel Zovatto G., Mercedes Diaz, et al. Washington, DC: Inter-American Development Bank and Harvard University.

Dickovick, Tyler. 2003. "Beyond Decentralization: Intergovernmental Relations in Brazil and South Africa." Paper presented at the annual meeting of the American Political Science Association, August 27, Philadelphia.

———. 2006. "Municipalization as a Central Government Strategy: Central-Regional-Local Politics in Peru, Brazil, and South Africa." *Publius: The Journal of Federalism* 37(1): 1–25.

———. 2012. *Decentralization and Recentralization in the Developing World: Comparative Studies from Africa and Latin America.* University Park: Pennsylvania State University Press.

Dillinger, William. 2002. "Brazil: Issues on Fiscal Federalism." Report # 22523-BR (June 4), 1–49. Washington, DC: World Bank.

Dillinger, William, and Steven Webb. 2002. "Fiscal Management in Federal Democracies: Argentina and Brazil." Washington, DC: World Bank.

Dixit, Avinash, and John Londregan. 1996. "The Determinants of Success of Special Interests in Redistributive Politics." *Journal of Politics* 58(4): 1132–55.

Draibe, Sonia. 2004. "Social Policy Reform." In *Reforming Brazil*, edited by Mauricio Font and Peter Spanakos, 71–93. Oxford: Lexington.

Dresser, Denise. 1991. "Neopopulist Solutions to Neoliberal Problems." San Diego: Centre for US-Mexico Relations.

Eaton, Kent. 2004a. "The Link between Political and Fiscal Decentralization in South America." In *Decentralization and Democracy in Latin America*, edited by Alfred Montero and David Samuels, 122–54. Notre Dame: University of Notre Dame Press.

———. 2004b. *Politics Beyond the Capital.* Stanford: Stanford University Press.

———. 2014. "Recentralization and the Left Turn in Latin America: Diverging Outcomes in Bolivia, Ecuador, and Venezuela." *Comparative Political Studies* 47(8): 1130–57.

Eaton, Kent, and Tyler Dickovick. 2004. "The Politics of Re-Centralization in Argentina and Brazil." *Latin American Research Review* 39(1): 90–122.

ECLAC (Economic Commission of Latin America and the Caribbean). [Various Years]. Statistical databases, "Bases de Datos y Publicaciones Estadísticas." Chile: United Nations. Available at http://www.eclac.org/estadisticas/.

Entin, Gabriel. 2004. "Peronsimo, Liderazgos Locales y Partidos Políticos: Las Elecciones de 2003 en La Mantanza." In *El Voto Liberado*, edited by Isidoro Cheresky and Inés Pousadela, 137–67. Buenos Aires: Editorial Biblos.

Esping-Andersen, Gøsta, Duncan Gallie, Anton Hemerijck, and John Myles. 2002. *Why We Need a New Welfare State.* Oxford: Oxford University Press.

Etchebarne, A., M. Ohlsson, and A. Jorgenson. 2012. "La Trampa de la Dependencia Economica." *Libertad y Progreso*: 1–53. Available online at http://

www.libertadyprogresonline.org/wp-content/uploads/2013/03/Trabajo
-Planes-Sociales_2.pdf.

Falleti, Tulia. 2003. "Governing Governors: Coalitions and Sequences of Decentralization in Argentina, Columbia, and Mexico." PhD diss., Northwestern University.

Fausto, Boris, and Fernando Devoto. 2004. *Brasil E Argentina: Um Ensaio de História Comparada*. São Paulo: Editora 34.

Fenwick, Tracy Beck. 2009. "Avoiding Governors: The Success of *Bolsa Família*." *Latin American Research Review* 44(1): 102–31.

———. 2010. "The Institutional Feasibility of National-Local Policy Collaboration: Insights from Brazil and Argentina." *Journal of Politics in Latin America* 2 (February): 155–85.

———. 2013. "Stuck Between the Past and the Future: Conditional Cash Transfer Programme Development and Policy Feedbacks in Brazil and Argentina." *Global Social Policy* 13(2): 144–67.

FGV (Fundação Getulio Vargas). 2006. "Miséria, Desigualdade e Estabilidade: O Segundo Real." São Paulo.

Figueiredo, Argelina. 2007. "Government Coalitions in Brazilian Democracy." *Brazilian Political Science Review* 1(2): 182–216.

Figueiredo, Argelina, and Fernando Limongi. 1999. *Executivo e Legislativo na Nova Ordem Constitucional*. Rio de Janeiro: Fundação Getulio Vargas.

Figueiredo, Argelina, Haroldo Torres, and Renata Bichir. 2006. "A Conjuntura Social Brasileira Revisitada." *Novos Estudos* 75 (July): 173–82.

Figueiredo, Rui, and Barry Weingast. 2005. "Self-Enforcing Federalism." *The Journal of Law, Economics, & Organization* 21(1): 103–35.

Filippov, Mikhail, Peter C. Ordeshook, and Olga Shvetsova. 2004. *Designing Federalism: A Theory of Self-Sustainable Federal Institutions*. Cambridge: Cambridge University Press.

Fleischer, David. 1998. "The Cardoso Government's Reform Agenda: A View from the National Congress, 1995–1998." *Journal of Interamerican Studies and World Affairs* 40(4): 119–36.

Folha de S.Paulo. São Paulo. Various issues. All back issues available at http://acervo.folha.com.br/.

Fox, Jonathan. 1994. "Latin America's Emerging Local Politics." *Journal of Democracy* 5(2): 105–16.

Gerchunoff, Pablo, and Juan Carlos Torre. 1998. "Argentina: The Politics of Economic Liberalization." In *The Changing Role of the State in Latin America*, edited by Menno Vellinga. Boulder, CO: Westview Press.

Gervasoni, Carlos. 2011. "A Rentier Theory of Subnational Democracy: The Politically Regressive Effects of Fiscal Federalism in Argentina." Phd diss., University of Notre Dame.

Gibson, Edward L. 1996. *Class and Conservative Politics: Argentina in Comparative Perspective*. Baltimore: Johns Hopkins University Press.

———. 1997. "The Populist Road to Market Reform Policy and Electoral Coalitions in Mexico and Argentina." *World Politics* 49(3): 339–70.

———, ed. 2004. *Federalism and Democracy in Latin America.* Baltimore: Johns Hopkins University Press.

———. 2008. "Subnational Authoritarianism and Territorial Politics: Charting the Theoretical Landscape." Paper presented at the American Political Science Association Annual Congress (APSA), August 28–31, Boston.

———. 2012. *Boundary Control: Subnational Authoritarianism in Federal Democracies.* Cambridge: Cambridge University Press.

Gibson, Edward, and Ernesto Calvo. 2000. "Federalism and Low-Maintenance Constituencies." *Comparative International Development* 35(3): 32–55.

Gibson, Edward, and Julieta Cao-Suarez. 2007. "Competition and Power in Federalized Party Systems." Working Paper 1 in the Program of Comparative Historical Social Science. Chicago: Northwestern University.

Gibson, Edward L., and Tulia Falleti. 2004. "Unity by the Stick: Regional Conflict and the Origins of Argentine Federalism." In *Federalism and Democracy in Latin America*, edited by Edward L. Gibson, 226–54. Baltimore: Johns Hopkins University Press.

Giddens, Anthony. 1998. *The Third Way: The Renewal of Social Democracy.* Cambridge: Polity Press.

Giraudy, Agustina. 2007. "The Distributive Politics of Emergency Employment Programs in Argentina (1993–2000)." *Latin American Research Review* 42(2): 33–56.

Golbert, Laura. 1996. "Viejos y Nuevos Problemas de las Políticas Asistenciales en Argentina." Working Paper 12. Buenos Aires: Centro de Estudios para el Cambio Estructural.

Gómez, Eduardo. 2003. "Decentralization and Municipal Governance: Suggested Approaches for Cross-Regional Analysis." *Studies in Comparative International Development* 38(3): 57–81.

González, Lucas. 2008. "Political Power, Fiscal Crises, and Decentralization in Latin America: Federal Countries in Latin America." *Publius: The Journal of Federalism* 38(2): 211–47.

Goodspeed, Timothy. 2002. "Bailouts in a Federation." *International Tax and Public Finance* 9(2): 409–21.

Gordin, Jorge. 2002. "The Political and Partisan Determinants of Patronage in Latin America." *European Journal of Political Research* 41(4): 513–49.

Government of Argentina. [Various Years]. "Legislative Database." Ministerio de Economía y Producción, www.infoleg.mecon.gov.ar.

———. [Various Years]. "Provincial Databases." Ministerio del Interior, www.mininterior.gov.ar.

———. [Various Years]. "Social Expenditure Databases." Dirección de Análisis de Gastos Públicos y Programas, Ministerio de Economía y Producción, www.mecon.gov.ar.

Government of Brazil. 1988. "Constitution of the Federal Republic of Brazil."
———. 2004. "Fiscal Accounts." Ministerio da Fazenda, www.receita.fazenda
.gov.br.
Government of La Matanza. 2007. "Ordenanza Presupuestaria." Secretaria de
Hacienda, www.lamatanza.gov.ar.
Graham, Lawrence, and Allison Rowland. 2006. "Two Centuries of Federalism
in Brazil, Mexico, and the USA." In *Governance in the Americas*, edited by
Robert Wilson, Peter Ward, Peter Spink, and Victoria Rodríguez, 30–62.
Notre Dame: University of Notre Dame Press.
Grindle, Merilee S. 2007. *Going Local: Decentralization, Democratization, and
the Promise of Good Governance*. Princeton: Princeton University Press.
Guigale, Marcelo, Fausto Trillo, and João Oliveira. 2000. "Subnational Borrow-
ing and Debt Management." In *Achievements and Challenges of Fiscal De-
centralization: Lessons from Mexico*, edited by Marcelo Guigale and Steven
Webb, 237–70. Washington, DC: World Bank.
Guigale, Marcelo, and Steven Webb, eds. 2000. *Achievements and Challenges
of Fiscal Decentralization: Lessons from Mexico*. Washington, DC: World
Bank.
Haggard, Stephan, and Steven B. Webb. 2004. "Political Incentives and Inter-
governmental Fiscal Relations: Argentina, Brazil, and Mexico Compared."
In *Decentralization and Democracy in Latin America*, edited by Alfred
Montero and David Samuels, 235–70. Notre Dame: University of Notre
Dame Press.
Hall, Anthony. 2007. "Social Policies at the World Bank: Paradigms and Chal-
lenges." *Global Social Policy* 7(2): 151–75.
Handa, Sudhanshu, and Benjamin Davis. 2006. "The Experience of Condi-
tional Cash Transfers in Latin America and the Caribbean." *Development
Policy Review* 24(5): 513–36.
Hemerijck, Anton. 2012. "Two or Three Waves of Welfare Transformation?" In
Towards a Social Investment Welfare State, edited by Natalie Morel, Bruno
Palier, and Joakim Palme, 33–61. Bristol: Policy Press.
Hoddinot, John, Emanuel Skoufias, and Robert Washburn. 2000. "The Impact
of PROGRESA on Consumption: A Final Report." International Food Pol-
icy Research Institute, Washington, DC.
Huber, Evelyne, and Juan Bogliaccini. 2010. "Emerging Welfare States: Latin
America." In *The Oxford Handbook of the Welfare State*, edited by Francis
Castles, Stephen Leibfried, Jane Lewis, Herbert Obinger, and Christopher
Pierson, 644–56. Oxford: Oxford University Press.
Huber, Evelyne, and John D. Stephens. 2012. *Democracy and the Left: Social
Policy and Inequality in Latin America*. Chicago: University of Chicago
Press.

Hunter, Wendy, and Timothy Power. 2007. "Rewarding Lula: Executive Power, Social Policy, and the Brazilian Elections of 2006." *Latin American Politics and Society* 49(1): 1–30.

Hunter, Wendy, and Natasha Sugiyama. 2013. "Whither Clientelism? Good Governance and Brazil's Bolsa Família Program." *Comparative Politics* 46(1): 43–62.

IBGE (Institute Brasileiro de Geografia e Estatística). 2010. National Census Results. Brasilía: Instituto Brasileiro de Geografia e Estatística." www.ibge .gov.br.

IBOPE (Instituto Brasileiro de Opinião Pública e Estatística). 2002. "Pesquisa de Opinião Pública #558." November 12. Available by request from the Centro de Estudos de Opinião Pública (CESOP). Campinas: Universidade de Campinas.

INDEC (Instituto Nacional Estadística y Censos Nacional). 1991. "Censo Na-cional." Buenos Aires: Government of Argentina. http://www.indec.mecon .ar/sen.asp.

———. 2001. "Censo Nacional." Buenos Aires: Government of Argentina. http://www.indec.gov.ar/micro_sitios/webcenso/.

———. 2006. "Base Usuaria Ampliada Encuestra Permanente de Hogares" (EPH) Puntual (1984–1994) and (1995–2006). Buenos Aires: Government of Argentina. http://www.indec.gov.ar/bases-de-datos.asp.

IPEA (Instituto de Pesquisa Econômico Aplicada). 2010. "Numeró de Indi-víduos Pobres Anual de 1976 até 2009," calculados com dados de PNAD/ IBGE. Brasilía: IPEA. www.ipeadata.gob.br.

Jaime, Fernando, and Félix Sabaté. 2013. "Gobernanza Multinivel Fragmentada en Politicas Sociales: Respuestas Locales Implementando la Asignación Universal por Hijo." Paper presented at the Annual Congress of the Latin American Studies Association, May 29–June 1, Washington, DC.

Jenson, Jane. 2010. "Diffusing Ideas for After Neoliberalism: The Social Invest-ment Perspective in Europe and Latin America." *Global Social Policy* 10(1): 59–84.

Jenson, Jane, and Denis San Martin. 2003. "New Routes to Social Cohesion? Citizenship and the Social Investment State." *The Canadian Journal of So-ciology/Cahiers Canadiens de Sociologie* 28(1): 77–99.

Jones, Mark. 1996. "Assessing the Public's Understanding of Constitutional Re-form: Evidence from Argentina." *Political Behaviour* 18(1): 25–49.

———. 1997. "Evaluating Argentina's Presidential Democracy 1983–1995." In *Presidentialism and Democracy in Latin America*, edited by Matthew Shugart, 259–99. Cambridge: University of Cambridge.

———. 2008. "The Recruitment and Selection of Legislative Candidates in Ar-gentina." In *Pathways to Power: Political Recruitment and Candidate Selec-tion in Latin America*, edited by Stephen Morgenstern and Peter Siavelis, 41–75. University Park: Pennsylvania State University Press.

Jones, Mark, and Wonjae Hwang. 2003. "Majority Cartels, Distributive Politics and Interparty Relations in a Unicameral Legislature." Paper presented at the Annual Conference of Latin American Studies Association, May 27–29, Dallas.

———. 2005. "Provincial Party Bosses." In *Argentine Democracy: The Politics of Institutional Weakness*, edited by Steven Levitsky and María Victoria Murillo, 115–38. University Park: Pennsylvania State University Press.

Jones, Mark, and Scott Mainwaring. 2008. "The Nationalization of Parties and Party Systems." *Party Politics* 9(2): 136–66.

Jones, Mark, Sebastian Saiegh, Pablo Spiller, and Mariano Tommasi. 2002. "Amateur Legislators-Professional Politicians: The Consequences of Party-Centered Electoral Rules in a Federal System." *American Journal of Political Science* 46(3): 656–69.

King, Gary, Robert Keohane, and Sidney Verba. 1994. *Designing Social Inquiry*. Princeton: Princeton University Press.

Kornai, Janos. 1980. *Economics of Shortage*. London: North-Holland.

Kornai, J., E. Maskin, and G. Roland. 2003. "Understanding the Soft Budget Constraint." *Journal of Economic Literature* 41 (December): 1095–1136.

Laakso, M., and R. Taagepera. 1979. "Effective Number of Parties: A Measure with Application to Western Europe." *Comparative Political Studies* 12(1): 3–27.

Lamounier, Bolivar. 1992. "Estrutura Institucional e Governabilidade na Década de 1990." In *O Brasil e as Reformas Políticas*, edited by João Paulo Reis Velloso, 23–49. Rio de Janeiro: José Olympio.

Latinobarómetre Public Opinion Survey. 2004. "Summary Report: Democracy and Ecnonomy." Latinobarómetre Corporation, www.latinobarometre.org.

Lavinas, Lena. 2013. "21st Century Welfare." *New Left Review* 84 (November–December): 5–40.

Leal, Victor Nunes. 1949. *Coronelismo, Enxada e Voto*. 3rd ed. São Paulo: Nova Fronteira.

Leiras, Marcelo. 2004. "Critica Partidista de los Partidos Políticos Argentinos." Working Paper. Buenos Aires: Departmento de Ciencia Política, Universidad de San Andrés.

———. 2008. "Cabinet Composition under Kirchner 2003–2007." Emailed to the author.

Levitsky, Steven. 2003. *Transforming Labor-Based Parties in Latin America: Argentine Peronism in Comparative Perspective*. Cambridge: Cambridge University Press.

Levitsky, Steven, and Victoria Murillo. 2003. "Argentina Weathers the Storm." *Journal of Democracy* 14(4): 153–66.

Levy, Santiago. 1991. "La Pobreza Extrema en México: Una Propuesta de Política." *Estudios Económicos* 6(1): 47–89.

————. 2006. *Progress against Poverty: Studying Mexico's Progresa*. Washington, DC: Brookings Institute.

Licio, Elaine. 2012. "Para Além de Recentralização: Os Caminhos da Coordenação Federativa do Programa Bolsa Família (2003-2010)." PhD diss., National University of Brasilia.

Lijphart, Arend. 1969. "Consociational Democracy." *World Politics* 21(2): 207-25.

————. 1984. *Democracies: Patterns of Majoritarian and Consensus Government in Twenty-One Countries*. New Haven and London: Yale University Press.

————. 1996. "The Puzzle of Indian Democracy: A Consociational Interpretation." *American Political Science Review* 90(2): 258-68.

————. 2002. "The Wave of Power-Sharing Democracy." In *The Architecture of Democracy*, edited by Andrew Reynolds, 15-37. Oxford: Oxford University Press.

————. 2008. *Thinking about Democracy*. New York: Routledge.

Limongi, Fernando. 2006. "Presidencialismo e Governo de Coalizão." In *Reforma Política no Brasil e na América Latina*, edited by Leonardo Avritzer and Fatima Anastasia, 237-57. Belo Horizonte (PNUD): Universidade Federal de Minas Gerais.

Lindert, Kathy, Emmanuel Skoufias, and Joseph Shapiro. 2006. "Redistributing Income to the Poor and the Rich: Public Transfers in Latin America and the Caribbean." Washington, DC: World Bank.

Lindert, Kathy, and Vanina Vincensini. 2010. "Social Policy, Perceptions and the Press: An Analysis of the Media's Treatment of Conditional Cash Transfers in Brazil." World Bank Discussion Paper 1008 (December), 1-122.

Lipton, Michael, and Martin Ravallion. 1995. "Poverty Policy." In *Handbook of Development Economics*, vol. 3, edited by Jere Behrman and T. N. Srinivasan, 2551-2657. Amsterdam: Elsevier.

Lloyd-Sherlock, Peter. 1997. "Policy, Distribution, and Poverty in Argentina since Redemocratization." *Latin American Perspectives* 24(6): 22-55.

Lodola, German. 2005. "Protesta Popular y Redes Clientelares en la Argentina: El Reparto Federal del Plan Trabajar." *Desarrollo Económico* 44: 176.

Lo Vuolo, Rubén. 2013. "The Argentine 'Universal Child Allowance': Not the Poor but the Unemployed and Informal Worker." In *Citizen's Income and Welfare Regimes in Latin America: From Cash Transfers to Rights*, edited by Rubén Lo Vuolo, 51-66. New York: Palgrave Macmillan.

Mainwaring, Scott. 1992. "Brazilian Party Underdevelopment in Comparative Perspective." *Political Science Quarterly* 107(4): 677-707.

————. 1995a. "Democracy in Brazil and the Southern Cone: Achievements and Problems." *Journal of Inter-American Studies and World Affairs* 37(1): 113-79.

———. 1995b. "Brazil: Weak Parties, Feckless Democracy." In *Building Democratic Institutions: Party Systems in Latin America,* edited by Scott Mainwaring and Timothy R. Scully, 354–99. Stanford: Stanford University Press.

Mainwaring, Scott, and Anibal Perez Linan. 1997. "Party Discipline in the Brazilian Constitutional Congress." *Legislative Studies Quarterly* 22(4): 453–83.

Mainwaring, Scott, Timothy Scully, and Jorge Vargas Cullell. 2007. "Measuring Successful Democratic Governance in Latin America." Paper presented at the Latin American Studies Association, September 5–8, Montreal.

Malamud, Andres, and Miguel de Luca. 2005. "The Anchors of Continuity: Party System Stability in Argentina 1983–2003." Paper presented at the European Consortium for Political Research, Granada.

Malloy, James. 1993. "Statecraft, Social Policy, and Governance in Latin America." *Governance* 6(2): 220–74.

Manzetti, Luigi. 1993. *Institutions, Parties, and Coalitions in Argentine Politics.* Pittsburgh: University of Pittsburgh Press.

Marques, Rosa. 2004. "A Importância do Bolsa Família nos Municípios Brasileiros." In Working Paper, Department of Economics. São Paulo: Pontificia Universidade Católica de São Paulo.

Marshall, T. H. (1950) 2006. "Citizenship and Social Class." In *The Welfare State Reader,* edited by Christopher Pierson and Francis G. Castles, 30–40. Cambridge: Polity Press.

MDS (Ministério de Desenvolvimento Social, Brazil). [Various years]. www .mds.gov.br.

———. 2015. "Plano Brasil Sem Miséria—Caderno de Resultados, 2011–2014." Brasilia: Government of Brazil. http://www.mds.gov.br/documentos /Caderno%20de%20Graficos%20BSM%20-%203%2C5%20anos2.pdf.

Medina, Juan, and Maria Ratto. 2006. "Tensiones y Desafíos del Sistema Partidario Argentino." Paper presented at the Annual Conference of Latin American Studies Association, March 15–18, Puerto Rico.

Medina, Luis Fernando, and Susan Stokes. 2002. "Clientelism as Political Monopoly." Paper presented at the Public Choice Society Meeting, San Antonio.

Melo, Marcus A., and Carlos Pereira. 2013. *Making Brazil Work: Checking the President in a Multiparty System.* New York: Palgrave Macmillan.

Menguello, Rachel. 2007. "Quem Apóia o Presidente." Paper presented at the Annual Conference of Latin American Studies Association, September 5–8, Montreal.

Ministerio de Desarrollo Social. 2007. "Programa Familias por la Inclusión Social: Resumen Ejecutivo 2007." Buenos Aires: Government of Argentina.

Ministry of Economy, Province of Buenos Aires. 2001. "Cuaderno de Económica 56."

Montero, Alfred. 2005. *Brazilian Politics.* Cambridge: Polity Press.

———. 2008. "Macroeconomic Deeds, Not Reform Words: The Determinants of Foreign Direct Investment in Latin America." *Latin American Research Review* 43(1): 55–83.

———. 2010. "No Country for Leftists? Clientelist Continuity and the 2006 Vote in the Brazilian Northeast." *Journal of Politics in Latin America* 2(2): 113–53.

Montero, Alfred, and David Samuels, eds. 2004. *Decentralization and Democracy in Latin America*. Notre Dame: University of Notre Dame Press.

Morel, Nathalie, Bruno Palier, and Joakim Palme, eds. 2012. *Towards a Social Investment Welfare State?* Bristol: Policy Press.

La Nacion. Buenos Aires. Various issues.

Neri, Marcelo. 2011. "Brasil Sem Miseria?" *Conjuntura Social*, Fundacão Getulio Vargas (Junho): 62–65.

Nickson, R. Andrew. 1995. *Local Government in Latin America*. Boulder, CO, and London: Lynne Rienner.

Nicolau, Jairo. [Various years]. Electoral Datasets. http://jaironicolau.iuperj.br/banco2004.html.

Nicolau, Jairo, and Vitor Peixoto. 2007. "Uma Disputa em Três Tempos: Uma Análise das Bases Municipais das Eleições Presidenciais de 2006." Paper presented at the Encontro Anual da ANPOCS, October 22–26, Caxambu.

Novaro, Marcos. 2004. "Los Incentivos a la Colaboración Interpartidaria de la Doble Vuelta: El Caso Argentino." In *Los Sistemas de Doble Vuelta*, edited by Rafael Gonzalez, 25–58. Barcelona: Institut de Ciénces Politiques i Socials.

Obinger, Herbert, Stephan Leibfried, and Francis G. Castles, eds. 2005. *Federalism and the Welfare State: New World and European Experiences*. Cambridge: Cambridge University Press.

O'Neill, Kathleen. 2004. *Decentralizing the State: Elections, Parties, and Local Power in the Andes*. New York: Cambridge University Press, 2005.

Oxhorn, Philip. 1995. "From Controlled Inclusion to Coerced Marginalization: The Struggle for Civil Society in Latin America." In *Civil Society: Theory, History and Comparison*, edited by John Hall, 250–77. Cambridge: Polity Press.

Oxhorn, Philip, Joseph Tulchin, and Andrew Selee, eds. 2004. *Decentralization, Democratization, and Civil Society in Comparative Perspective*. Baltimore: Johns Hopkins University Press.

Parker, Susan W., Luis Rubalcava, and Graciela Terurel. 2008. "Evaluating Conditional Schooling and Health Programs." In *Handbook of Development Economics*, vol. 4, edited by Schultz T. Paul and John Strauss, 3963–4020. Amsterdam: Elsevier.

Pereira, Carlos, and Bernardo Mueller. 2004. "Strategic Behaviour of the President and Legislators in Brazil's Budgetary Process." *Comparative Political Studies* 37(9): 781–815.

Porto, Alberto. 2004. *Disparidades Regionales y Federalismo Fiscal.* La Plata: Editorial de la Universidad de La Plata.

Porto, Alberto, and Pablo Sanguinetti. 2001. "Political Determinants of Intergovernmental Grants: Evidence from Argentina." *Economics and Politics* 13(3): 237–55.

Power, Timothy. 2010. "Optimism, Pessimism, and Coalitional Presidentialism: Debating the Institutional Design of Brazilian Democracy." *Bulletin of Latin American Research* 29(1): 18–33.

Power, Timothy, and Cesar Zucco. 2013. "Bolsa Família and the Shift in Lula's Electoral Base, 2002–2006: A Reply to Bohn." *Latin American Research Review* 48(2): 3–25.

Razavi, Shahra. 2012. "World Development Report 2012: Gender Equality and Development—A Commentary." *Development and Change* 43(1): 423–37.

Remmer, Karen. 2007. "The Political Economy of Patronage." *Journal of Politics* 69(2): 363–77.

Repetto, Fabian, and Langou Diaz. 2010. "Desafíos y Enseñanzas de la Asignación Universal por Hijo para Protección Social a un año de su Creación." *Documento de Políticas Publicas* no. 88. CIPPEC (Centro de Implementación de Políticas Públicas para la Equidad y el Crecimiento), Buenos Aires. Available at www.cippec.org.

Requejo, Ferran. 2001. "Political Liberalism in Multinational States: The Legitimacy of Plural and Asymmetrical Federalism." In *Multinational Democracies*, edited by Alain Gagnon and James Tully, 110–33. Cambridge: Cambridge University Press.

Rezende, Fernando. 2007. "Federal Republic of Brazil." In *The Practice of Fiscal Federalism*, edited by Anwar Shah, 74–97. Montreal: McGill-Queens University Press.

Rezk, Ernesto. 2000. "Federalism and Decentralization under Convertibility." Working Paper, Institute of Economics and Finance. Cordoba: National University of Córdoba. Available at https://www.imf.org/external/pubs/ft /seminar/2000/fiscal/rezk.pdf.

Rice, James J., and Michael J. Prince. 2013. *Changing Politics of Canadian Social Policy.* 2nd ed. Toronto: University of Toronto Press.

Richardson, Neal P. 2009. "Export-Oriented Populism: Commodities and Coalitions in Argentina." *Studies in Comparative International Development* 44(3): 228–55.

Riker, William H. 1964. *Federalism: Origin, Operation, Significance.* Basic Studies in Politics. Boston: Little, Brown.

Riker, William H., and Ronald Schaps. 1987. "Disharmony in Federal Government." In *The Development of American Federalism*, by William H. Riker [some essays co-authored], 73–79. Boston: Kluwer.

Rodden, Jonathan. 2001. "Creating a More Perfect Union: Electoral Incentives and the Reform of Federal Systems." Unpublished paper. Boston, MIT.

————. 2003. "Federalism and Bailouts in Brazil." In *Fiscal Decentralization and Challenge of Hard Budget Constraints*, ed. Jonathan Rodden, Gunnar Eskeland, and Jennie Litvack, 213–48. Boston: MIT Press.

————. 2004. "Comparative Federalism and Decentralization: On Meaning and Measurement." *Comparative Politics* (July): 481–500.

————. 2006. *Hamilton's Paradox: The Promise and Peril of Fiscal Federalism.* New York: Cambridge University Press.

Rodden, Jonathan, Gunnar Eskeland, and Jennie Litvack, eds. 2003. *Fiscal Decentralization and Challenge of Hard Budget Constraints.* Boston: MIT Press.

Rodden, Jonathan, and Eric Wibbels. 2002. "Beyond the Fiction of Federalism." *World Politics* 54(4): 494–531.

Ronconi, Lucas. 2002. "El Programa Trabajar." In *Documento 63.* Buenos Aires: Centro de Estudios para el Desarrollo Institucional Fundación, Fundación Gobierno y Sociedad.

Ronconi, Lucas, Pablo Sanguinetti, Sandra Fachelli, Virginia Casazza, and Ignacio Franceschelli. 2006. "Poverty and Employablity Effects of Workfare Programs in Argentina." In Poverty and Economy Policy Working Paper, 1–33. Buenos Aires: Ministry of Economy, Argentina.

Rondinelli, Dennis. 1980. "Government Decentralization in Comparative Perspective." *International Review of Public Administration* 47(2): 133.

Rueschemeyer, Dietrich. 2004. "Addressing Inequality." *Journal of Democracy* 15(4): 76–90.

Saiegh, Sebastian, and Mariano Tommasi. 1998. "Argentina's Federal Fiscal Institutions: A Case Study in the Transaction-Cost Theory of Politics." Working Paper 11. Buenos Aires, Centro de Estudios para el Desarrollo Institucional.

Salinas, Carlos. 1978. "Public Investment, Political Participation and System Support: Study of Three Rural Communities in Central Mexico." PhD diss., Harvard University.

Samuels, David. 2003. *Ambition, Federalism, and Legislative Politics in Brazil.* Cambridge: Cambridge University Press.

Samuels, David, and Scott Mainwaring. 2004. "Strong Federalism, Constraints on the Central Government, and Economic Reform in Brazil." In *Federalism and Democracy in Latin America*, edited by Edward L. Gibson, 85–130. Baltimore: Johns Hopkins University Press.

Samuels, David, and Richard Snyder. 2004. "Legislative Malapportionment in Latin America: Historical and Comparative Perspectives." In *Federalism and Democracy in Latin America*, edited by Edward L. Gibson, 131–72. Baltimore: Johns Hopkins University Press.

Saunders, Peter. 2010. "Inequality and Poverty." In *The Oxford Handbook of the Welfare State*, edited by Francis Castles, Stephen Leibfried, Jane Lewis,

Herbert Obinger, and Christopher Pierson, 526–39. Oxford: Oxford University Press.

Schamis, Hector. 2002. "Argentina: Crisis and Democratic Consolidation." *Journal of Democracy* 13(2): 81–94.

Schneider, Aaron. 2003. "Decentralization: Conceptualization and Measurement." *Studies in Comparative International Development* 38(3): 32–56.

Shah, Anwar. 2007. "Comparative Conclusions on Fiscal Federalism." In *The Practice of Fiscal Federalism: Comparative Perspectives*, edited by Anwar Shah, 370–95. Montreal: McGill-Queen's University Press.

Shugart, Matthew. 1999. "Presidentialism, Parliamentarism, and the Provision of Collected Goods in Less-Developed Countries." *Constitutional Political Economy* 10: 53–88.

Silva, Nelson do Valle. 2008. "Brazilian Society: Continuity and Change, 1930–2000." In *The Cambridge History of Latin America*, edited by Leslie Bethell, 9:455–544. Cambridge: Cambridge University Press.

Singer, Matthew. 2004. "Local Parties and Local Politics: Electoral Fragmentation and Municipal Budget Choices in Bolivia and Mexico." Paper presented at the Annual Meeting of the American Political Science Association, September 2–5, Chicago.

SIOP (Sistema Integrado de Planéjamento e Orçamento). 2014. "Rélatorio de Acompanhamento de Despesas do Plano Brasil Sem Misería (Execuçao 2014)." Brasilía: Ministerio do Planejamento, Orçamento, e Gestão. www.siop.planejamento.gov.br.

Snyder, Richard. 2001. "Scaling Down: The Subnational Comparative Method." *Studies in Comparative International Development* 36(1): 93–110.

Soares, Fabio V., Rafael P. Ribas, and Rafael G. Osório. 2010. "Evaluating The Impact of Brazil's Bolsa Família: Cash Transfer Programs in Comparative Perspective." *Latin American Research Review* 45(2): 173–90.

Soares, Glaucio A. D., and Sonia L. Terron. 2008. "Dois Lulas: A Geografia Eleitoral da Reeleição." *Opinião Pública* 14(2): 269–301.

Soares, Sergei, and Natalia Sátyro. 2010. "Infraestrutura das Escolas Brasileiras e Desempenho Escolar." In *Infraestrutura Social e Urbana no Brasil: Subsídios para uma Agenda de Pesquisa e Formulação de Políticas Públicas*, edited by Costa M. and M. P. Morais, 151–92. Brasília: IPEA.

Soares, Sergei, Pedro H. G, Ferreira de Souza, Rafael G. Osório, and Fernando G. Silveira. 2010. "Os Impactos do Benefício do Programa Bolsa Família Sobre a Desigualdade e a Probreza. In *Bolsa Familia 2003–2010: Avanços y Desafios*, vol. 2, edited by Jorge Abrahão and Lucia Modesto, 25–53. Brasília: IPEA.

Souza, Celina. 1997. *Constitutional Engineering in Brazil*. London: St. Martin's Press.

——. 2000. "Participatory Budgeting in Brazilian Cities: Limits and Possibilities in Building Democratic Institutions." Urban Governance, Partnership and Poverty Working Paper 28. Birmingham: University of Birmingham.

——. 2002. "Brazil: The Prospects of a Centre-Constraining Federation in a Fragmented Polity." *Publius: The Journal of Federalism* 32(2): 23–48.

——. 2003. "Building Municipal Capacity for Finance and Budgeting in Brazil." Working Paper 2. Birmingham: University of Birmingham.

——. 2004. "Governos Locais e Gestão de Políticas Sociais Universais." *São Paulo em Perspectiva* 18(2): 27–41.

Spiller, Pablo T., Ernesto Stein, and Mariano Tommasi. 2008. "Political Institutions, Policymaking, and Policy: An Introduction." In *Policymaking in Latin America: How Politics Shapes Policies*, edited by Ernesto Stein and Mariano Tommasi, with Pablo T. Spiller and Carlos Scartascini, 1–28. New York: Inter-American Development Bank; Cambridge, MA: David Rockefeller Center for Latin American Studies, Harvard University.

Spiller, Pablo T., and Mariano Tommasi. 2007. *The Institutional Foundations of Public Policy in Argentina*. Political Economy of Institutions and Decisions. New York: Cambridge University Press.

——. 2008. "Political Institutions, Policymaking Processes, and Policy Outcomes in Argentina." In *Policymaking in Latin America: How Politics Shapes Policies*, edited by Ernesto Stein and Mariano Tommasi, with Pablo T. Spiller and Carlos Scartascini, 69–110. New York: Inter-American Development Bank; Cambridge, MA: David Rockefeller Center for Latin American Studies, Harvard University.

Stein, Ernesto, Mariano Tommasi, J. Mark Payne, Eduardo Lora, and Koldo Echebarria, eds. 2005. *The Politics of Policies*. Washington, DC: Inter-American Development Bank.

Stepan, Alfred. 2001. *Arguing Comparative Politics*. Oxford: Oxford University Press.

——. 2004. "Electorally Generated Veto Players in Unitary and Federal Systems." In *Federalism and Democracy in Latin America*, edited by Edward L. Gibson, 323–63. Baltimore: Johns Hopkins University Press.

Stephens, John. D. 2010. "The Social Rights of Citizenship." In *The Oxford Handbook of the Welfare State*, edited by Francis Castles, Stephen Leibfried, Jane Lewis, Herbert Obinger, and Christopher Pierson, 511–26. Oxford: Oxford University Press.

Stoker, Gerry. 1988. *The Politics of Local Governments*. London: Macmillan.

Strom, Kaare. 1990. "Behavioural Theory of Competitive Political Parties." *American Journal of Political Science* 34(2): 565–98.

Sugiyama, Natasha, Borges. 2011. "The Diffusion of Conditional Cash Transfer Programs in the Americas." *Global Social Policy* 11(2–3): 250–78.

——. 2012. "Bottom-Up Policy Diffusion: National Emulation of a Conditional Cash Transfer Program in Brazil." *Publius: The Journal of Federalism* 42(1): 25–51.

——. 2013. *Diffusion of Good Government: Social Sector Reforms in Brazil.* Notre Dame: University of Notre Dame Press.

Suplicy, Eduardo Matarazzo. 2002. *Renda de Cidadania.* São Paulo: Cortez Editora.

Tanzi, Vito. 1995. "Taxation in an Integrating World." Washington, DC: Brookings Institution.

Tarrow, Sidney. 2010. "The Strategy of Paired Comparison: Toward a Theory of Practice." *Comparative Political Studies* 43(2): 230–59.

Tommasi, Mariano, Sebastian Saiegh, and Pablo Sanguinetti. 2001. "Fiscal Federalism in Argentina: Policies, Politics, and Institutional Reform." *Economia* (Spring): 147–201.

Tonelli, Luis. 2011. Preface. In *La Política en tiempos de los Kirchner*, edited by Andrés Malamud and Miguel de Luca, 9–15. Buenos Aires: Eudeba.

Torre, Juan Carlos. 1998. "Critical Junctures and Economic Change." In *Argentina: The Challenges of Modernization*, edited by Joseph Tulchin and Alison Garland. Wilmington, DE: Scholarly Resources.

Torre, Juan Carlos, and Elisa Pastoriza. 2002. "La Democratización del Bienestar." In *Nueva Historia Argentina: Los Años Peronistas*, edited by Juan Carlos Torre, 257–313. Buenos Aires: Editorial Sudamericana.

Treisman, Daniel. 2004. "Stabilization Tactics in Latin America." *Comparative Politics* 36(4): 399–420.

——. 2007. *The Architecture of Government: Rethinking Political Decentralization.* Cambridge: University of Cambridge Press.

Trudeau, Pierre Elliott. 1968. *Federalism and the French Canadians.* Toronto: Macmillan.

TSE (Tribunal Superior Eleitoral Brasileira). 2006 and 2002. Resultados das Eleições. Brasília: TSE. Available at www.tse.jus.br.

Tsebelis, George. 1995. "Decision Making in Political Systems: Veto Players in Presidentialism, Parliamentarism, Multicameralism and Multipartyism." *British Journal of Political Science* 25(3): 289–325.

——. 2000. "Veto Players and Institutional Analysis." *Governance* 13(4): 441–74.

UNDP (United Nations Development Program). 2006. "Human Development Report." New York.

Veja (magazine). São Paulo. Various issues.

Vinocur, Pablo, and Leopoldo Halperin. 2004. "Pobreza y Políticas Sociales en Argentina de los Anos Noventa." In Working Paper 85, 14–66. Santiago: Economic Commission of Latin America (ECLAC).

Ward, Peter, Victoria Rodriguez, and Enrique Mendoza. 1999. *New Federalism and State Government in Mexico: Bringing the States Back.* Austin: University of Austin Press.

Weaver, Kent. 2002. "Electoral Rules and Governability." *Journal of Democracy* 13(2): 111–25.

Webb, Steven. 2003. "Hardening the Provincial Budget Constraints in Argentina." In *Fiscal Decentralization and the Challenge of Hard Budget Constraints,* edited by Jonathan Rodden, Gunnar Eskeland, and Jennie Litvack, 189–211. Boston: MIT Press.

Weitz-Shapiro, Rebecca. 2006. "Partisanship and Protest." *Latin American Research Review* 41(3): 122–49.

Weyland, Kurt. 1996. "Neopopulism and Neoliberalism in Latin America: Unexpected Affinities." *Studies in Comparative International Development* 31 (Fall): 3–31.

———. 2007. *Bounded Rationality and Policy Diffusion: Social Sector Reform in Latin America.* Princeton: Princeton University Press.

Whitehead, Laurence. 1996. "Democracy and Decolonization." In *The International Dimensions of Democratization,* edited by Laurence Whitehead, 356–93. Oxford: Oxford University Press.

Wibbels, Eric. 2005. *Federalism and the Market: Intergovernmental Conflict and Economic Reform in the Developing World.* Cambridge: Cambridge University Press.

Willis, Eliza, Christopher da C. B. Garman, and Stephan Haggard. 1999. "The Politics of Decentralization in Latin America." *Latin American Research Review* 34(1): 7–56.

Wilson, Robert, Peter Ward, Peter Spink, and Victoria Rodríguez. 2006. *Governance in the Americas.* Notre Dame: University of Notre Dame Press.

World Bank. [Various Years]. "GINI Index" and "Annual Growth Index" Global Summary Statistics. Available at www.data.worldbank.org.

World Values Survey Wave 3. 1995–1998. OFFICIAL AGGREGATE v.20140921. World Values Survey Association (www.worldvaluessurvey.org). Aggregate File Producer: Asep/JDS, Madrid SPAIN.

Yanes, Pablo. 2013. "Targeting and Conditionalities in Mexico: The End of a Cash Transfer Model?" In *Citizen's Income and Welfare Regimes in Latin America: From Cash Transfers to Rights,* edited by Rubén Lo Vuolo, 67–87. New York: Palgrave Macmillan.

Zucco, Cesar. 2008. "The President's 'New' Constituency: Lula and the Pragmatic Vote in Brazil's 2006 Presidential Elections." *Journal of Latin American Studies* 40: 29–49.

———. 2013. "When Payouts Pay Off: Conditional Cash Transfers and Voting Behavior in Brazil, 2002–10." *American Journal of Political Science* 57(4): 810–22.

INDEX

Figures and tables are referred to with *f* and *t*, respectively.

Mexico (*continued*)
  foreign debt payments in, 234n15
  peso devaluation in, 123
  Progresa-Opportunidades-
    Prospera and, 5, 29, 32, 133, 134,
    148, 224
middleman, 72
Minha Casa, Minha Vida, 81
minimum wage, 65
Ministério de Desenvolvimento
  Social (Ministry of Social
  Development) (MDS), 68, 69,
  111
Ministry of Cities, 96
Ministry of Economy, 137, 170, 171,
  176, 182
Ministry of Health, 64
Ministry of Health and Social Action,
  122
Ministry of Labor, 123, 128, 133, 137,
  192, 237n1
Ministry of Labor and Welfare, 119,
  120
Ministry of Mines and Energy, 64
Ministry of Social Development
  (Desarrollo Social), 133, 137–38,
  140, 142, 148, 195, 208
Ministry of Social Development
  (Ministério de Desenvolvimento
  Social), 68
Moreno, Buenos Aires, 140
multilevel governance, 33, 101
municipal autonomy, 89, 163t, 195
municipal collaboration, 41–53, 42t,
  113
municipal decentralization, 170
municipal heterogeneity, 68
municipalization, 10, 45, 93, 103, 113
  Bolsa Família and, 94–101
  top-down, 206
municipal participation, 73–74
municipal social spending, 177f

municipios libres, 44
Murillo, Victoria, 127, 145

National Administration of Social
  Security (ANSES), 147–48, 151,
  179, 199, 225, 239n29
National Census (2010), 80, 93
national collective goods, 11, 35
National Constituent Assembly, 59
National Constitution, 156, 161–62,
  163, 165, 170, 194
National Coordinative Council of
  Social Policy, 138
National Council of Social Policy
  Coordination, 128
national food programs, 171
national hospitals, 171
National Institute of Statistics and
  Census, 144
nationalization
  of Bolsa Família, 113
  of CCTs, 62–67
National Microcredit program
  (MEI), 81
National Minimum Income
  Guarantee Program, 62
national policy objectives, 40–53,
  42t, 85
  political regime type and, 50–52,
    213–17
  subnational finances and, 45–50,
    209–13
  subnational government and,
    41–45, 205–9
National Secretariat of Social
  Assistance (SNAS), 60
national security, 89
National Solidarity Program, 32
neoliberalism, 3, 25, 38, 238n7
neopopulism, 123, 238n7
Network on Public Policy Management and Transparency, 17

TRACY BECK FENWICK

is director of the Australian Centre for Federalism and lecturer
in political science at the School of Politics and International Relations,
Australian National University.